NON-CHRISTIAN RELIGIOUS SYSTEMS
BUDDHISM

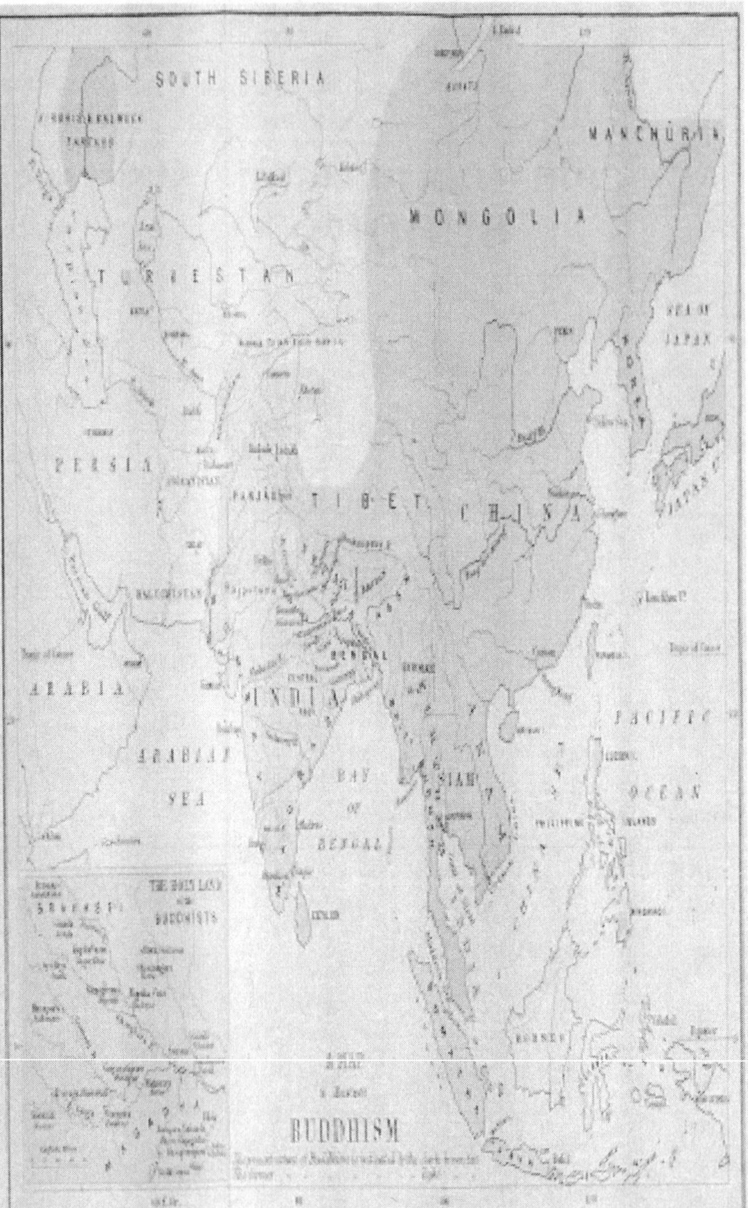

London: Published by the Society for Promoting Christian Knowledge.

NON-CHRISTIAN RELIGIOUS SYSTEMS

BUDDHISM:

BEING

A SKETCH OF THE LIFE AND TEACHINGS OF GAUTAMA, THE BUDDHA

BY

T. W. RHYS DAVIDS,

OF THE MIDDLE TEMPLE, BARRISTER-AT-LAW, AND LATE OF THE CEYLON CIVIL SERVICE

PUBLISHED UNDER THE DIRECTION OF
THE COMMITTEE OF GENERAL LITERATURE AND
EDUCATION APPOINTED BY THE SOCIETY FOR PROMOTING
CHRISTIAN KNOWLEDGE.

GYAN

Published by

GYAN

Gyan Publishing House
5, Ansari Road
Daryaganj, New Delhi-110002
Phone: 011-47034999, 9811692060
E-mail: books@gyanbooks.com

Distribution Network
gyanbooks.com
India, USA, Canada, UK, Australia, France

ISBN : 978-81-212-4501-2 (HB)
First Published, 1870

2nd Impression 2020

Printed at: Gyan Press, Delhi.

Non-Christian Religious Systems, Buddhism
Author: T. W. Rhys Davids

NON-CHRISTIAN RELIGIOUS SYSTEMS.

BUDDHISM:

BEING

A SKETCH OF THE LIFE AND TEACHINGS OF GAUTAMA, THE BUDDHA.

BY

T. W. RHYS DAVIDS,

OF THE MIDDLE TEMPLE, BARRISTER-AT-LAW, AND LATE OF THE CEYLON CIVIL SERVICE.

PUBLISHED UNDER THE DIRECTION OF
THE COMMITTEE OF GENERAL LITERATURE AND EDUCATION
APPOINTED BY THE SOCIETY FOR PROMOTING
CHRISTIAN KNOWLEDGE.

LONDON:
SOCIETY FOR PROMOTING CHRISTIAN KNOWLEDGE.
SOLD AT THE DEPOSITORIES,
77, GREAT QUEEN STREET, LINCOLN'S-INN FIELDS;
ROYAL EXCHANGE; 48, PICCADILLY;
AND BY ALL BOOKSELLERS.
New York: Pott, Young, & Co.

TABLE OF CONTENTS.

CHAPTER I.—INTRODUCTION.

Statistics of Buddhism, 3; of other religions, 6; extent of the subject and limits of this work, 8; sources of information, 9; authorities relating to the life of Gautama, 11; estimate of their value, 15.

APPENDIX: List of the Pitakas, 18; size of the Pitakas, 19.

CHAPTER II.—THE LIFE OF GAUTAMA (PART I.).

The Āryans in the sixth century B.C., 22; the Sākyas, 25; Gautama's birth, 26; his names, 27; his marriage, 28; the four visions, 29; birth of his son Rāhula, 30; he abandons his home, 31; studies under the Brahmans, 33; his self-mortification, 34; he gives up penance, and his disciples desert him, 35; the temptation, 36; the victory, the attainment of Buddha-hood, 39; the after-doubt, 41; his meeting with Upaka, 42; reception by his former disciples, 43; the foundation of the Kingdom of Righteousness, 45; the first sermon, 47; the first converts, 49.

APPENDIX: Gautama's wife and relations, 50.

CHAPTER III.—THE LIFE OF GAUTAMA (PART II.).

The first lay disciples, 53; sending out the sixty, 55; the season of *was*, 57; conversion of Kāṣyapa, 58, sermon on fire, 59; return to Rājagriha, 61; Bimbisāra's gift of Veluvana, 62; the Sāvaka Sannipāta, 63; discontent of the people, 63; return home, 64; interview with his father, 65; interview with his wife, 66; Rāhula admitted to the Order, 67; other accessions to the Order, 68; the gift of Jetavana, 69; chronicle of the ministry, 70; Dewadatta, 75; Gautama's last days, 77; Buddhism and Brahmanism, 83.

CHAPTER IV.—THE ESSENTIAL DOCTRINES OF BUDDHISM.

The Pitakas, our oldest authority, 86; ultimate facts, 87; the Skandhas, 90; Buddhism denies the existence of the soul, 93; transmigration, 99; Karma, 101; the Four Truths, 106; the Four Paths, 108; the Ten Fetters, 109; Nirvāna, 110.

APPENDIX: Passages in which Nirvāna is mentioned, 120.

Chapter V.—Buddhist Morality.

The Fruit of the Noble Path, 124; Buddhist Beatitudes, 125; the true treasure, 127; Scripture verses, 128; parable of the mustard-seed, 133; parable of the sower, 134; other parables, 135; summary of lay duty from the Dhammika Sutta, 137; the Ten Sins, 142; the Sigālovāda Sutta, 143; concluding remarks, 148.

Chapter VI.—The Order of Mendicants.

Cause of the foundation of the Order, and its results, 150; Scripture verses, 153; form of admission to the Order, 158; rules of the Order as to food, 163; residence, 164; clothing, 165; poverty, 166; obedience, 168; daily life of the mendicants, 169; summary, 170; mystic trance, 174.

Chapter VII.—The Legend of the Buddha.

The Buddhas, 179; miraculous birth of Gautama, 182; prophecies regarding the child, 183; the holy child, 184; the Chakravartī parallel, 188; wonders at Gautama's death, 189; the legend as sun-myth, 190; local legends, 194; Buddha as Catholic saint, 196; the Buddha as the Man in the Moon, 197.

Chapter VIII.—Northern Buddhism.

Theory of the Buddhas, 199; Manjusrī, 201; Avalokiteṣvara, 203; Vajrapāṇī, 203; the Dhyāni-Buddhas, 204; Ādi-Buddha, 206; the Tantra system, 208; praying wheels and flags, 210.

Chapter IX.—Spread of Buddhism.

Date of Gautama's death, 212; the First Council, 213; the Second Council, 215; Chandragupta, 220; Asoka, 222; the Third Council, 224; Asoka's missionaries, 226; Mahinda, 228; Sanghamittā, 230; the Bo tree, 231; the Pitakas reduced to writing, 233; Buddhaghosha, 235; Java and Sumatra, 236; Kanishka, 237; Kanishka's Council, 238; Chinese Buddhism, 240; the Korea and Japan, 241; Chinese pilgrims, 242; Buddhism expelled from India, 245; the Lāmāism of Tibet, 246.

TRANSLITERATION OF PĀLI WORDS.

THE earliest form of the Pāli language for which an alphabet was made, was written in the square letters of which the earliest forms preserved to us are found in Asoka's inscriptions. But Pāli writers learnt very early to distinguish between the language and its alphabet, and the square letters fell out of use, the language being written in the alphabets in use in the different countries—Ceylon, Burma, and Siam—where the language was till studied. European writers on Pāli have also followed the excellent practice of printing Pāli texts in European characters; disregarding, of course, the peculiarities of the present unscientific, and unpractical English system.[1] In this work Pāli words are accordingly printed in English letters, subject to the following remarks on pronunciation :—

VOWELS.—A, when the accent falls upon it, represents the sound of short a in the French or German: when the accent does not fall upon it, the sound of the u in our word *hut*. Ā represents the former sound doubled—our a in *father*.

I represents our i in *hit*; ī, the same sound doubled.

U represents our oo in *foot*; ū, the same sound doubled.

E and O are always long when they close a syllable, always short when they do not. Hence the long mark is needless, and is not used. Short e is pronounced as our e in *met*; long e, as our a in *mate*; short o, as our o in *lot*; long o, as our oa in *boat*.

Ai and au, as in our words '*eye*' and '*how*.'

CONSONANTS.—The h is always fully audible; for instance kh, as in '*seek him*'; th, as in '*at home*.'

ṁ is our *ng*. It is a pity there is not a more distinct sign for this sound, which contains neither an *m* nor an *n*, nor a *g*.

c is our ch (tsh).

ñ is the Spanish ñ, our ny.

---

[1] See the strongly-expressed opinion of Mr. Fausböll at the end of the preface to his edition of the Jātakas—an opinion with which I heartily concur.

ṭ represents the first part of the compound sound represented by c. The ṭh, ḍ, ḍh, ṇ and s follow it; *i.e.*, they are all pronounced by placing the tongue against the point where the palate passes into the gum, a quarter of an inch or more *behind* the teeth.

t, th, d, dh, n, and l are pure dentals; that is, they are pronounced by placing the tongue at the root of the teeth, or against the teeth, so that t and d are very slightly aspirate. We do not in English make this distinction between ṭ and t, but our t is much more often ṭ than t, and care is therefore necessary in pronouncing all the dentals.

v (or rather the corresponding native character) is always pronounced w by native scholars. Formerly it may have been v or either v or w, except after a consonant, when it was certainly w, as in dve (pronounced dwē).

The other consonants call for no remark; but it should be noticed that double consonants are pronounced double, one of the chief beauties of Pāli, as of Italian. Patta is pat-ta not pata. If the double consonant already represents a compound sound, only the former of the two can be doubled, saññā = san-nyā; kukucca, pronounced, koo-koot-tsher.

There is great difficulty in choosing between the use of the Sanskrit and the Pāli forms of names and technical terms; a difficulty already pointed out by Professor Max Müller (in his preface to Captain Rogers's 'Buddhaghosha's Parables,' pp. l. liii.). I have much doubt, for instance, whether I have done right to use the Sanskrit form Gautama[1] instead of the Pāli Gotama. When either of the forms would be particularly uncouth, or difficult for Englishmen to pronounce, I have chosen the other: writing, therefore, Moggallāna, not Maudgalyāyana; and Karma, not Kamma; which Englishmen would inevitably pronounce Kama. I have kept the Pāli forms of a few words distinctively Pāli, and have used forms neither Sanskrit nor Pāli for one or two words (Nirvāna and Pitaka for instance) which may be considered to have become English. In other respects I have followed the rules suggested by Professor Max Müller.

---

[1] Pronounce the first syllable as in 'how,' the second and third exactly as in 'handsomer.' The accent falls on the first syllable.

BUDDHISM.

CHAPTER I.

INTRODUCTION.

SEVERAL writers have commenced their remarks on Buddhism by reminding their readers of the enormous number of its adherents; and it is, indeed, a most striking fact, that the living Buddhists far outnumber the followers of the Roman Church, the Greek Church, and all other Christian Churches put together. From such summary statements, however, great misconceptions may possibly arise, quite apart from the fact that numbers are no test of truth, but rather the contrary. Before comparing the numbers of Christians and Buddhists, it is necessary to decide, not only what Christianity is, and what is Buddhism; but also, as regards the Buddhists, whether a firm belief in one religion should or should not, as far as statistics are concerned, be nullified by an equally firm belief in another. The numbers are only interesting in so far as they afford a very rough test of the influence which Buddhism has had in the development of the human race; and for this purpose they err both by excess and by defect. In the following tables no allowance has been made for India, which has been and is profoundly influenced by the results of the rise and fall within it of the Buddhist church, and too much allowance has been made for China, where there religions hold to one another an anomalous relation quite unexampled in history; for almost every Chinaman would probably profess himself a believer in the philosophy of Konfucius, while he would also worship at both Buddhist and Tao temples. It would, however, be as impossible to express numerically the influence of Buddhism in India, as it would be to subtract from the Chinese numbers so as to show how much of the average Chinaman was Buddhist, and how much Taossean or Konfucian. Perhaps the deficiency is balanced by the excess; in any case, we must leave the numbers as they are. The following are the tables referred to, giving the nearest approximation possible to the actual number of living Buddhists as compared with the number of the adherents of other religions:—

Southern Buddhists.

In Ceylon[1]	1,520,575
,, British Burmah[2]	2,447,831
,, Burma[3]	3,000,000
,, Siam[3]	10,000,000
,, Anam[3]	12,000,000
,, (Jains)[4]	485,020
Total about	30,000,000

[1] According to the Ceylon census, 1872, the total number of inhabitants was 2,405,287. About 500,000 were Muhammadans.

[2] From the census of 1871. The total was 2,747,148, the remainder being mostly Hindus.

[3] According to native military returns, which give only the number of males. The totals are therefore conjectural.

[4] This is the number of 'Buddhists' given in the Indian census of 1871 (Bombay, 191,137; Bengal, 84,974; Panjāb, 36,190; Central Provinces, 36,569; Maisūr, 13,263; and a few in Kurg Manadd ras). I presume 'Buddhists' means Jains; if so, I doubt

Northern Buddhists.

Dutch possessions and Bali[1]	50,000
British possessions[2]	500,000
Russian possessions[3]	600,000
Lieu Khen Islands[4]	1,000,000
Korea[4]	8,000,000
Bhutan and Sikhim[5]	1,000,000
Kashmīr[6]	200,000
Tibet[4]	6,000,000
Mongolia[4]	2,000,000
Mantchūria[4]	3,000,000
Japan[7]	32,794,897
Nepāl[8]	500,000
China proper[9] (18 prov.)	414,686,994
Total about	470,000,000

whether it includes them all, and it is not known how far they are Buddhists. There are about 4,000 Buddhists in Bakarganj.

[1] The Javanese are now Muhammadans. The Buddhists in the island are from China or Siam. For Bali, see Dr. Friedrich's paper in the Journal of the R. A. Soc., 1876, viii. p. 196.

[2] Chiefly in Spiti, Assam, Further India, and Hong Kong.

[3] There are rather more than 200,000 Kirghis and Kalmuk Tartars on the lower banks of the Volga in Europe, and an increasing number of Buriats and others in South Siberia, where Buddhism is still extending (Schlagintweit, 'Buddhism in Tibet,' p. 12; Keith-Johnston, 'Physical Atlas,' pl. 34).

[4] Keith-Johnston, 'Physical Atlas,' ed. 1856, estimates these states tributary to China to contain 35,000,000 inhabitants. So far as I can gather, this seems to be too much. The total of the above estimate is 20,000,000.

[5] The 'Allgemeine Zeitung,' Jan. 1862, *apud* Schlagintweit *loc. cit.*, gives one and a half million.

[6] The inhabitants of Kashmīr proper are almost entirely Muhammadans. The Buddhists are nearly confined to Ladāk.

[7] From a census, year not stated, quoted in Martin's 'Statesman's Year-book,' 1876.

[8] The total population is about two and a half millions, of whom the majority are now Hindus.

[9] Schopenhauer says ('Parerga et Paralipomena,' p. 128),

The following table will show at a glance the relative numbers of the different religions, and the percentage each bears to the whole:—

Parsees [1]	150,000	
Sikhs [2]	1,200,000	
Jews [3]	7,000,000	being about ½ per cent of the total.
Greek Catholics [4]	75,000,000	about 6 pr. cent.
Roman Catholics [4]	152,000,000	,, 12 ,,
Other Christians [4]	100,000,000	,, 8 ,,
Hindus [5]	160,000,000	,, 13 ,,
Muhammadans [4]	155,000,000	,, 12½ ,,
Buddhists	500,000,000	,, 40 ,,
Not included in the above [4]	100,000,000	,, 8 ,,
Total	1,250,350,000	

---

that according to the 'Moniteur de la Flotte,' May, 1857, the allied armies found, on taking Nanking in 1842, returns which gave the population at 396,000,000, and that the 'Post Zeitung' of 1858 contains a report from the Russian mission in Peking giving the numbers, on authority of state papers, at 414,687,000. The numbers above are those of the Chinese census of 1842, and their large total has caused some doubts. They give, however, a smaller number to the square mile than the English census gives to Bengal; while all accounts agree in representing the population as in many parts extremely dense, and the Chinese are quite capable of taking a census. I should fancy there has been very little increase, taking the eighteen provinces together, during the quarter of a century since 1842.

[1] Dosabhoi Framjee, 'The Parsees,' 1858, pp. 52, 56, and the Indian census.

[2] Indian census. It would be incorrect to include them under Hindus.

[3] The Rev. Hugh Miller 'On the Numbers of the Jews in all Ages' (Trans. of the Society of Biblical Archæology, vol. iv. part 2, 1876, pp. 325–331), where full details may be seen.

[4] From the estimates by Berghaus and Keith-Johnston.

[5] By the Indian census of 1872 there were 139,248,568 Hindus

Looked at solely as statistics of actual religious belief, the foregoing calculations may be utterly misleading, unless used with great care; they are vitiated by the attempt to class each man's religion under one word. In point of fact, each item lies open to an objection similar to that made above against the Chinese figures: many of the Ceylonese so-called Buddhists, for instance, take their oaths in court as Christians, and most of them believe also in devil-worship, and in the power of the stars. Their whole belief is not Buddhist; many of their ideas are altogether outside of Buddhism; their minds do not run only on Buddhist lines. On the other hand, such statistics are full of value if they enable us to realize in any degree the enormous numbers of those who are born and live and die without even once experiencing those thoughts which make up so much of our life, and afford us so much of guidance and support. Not one of the five hundred millions who offer flowers now and then on Buddhist shrines, who are more or less moulded by Buddhist teaching, is only or altogether a Buddhist; but these figures cannot fail to show how great is the claim on our attention of that system whose influence over living men they roughly express.

It is not incorrect to say 'that system.' It may be true that Buddhism having been adopted by very savage and very civilized peoples—the wild hordes on the cold table-lands of Nepal, Tartary, and Tibet; the cultured Chinese and Japanese in their varying

in British India. There must be about 20,000,000 more in the native states, Nepal, Further India, Bali, Ceylon, Mauritius, the West Indies, and elsewhere.

climes; and the quiet Sinhalese and Siamese, under the palm groves of the South—it has been so modified by the national characteristics of its converts, that it has developed under these different conditions into strangely inconsistent, and even antagonistic beliefs. But, nevertheless, each of these beliefs breathes more or less of the spirit of the system out of which they all alike have grown, and can only be rightly understood by those who have first realized what that system really was.

To trace all the developments of Buddhism, from its rise in India in the fifth century B.C., through its various fortunes there, and its progress in the countries to which it spread, down to the present time, would be to write the history of nearly half the human race during the greater part of that period within which anything worthy of the name of history is possible at all. To prepare even the materials for such a history, the labours of many scholars will be required for many years to come; and without a clear knowledge of the earliest phase of the religion, those labours would run great danger of being wrongly directed, and would certainly be constantly spent in the dark. The following pages will, therefore, be chiefly devoted to a consideration of Buddhism as it appears in its earliest records; with a rapid summary of the principal lines along which in after-times the most vital changes, and the most essential developments took place.

It may, perhaps, be doubted whether our knowledge is sufficiently advanced to be stated in that clear and precise way which a popular treatise requires. Happily or unhappily, however, there is already a by no means small quantity of popular literature on the subject; and it will be seen that enough at least, is known, to correct several of the most popular conceptions, both about Buddhism, and about the person of Gautama. Of early Buddhism, indeed, it is already possible to form an idea, which in its main features is certainly accurate; and as regards Gautama himself, though we know very little, we know, perhaps, nearly as much regarding the principal crises in his life as we are ever likely to ascertain. Future investigations will give us fuller details regarding early Buddhism, and both greater exactness and greater certainty regarding the life of its founder, and they will above all enable us to follow clearly the development of Buddhism, which runs so remarkably parallel with that of Christianity.

As to the two former subjects our information is at present derived from the same ultimate sources—the three *Piṭakas* or Collections, as the canonical books of the Southern Buddhists are called; the *Commentaries* on the Pitakas; and the sacred books of the Northern Buddhists, which have hitherto received no inclusive name. It will be seen hereafter that Gautama Buddha left behind him no written works,—indeed, it is very doubtful whether at the time when he lived the art of writing was known in the southern valley of the Ganges; but the Buddhists believe that he composed works which his immediate disciples learned by heart in his lifetime, and which were handed down by memory in their original state until they were committed to writing. This is not impossible: it is known that the Vedas were handed down in this manner for many hundreds of years, and none would now dispute the enormous powers of memory to which Indian priests and monks attained, when written books were not invented, or only used as helps to memory: when they could calmly devote their lives to learning and repeating one or more of those scriptures which they held to be sacred; and round which all their other meagre knowledge centred.[1] But it is quite clear from internal evidence alone, that this cannot have been the case with any of the books of the Northern Buddhists as yet known to us, or with those parts of the Pitakas which relate to the life of Gautama. The orthodox Buddhist belief therefore falls to the ground, and we are left to our own researches to ascertain the time when their sacred books were composed. This has as yet been very imperfectly done, but it may be stated generally that some of the Northern books are known to have been translated into Chinese shortly after the commencement of our era, and that there is every reason to believe that the Pitakas now extant in Ceylon are substantially identical with the books of the Southern Canon, as settled at the Council of Patna about the year 250 B.C.[2] As no works would have been received into the canon which were not then believed to be very old, the Pitakas may be approximately placed in the fourth century B.C., and parts of them possibly reach back very nearly, if not quite, to the time of Gautama himself.

[1] Even though they are well acquainted with writing, the monks in Ceylon do not use books in their religious services, but repeat, for instance, the whole of the Pātimokkha on Uposatha (Sabbath) days by heart.

[2] On this council, see below, p. 224. A list of these scriptures is given at the end of this chapter.

But of this canon, only a very small part has been published; and we have as yet to rely a good deal on later works. Those, both Northern and Southern, treating of Buddhist ethics and philosophy, will be considered further on; those relating to the life of Gautama are more especially the following:—

I. The 'Lalita Vistara,' the standard *Sanskrit* work of the Northern Buddhists on this subject, which, however, only carries the life down to the time when Gautama came openly forward as a Teacher. It is partly in prose, and partly in verse, the poetical passages being older than the others. M. Foucaux has published a translation into French of a translation of this work into Tibetan. He holds the Tibetan version to have existed in the 6th century A.D. How much older the present form of the Sanskrit work may be is quite uncertain.[1] The Sanskrit text and part of an English translation by Rājendra Lāl Mitra has been published at Calcutta, and Professor Lefmann, of Heidelberg, is now publishing a translation into German. The 'Lalita vistara' is full of extravagant poetical fictions in honour of Gautama, some of which are not without literary value; and it is just as much a poem on the birth and temptation of Gautama, based on earlier lives of the Teacher, as Milton's 'Paradise Regained' is a poem on the birth and temptation of Christ, based on the accounts found in the Gospels. Such historical value as it possesses is derived therefore from the comparison which it enables us to draw between the later Northern and the earlier Southern traditions, and from the light which it throws on the development of the religious beliefs which sprang up regarding the person of 'the Buddha.' It is much to be regretted that the earlier Northern accounts are not at present accessible.

II. The *Tibetan* accounts, which have been analyzed by two scholars; by Alexander Csoma in his 'Notices on the Life of

---

[1] M. Foucaux's work was published in 1847, under the title 'rGya Tcher Rol Pa,' (the *r* is silent). Foucaux, without any evidence whatever, assigns the Sanskrit original to Kanishka's Council (see below p. 239). For other opinions see Senart 496, and Feer, 'Journal Asiatique,' 1866, p. 275.

Shakya extracted from the Tibetan authorities,' 1839,[1] and, at greater length, by Anton Schiefner, in his abridged translation[2] of a work written in Tibetan in 1734 A.D., by a Buddhist monk named Ratna-dharma-rāja. Both these accounts are based chiefly on the 'Lalita Vistara,' the conclusion only of the latter being drawn from the Sanskrit work mentioned below (No. III.). Csoma's 'Notices' have been superseded by the works of Foucaux and Schiefner, but the latter contains a good deal which still has independent value.

III. An abbreviated translation into English of a translation into *Chinese* of a Sanskrit work called 'Mahābhinishkramana Sūtra' (the Book of the Great Renunciation, referring to Gautama's having renounced his home in order to become an ascetic). The date of the Sanskrit work is unknown; the translation into Chinese was made in the sixth century A.D.; the English version by the Rev. Samuel Beal was published in 1875, under the title 'Romantic Legend of Śākya Buddha.'[3]

IV. A translation into English of a translation into *Burmese* of a Pāli work called by Bigandet 'Mallalingara Wouttoo.' Neither date nor author is known of either the Pāli or the Burmese work. Two editions of the English version by Bishop Bigandet have appeared at Rangoon in 1858 and 1866, under the title 'The Life or Legend of Gaudama, the Budha of the Burmese.' This life agrees not only throughout in its main features, but even word for word in many passages with the Jātaka commentary, to be mentioned below, written in Ceylon,

---

[1] In vol. xx. of the 'Asiatic Researches,' pp. 285–296, to which notes are added.

[2] Read 31st May, 1848, before the Academy at St. Petersburg, and published in the 'Mémoires présentés par divers Savants à l'Académie Impériale de St. Péterbourg,' vol. vi. livraison 3, 1851, pp. 231–332, 4to. Also published separately, under the title 'Eine Tibetische Lebensbeschreibung Çakyamuni's. St. Petersburg. 1849, 8vo.'

[3] It is based on Chinese amplified versions of Sanskrit texts, giving a very legendary account of Gautama's life down to the time when, in his thirty-sixth year, he revisited his father's home after openly coming forward as a Teacher.

in the fifth century. It follows that its original author usually adhered very closely to the orthodox books and traditions of the Southern church; which were introduced into Burma from Ceylon in the fifth century.

V. The account published in 1860 by the Rev. Spence Hardy in his 'Manual of Buddhism,' based on various *Ceylonese* books, most of which date after the twelfth century of our era. As might be expected, this account is more ample and less reliable than the last.

VI. The original *Pāli* text of the 'Commentary on the Jātakas,' written in Ceylon probably about the middle of the fifth century of our era. The first part of this commentary, published by Mr. Fausböll in Copenhagen in 1875, contains a life of Gautama down to the time when he revisited his home after his appearance as a public teacher; and down to that time it is the best authority we have. It contains word for word almost the whole of the life of Gautama given by Turnour, in his 'Pāli Buddhistical Annals,'[1] from the 'Madurattha-vilāsinī,' a commentary on the 'Buddhavansa,' which is the account of the Buddhas contained in the second Pitaka. The light it throws on the other accounts is often exceedingly interesting and instructive, especially as showing the gradual growth of the supernatural parts of the biography.

The following instance is a fair sample of the value of the different authorities. When his relations complain of the future Buddha that he is remiss in martial and manly exercises, the Jātaka says, that on a day fixed by him he showed his proficiency in the twelve arts, and his superiority over other archers. Bigandet's account is equally simple, but the number of 'arts and sciences' is eighteen. The later Sinhalese books make him do wonders with a bow which 1,000 men could not bend, and

---

[1] 'Journal of the Bengal Asiatic Soc.,' vol. vii. pp. 797, *et seq.* The Jātaka omits only a few very unimportant words in eleven places; it gives slightly different versions of six short passages, and adds other paragraphs throughout. The solitary discrepancy is in the account of the 'competition' referred to below, p. 29. (Jātaka, 58, 19-30, compared with Turnour, J. B. A. S. vii. 803, 4.)

the twang of whose string was heard for 7,000 miles, and they say, "The prince also proved that he knew perfectly the eighteen arts, though he had never had a teacher, and he was equally well acquainted with many other sciences." Lastly, the Northern Buddhists place the whole occurrence at a different time. Beal has eight pages full of the miracles ascribed to Gautama on that occasion, and the account in the 'Lalita Vistara,' in M. Foucaux's translation, is more lengthy and more miraculous still.

VII. The account in *Pāli* of the death of Gautama from the second Pitaka. It is called the 'Mahāparinibbāna Sutta.' Copious extracts from it have been given by Turnour,[1] and a complete edition of it has just been published in the 'Journal of the Royal Asiatic Society' (vols. vii. and viii., N.S.) by Prof. Childers.

This, the oldest and most reliable of all our authorities, cannot be dated later than the end of the fourth century B.C., nor earlier than the time when Patna had become an important town and relic-worship had become general in the Buddhist church. It exaggerates the events which are said to have happened after the death took place, and most of the long sermons it ascribes to Gautama just before he died are probably compositions of the author, including much that was said at other times, rather than what Gautama then actually said: but in its main facts the recital bears the impress of truth.

VIII. The Siamese account as given by Mr. Alabaster in his 'Wheel of the Law';[2] being a translation of a Siamese work of unknown author and date, called 'Pathama Sambodhiyan, the attainment of Buddhahood, or Supreme Wisdom.' The translation unfortunately does not pretend to be accurate. The author says,[3] "My translation is free or literal according to my

---

[1] In the 'Journal of the Bengal Asiatic Society,' vol. vii. pp. 991—1014. It is the third Sutta of the Mahāvagga in the Dīgha-nikāya of the Sutta Piṭaka.

[2] London, Trübner: 1871, pp. 76–162.

[3] Preface, pp. xiv, xxvi. In quoting the author's own opinion of this portion of his book, a wrong impression might be produced, unless it be added that the work, as a whole, has admirably

judgment; in many parts I have cut out tedious descriptive passages; in one or two places, duly referred to in the notes, I have corrected presumed errors in my Siamese MS.; and in ch. x. I have substituted a simple for a confused arrangement. I do not expect to supply fresh materials to scholars." Mr. Alabaster's object was to produce a readable narrative, rather than to adhere strictly to his Siamese authority; which is evidently much more modern than the other accounts of the same school, and, as the title implies, only carries the life down to the crisis under the Bo Tree.

The first three of these accounts depend ultimately on the Sanskrit works of the Northern Buddhists, the last five on the Pāli text of the Southern canon. These are much the more reliable and complete; the former being inflated to a greater length by absurd and miraculous legends, shorter forms of which occur in the Southern books. The basis of fact underlying all the various accounts is sometimes clearly enough, and sometimes not at all, and more often doubtfully, recognizable.[1] As there has been very little communication between the two churches since the third century B.C., great reliance may reasonably be placed on those statements in which they agree; not indeed as to the actual facts of Gautama's life, but as to the belief of the early Buddhists concerning it. The following account is based on that belief, as far as it can be at present ascertained by

fulfilled the purpose with which it was written, and is a valuable addition to our small Buddhistic library.

[1] M. Senart, in his interesting work 'La Légende du Buddha,' attempts to trace the origin of many of the latter legends of both churches,—as also of the stories about Vishnu and Krishna, with which he compares them—in the old worship of the powers of nature, and especially of the sun.

a critical comparison of the different authorities. In endeavouring by such comparison to arrive at an approximation to the truth, it has not seemed necessary to me to reject entirely the evidence of any witness who believes in the miraculous. It is true that these early writers were not capable of making due distinction between that which they thought ought to have happened and that which actually occurred; it is true, even, that what they thought highly edifying is often miraculous, and not seldom absurd or childish. But it is no less absurd to lose all patience with them on that account; and to imagine that the life of Gautama is all a fiction, and that the Buddhist philosophy, or the still powerful Order of Buddhist mendicant friars, could have arisen from the misunderstood development of some solar myth.

There was certainly an historical basis for the Buddhist legend; and if it be asked whether it is at all possible to separate the true from the false, I would reply, that the difficulty, though great, is apt to be exaggerated. The retailers of these legends are not cunning forgers, but simple-minded men, with whose modes of thought we can put ourselves more or less *en rapport;* we are getting to know what kind of things to expect from their hero-worship and religious reverence, and delight in the physically marvellous; and we are not without information as to what was, and what was not, historically possible in the fifth century B.C. in the eastern valley of the Ganges. Scholars will never become unanimously agreed on all points; but they will agree in rejecting many things, and after allowing for all reasonable doubts they will agree that there still remain small portions of the narrative whose existence can only be explained on the hypothesis that they relate to actual events. I would maintain, therefore, that some parts of the story—few indeed, but very important, and sufficient to throw great light on the origin of Buddhism—may already be regarded as historical; other parts may be as certainly rejected; and many episodes remain, which may be altogether or partly fictitious.

The legends group themselves round a number of very distinct occurrences; and, properly speaking, each such episode should be judged separately, though of course by the same general rules of criticism. A complete work on the life of Gautama would thus compare the different versions of each episode so as to arrive at its earliest form: it would then discuss that account in order to ascertain whether all, or if not, how much of it, could be explained by religious hero-worship, mere poetical imagery, misapprehension, the desire to edify, applications to Gautama of previously existing stories, or sun myths, and so on. It would be in this, the most difficult part of the inquiry, that there would always be much difference of opinion; but some substantial progress could certainly be made. The size and aim of this little work quite preclude any such thorough examination. I shall therefore pass over almost in silence the later forms of the legend, and such portions of the earlier accounts as are in my opinion certainly due to one or other of the causes just referred to.

APPENDIX TO CHAPTER I.

LIST OF THE THREE PITAKAS, THE SACRED BOOKS OF THE SOUTHERN BUDDHISTS.

Vinaya Piṭaka (Discipline, for the Order).

1. Pārājika. On sins involving expulsion.
2. Pācitti. On sins requiring forgiveness.
3. Mahāvagga. } These are collectively called Khandaka, and contain rules for the daily life of the monks.
4. Cūla-vagga. }
5. Parivāra-pāṭha. A résumé of the preceding books.

Sutta Piṭaka (Discourses, for the Laity).

1. Dīgha-nikāya. The collection of 34 long treatises; one of which is the Parinibbāna Sutta (see p. 13). Seven others have been edited, with the translations of Burnouf and Gogerly, by M. and Mad. Grimblot, in the important work 'Sept Suttas Pālis.' Paris, 1876.
2 Majjhima-nikāya. The collection of 152 treatises of moderate size.
3. Saṁyutta-nikāya. Continuation.
4. Aṁguttara-nikāya. Miscellaneous, the largest book in the three Piṭakas.
5. Khuddaka-nikāya. The collection of short treatises. This is added by one school to the next Piṭaka. It contains the following short books.[1]
    1. Khuddaka-pāṭha. 'Short passages,' published by Mr. Childers, with English translation, in the Journal of the Royal Asiatic Society for 1869.

---

[1] I follow the order given by Turnour, 'Mahāvansa,' p. lxxv., which is presumably that adopted at the Council of Pātaliputra. Buddhaghosha, as quoted in Childers's Dictionary, under the word Nikāya, gives another order in his account of the

2. Dhamma-pada. 'Scripture verses,' published by Mr. Fausböll in Copenhagan, 1855, with Latin translation. Translated into German by Professor Weber, 'Zeitschrift der deutschen morgenländischen Gesellschaft, vol. xiv. 1860; reprinted in 'Indische Streifen,' vol. i. Translated into English by Professor Max Müller, as

---

first Council at Rājagriha. The first five are merely a collection of edifying extracts from the other sacred books. In the 'Annual Report of the Philological Society' for 1875 I have given a full account of the work hitherto accomplished in the publication of Pāli texts, and of dictionaries or grammars of the Pāli language in which the Pitakas are written. Great misconceptions have prevailed with regard to the supposed enormous extent of these scriptures: thus Spence Hardy says,[1] "in size the Pitakas surpass all Western compositions," and Sir Coomāra Swāmy[2] talks of "the vast mass of original writings, irrespective of the commentaries, in which the doctrines of Buddhism are embodied." This is much exaggerated, and as it tends to discourage research, I have made such calculations as will, I hope, settle the point. By counting the words in ten pages of our Bible I find that it, exclusive of the Apocrypha, contains between 900,000 and 950,000 words. The number of words in the first 221 verses of the Dhamma-pada, which are a fair sample of the whole, is 3,001; the 431 verses of that book ought therefore to contain rather less than 6,000 words. Now, the Dhamma-pada, according to Turnour's list,[3] is written on fifteen leaves, and the whole three Pitakas, exclusive of Nos. 10 and 11 of the Khuddaka Nikāya, whose extent is uncertain, are written on 4,382 leaves of about the same size. This would give 1,752,800 words for the whole text. To ascertain the relative number of words required to express the same ideas in English and Pāli, I have also counted the words in Professor Childers's edition of the Khuddaka Pātha, and in his translation. They are respectively 1,242 and 2,344. The Buddhist scriptures

---

[1] 'Eastern Monachism,' p. 190. [2] 'Sutta Nipāta,' p. 10.
[3] Mahāvansa, p. lxxv.

introduction to 'Buddhaghosha's Parables,' 1870. A few verses are rè-translated below. See the Index under Dhamma-pada.

3. Udāna. 'Songs of exultation.' Eighty-two short lyrics, supposed to have been uttered by Gautama under strong emotion, at important crises in his life. Each lyric is accompanied by details of the circumstances under which it arose.
4. Iti-vuttaka. One hundred and ten extracts beginning, "Thus it was spoken by the Blessed One."
5. Sutta-nipāta. A collection of 70 didactic poems, 30 of which have been translated by Sir Coomāra Swāmy in his 'Sutta Nipāta,' 1874.
6. Vimāna-vatthu. On the celestial mansions.

---

therefore,—including all the repetitions,[1] and all those books which consist of extracts from the others,—contain rather less than twice as many words as are found in our Bible; and a translation of them into English would be about four times as long. Such a literature is by no means unmanageable; but though the untiring genius and self-sacrificing zeal of the late Professor Childers, whose premature death has inflicted so irreparable a loss on Pāli scholarship, gave a new start to Pāli philology, no one in England seems to follow in his steps. Considering the importance of the inquiry, and the ease with which a student in this department can add to the sum of existing knowledge, I venture to express a hope that some of that passionate patience with which older and well-worn studies are pursued may soon be diverted to this most promising field.

---

[1] These are so numerous, that without them the Buddhist Bible is probably even shorter than ours. Thus the whole of the Dhamma-pada and the Sutta Piṭaka, are believed to be taken from other books; and even in the Nikāyas whole paragraphs and chapters are repeated under different heads, (the Subha Sutta, for instance, contains almost the whole of the Sāmañña-phala Sutta, and a great part of the Brahmajāla Sutta. (Burnouf, 'Lotus,' 448, 465, note 5.)

7. Petavatthu. On disembodied spirits.
8. Thera-gāthā. Poems by monks.
9. Theri-gāthā. Poems by nuns.
10. Jātaka. Five hundred and fifty old stories, fairy tales and fables, the most important collection of ancient folk-lore extant. The Pāli text and commentary is now being edited by Mr. Fausböll of Copenhagen, with an English translation by the present writer (comp. No. 15).
11. Niddeesa. A commentary ascribed to Ṣāriputra, on the latter half of Sutta Nipāta (No. 5).
12. Paṭisambhidā. On the powers of intuitive insight possessed by Buddhist saints.
13. Apadāna. Stories about Buddhist saints.
14. Buddha-vaysa. Short lives of the 24 preceding Buddhas and of Gautama, the historical Buddha.
15. Cariyā-piṭaka. Short poetical versions of some of the Jātaka stories, illustrating Gautama's virtue in former births. M. Gogerly has translated part of this in the Ceylon Asiatic Society's Journal, 1852.

Abhidhamma (Metaphysics).

1. Dhamma-sangaṇi. 'On conditions of life in different worlds.' The first paragraph translated by Gogerly, Cey. As. Soc. J. 1848, p. 7.
2. Vibhanga. Eighteen treatises of various contents.
3. Kathā-vatthu. On 1,000 controverted points.
4. Puggala-paññatti. Regulations for those who have entered the Paths. The shortest book of this Piṭaka, consisting of about 10,000 words.
5. Dhātu-kathā. On the Elements, a short book containing about 12,000 words.
6. Yamaka. 'The Pairs,' that is, on apparent contradictions or contrasts.
7. Paṭṭhāna. 'The Book of Origins.' On the causes of existence.

CHAPTER II.

THE LIFE OF GAUTAMA, DOWN TO THE TIME OF HIS APPEARANCE AS A TEACHER.

At the end of the sixth century B.C. those Aryan tribes, sprung from the same stem as our own ancestors, who have preserved for us in their Vedic songs so precious a relic of ancient thought and life, had pushed on beyond the five rivers of the Panjāb, and were settled all along the plains far down into the valley of the Ganges. Their progress had been very gradual, and though they had doubtless displaced many of the Dravidian tribes who previously half-occupied the land, they had also absorbed many of the foreigners into their own social organization as slaves or servants. They had meanwhile given up their nomadic habits; they dwelt in villages, here and there large enough to be called towns; and their chief wealth was in land and agricultural produce, as well as in cattle. They were still divided into clans; but the old democratic spirit which made each householder king and priest in his own family, had long ago yielded to the inroads of class feeling. Their settled life had given rise to customs which had hardened into unwritten laws; and with them, as elsewhere, these early institutions, though most useful, even necessary to society, were often productive of great personal hardship, and always a restraint on individual freedom.

The pride of race had put an impassable barrier between the Aryans and the conquered aborigines; the pride of birth had built up another between the chiefs or nobles and the mass of the Aryan people. The superstitious fears of all yielded to the priesthood an unquestioned and profitable supremacy; while the exigences of occupation, and the ties of family had further separated each class into smaller communities, until the whole nation had become gradually bound by an iron system of caste.

The old childlike joy in life, so manifest in the Vedas, had died away, the worship of nature had developed or degenerated into the worship of new and less pure divinities, and the Vedic songs themselves, whose freedom was little compatible with the spirit of the age, had faded into an obscurity, which did not lessen their value to the priests. The country was politically split up into little principalities, each governed by some petty despot, whose interests were not often the same as those of the community. The inspiriting wars against the enemies of the Aryan people, the infidel deniers of the Aryan gods, had given place to a succession of internecine feuds between the chiefs of neighbouring clans; and in literature, an age of poets had long since made way for an age of commentators and grammarians, who thought that the old poems must have been the work of gods.

The simple feeling of awe and wonder at the glorious battles of the storm, and the recurring victories of the sun, had given way before a debasing ritualism, before the growing belief in the efficacy of carefully conducted rites and ceremonies, and charms, and incantations; before the growing fear of the actual power of the stars over the lives and destinies of men; before the growing dependence on dreams, and omens, and divinations. A belief in the existence of a soul was probably universal, and the curious doctrine of transmigration satisfied the unfortunate that their present woes were the result of their own actions in some former birth, and would be avoided in future ones by present liberality to the priests. Every man's position and occupation were decided for him by his birth; there was plenty for all of the few necessaries of life; and the struggles and hopes and grinding poverty of a crowded country with the social arrangements of other times, were quite unknown. The village lands were usually held in common by an irrevocable tenure, and the thoughtless peasantry led, on the whole, quiet and not unhappy lives under the influence of a social despotism irresistible but not unkindly.

The priests were mostly well-meaning, well-conducted, ignorant, superstitious, and inflated with a sincere belief in their own divinity; and they inculcated a sense of duty, which tempered the despotism of the petty rājas, while it bound all the community in an equal slavery to the 'twice-born' Brahmans. A few of them also were really learned, a still smaller number earnestly thoughtful, and there was no little philosophical or sophistical discussion in the schools where the younger priests were trained. The religious use of the Vedas, and the right to sacrifice, were strictly confined to the Brahmans; but they were not the exclusive possessors of such secular knowledge as could then be acquired, and they divided the odour of sanctity with ascetics from other castes. Here and there travelling logicians were willing to maintain theses against all the world; anchorites had their schemes of universal knowledge and salvation; ascetics with unwavering faith practised self-torture and self-repression, in the hope of becoming more powerful than the gods; and solitary hermits sought for some satisfactory solution of the mysteries of life. The ranks of the officiating priesthood were for ever firmly closed against intruders; but a man of lower caste, a Kshatriya or a Vaisya, whose mind revolted against the orthodox creed, or whose heart was stirred by mingled zeal and ambition, might find through these irregular openings an entrance to the career of religious teacher and reformer.

Under some such conditions as these, thus rudely sketched in outline, an Aryan tribe, named the Ṣākyas, were seated, about 500 years before the birth of Christ, at a place called Kapila-vastu, on the banks of the river Rohini, the modern Kohāna, about 100 miles north-east of the city of Benāres. That insignificant stream rose thirty or forty miles to the north of their settlement, in the spurs of the mighty Himālayas, whose giant peaks loomed up in the distance against the clear blue of the Indian sky. The Ṣākyas had penetrated further to the east than most of their fellow-Aryans, but beyond them in that direction was the powerful confederation of the Lichchavis, and the rising kingdom of Magadha. To their north were rude hill tribes of Mongolian extraction; while behind them to the west lay those lands which the Brahmans held most sacred. Their nearest neighbours to be feared in that direction were the subjects of the king of Ṣrāvasti,[1] the rival of the king of Magadha. It was this rivalry of their neighbours more than their own strength which secured for the Ṣākyas a precarious independence; but their own hand was strong enough to protect them against the incursions of roving bands from the hills, and to sustain them in their quarrels with neighbouring clans of the same standing as themselves. They lived from the produce of their cattle and their rice-fields; their supplies of water being drawn from the Kohāna, on the other side of which stream lived the Koliyans, a kindred tribe.

With them the Ṣākyas sometimes quarrelled for the possession of the precious liquid, but just then the two clans were at peace, and two daughters of the rāja or chief of the Koliyans were the wives of Suddhodana, the rāja of the Sākyas. The story tells us that both were childless; a misfortune great enough in other times and in other countries, but especially then among the Aryans, who thought that the state of a man's existence after death depended upon ceremonies to be performed by his heir. The rejoicing, therefore, was great when in about the forty-fifth year of her age the elder sister,[2] promised her husband a son. In accordance with custom, she started in due time with the intention of being confined at her parents' house, but it was on the way under the shade of some lofty satin-trees in a pleasant grove called Lumbini, that her

[1] See below, p. 69.

[2] On the names, see Appendix to Chapter II., p. 51.

son, the future Buddha, was unexpectedly born. The mother and child were carried back to Suddhodana's house, and there, seven days afterwards, the mother died; but the boy found a careful nurse in his mother's sister, his father's other wife.

As with other men who afterwards became famous, many marvellous stories have been told about the miraculous birth and precocious wisdom and power of Gautama; and these are not without value, as showing the spirit of the times in which they arose and grew. It is probable that his having been an only child, born, as it were, out of due time, the subsequent death of his mother, and other details of the story may be due to this instinctive feeling that his birth must have been different from that of ordinary men.

Even the name Siddhārtha, said to have been given him as a child, may have been a subsequent invention, for it means 'he who has accomplished his aim.' But parents of Suddhodana's rank have never shown much aversion for grand names, and other Siddhārthas are mentioned[1] who were not at all peculiarly successful in accomplishing their desires. However this may be, his family name was certainly Gautama, and as this was the name by which he was usually known in after-life, we shall use it throughout this book.[2] Any other names given to the founder of

[1] Perhaps only in post-Buddhistic writings. The name occurs in works of the Northern Buddhists, and in Jaina books: but also in the Rāmāyana and Mahābhārata.

[2] It is a curious fact that Gautama is still the family name of the Rājput chiefs of Nagara, the village which has been identified with Kapilavastu (Cunningham's 'Ancient Geography of India,' vol. i. p. 417). Gautama is often called simply 'the

Buddhism are not names at all, but titles. To the pious Buddhist it seems irreverent to speak of Gautama by his mere ordinary and human name, and he makes use, therefore, of one of those numerous epithets which are used only of the Buddha, the Enlightened One. Such are Ṣākya-siṇha, 'the lion of the tribe of Ṣākya;' Ṣākya-muni, 'the Ṣākya sage;' Sugata, 'the happy one;' Satthā, 'the teacher;' Jina, 'the conqueror;' Bhagavā, 'the blessed one;' Loka-nātha, 'the Lord of the world;' Sarvajñā, 'the omniscient one;' Dharma-rāja, 'the king of righteousness,' and many others. These expressions, like the Swan of Avon, may have had very real significance in moments of poetic fire; but their constant use among the Buddhists tended not to bring into clearer vision, but to veil the personality of Gautama, and their constant use as names by modern writers arises simply from mistake.

There seems to be no reason to doubt that Gautama was very early married to his cousin the daughter of the rāja of Koli (see p. 50); but the next episode in the biographies is probably due to the influences just referred to. According to most of the southern accounts, his relations soon after complained in a body to the rāja Suddhodana that his son, devoted to home pleasures, neglected those manly exercises necessary for one who might hereafter have to lead his kinsmen in case of war. Gautama, being told of this, is said to have appointed a day by beat of drum to prove his skill against all comers, and by surpassing even the cleverest bowmen, and showing his mastery in 'the twelve arts,' to have won back the good opinion of

Rājput' in the earlier portions of the Northern biographies (Klaproth's note in 'Foe Koue Ki,' p. 203).

the complaining clansmen.[1] The Northern accounts, and the Madhurattha-vilāsinī make this competition take place before his marriage, and for the hand of his wife; and there are other discrepancies. No reliance can therefore be placed on the actual occurrence of this episode, the rise of the story being easily explicable, as suggested above, by the universal desire to relate wonderful things of the boyhood of men afterwards famous. It is instructive to notice that we find most discrepancies in the accounts of those parts of the story which are most improbable, a consideration which confirms, I think, the authority of those other parts, in themselves not improbable, in which all the accounts agree.

This is the solitary record of his youth. We hear nothing more until in his 29th year, Gautama suddenly abandoned his home to devote himself entirely to the study of religion and philosophy. All our authorities agree in the reason they assign for this momentous step. An angel appeared to him in four visions,—under the forms of a man broken down by age, of a sick man, of a decaying corpse, and lastly, of a dignified hermit—the visions appearing only to Gautama and his attendant Channa, who was each time specially inspired to explain to his deeply moved master the meaning of the sight. The different versions of this story contain various discrepancies in minor details, and the mere sight of an old or diseased stranger, or even of a dead body, would be insufficient of itself to work so powerful an effect on the mind of one who was not already keenly

[1] On the later versions of the story see above, p. 13.

sensible to the mysteries of sorrow and of death; but we find in this ancient tradition an expression—inadequate it may be, and even childish—of what in the main we must ourselves believe to be the true explanation of the cause which induced Gautama to abandon his family and his home. He was probably not the first—he was certainly not the last—who, in the midst of prosperity and comfort, has felt a yearning and a want which nothing could satisfy, and which have robbed of their charm all earthly gains and hopes. This vague dissatisfaction deepens with every fresh proof of the apparent vanity of life, and does not lose but gains in power when, as is reported in the case of Gautama, it arises more from sympathy with the sorrows of others than from any personal sorrow of one's own. At last, the details of daily life become insupportable; and the calm life of the hermit troubled with none of these things seems a haven of peace, where a life of self-denial and earnest meditation may lead to some solution of the strange enigmas of life.

Such feelings must have become more and more ascendant in Gautama's mind, when about ten years after his marriage, his wife bore him their only child, a son named Rāhula; and the idea that this new tie might become too strong for him to break, seems to have been the immediate cause of his flight. According to the oldest authorities of the Southern Buddhists, the birth of his son was announced to him in a garden on the river-side, whither he had gone after seeing the fourth vision,—that of the hermit. The event was not then expected, but he only said quietly, 'This is a new and strong tie I shall have to break,' and returned home thoughtful and sad. But the villagers were delighted at the birth of the child, their rāja's only grandson. Gautama's return became an ovation, and he entered Kapilavastu amidst a crowd of rejoicing clansmen. Among the sounds of triumph which greeted his ear, one especially is said to have attracted his attention—A young girl, his cousin, sang a stanza, "Happy the father, happy the mother, happy the wife of such a son and husband."[1] In the word 'happy' lay a double meaning; it meant also 'freed,' delivered from the chains of sin and of transmigration saved.[2] Grateful to one who at such a time reminded him of his highest thoughts, he took off his necklace of pearls, and sent it to her, saying, 'Let this be her fee as a teacher.' She began to build castles in the air thinking 'Young Siddhārtha is falling in love with me, and has sent me a present,' but he took no further notice of her, and passed on.

That night at midnight he sent his charioteer Channa for his horse, and whilst he was gone he went to the threshold of his wife's chamber, and there by the light of the flickering lamp, he watched her sleeping, surrounded by flowers, with one hand on the head of their child. He had wished for the last time to take the babe in his arms before he left, but he now saw that he could not do so without awaking the mother. As this might frustrate all his intentions, the fear of waking Yasodharā at last prevailed; he reluctantly tore himself away, and, accompanied only by Channa, left his father's home, his wealth and power, his young wife and only

[1] Fausböll's Jātaka, p. 60. Dhamma-pada, p. 118.

[2] The Pāli word is Nibbuta, which is derived from the same word as Nibbāna, in Sanskrit Nirvāna, the Buddhist salvation.

child, behind him; and rode away into the night to become a penniless and despised student, and a homeless wanderer. This is the circumstance which has given its name to the Sanskrit original of the Chinese work, of which Mr. Beal has given us the translation mentioned above—the 'Mahābhinishkramana Sūtra,' or 'Sūtra of the Great Renunciation.'

How much of this graceful story is historically true it is as yet impossible to say; but it certainly belongs to the very earliest form of Buddhist belief.

We next find another endeavour to relate, under the form of a real material vision, what is supposed to have passed in Gautama's mind. Māra, the spirit of Evil, appears in the sky, and urges Gautama to stop, promising him in seven days a universal kingdom over the four great continents, if he will but give up his enterprise. When his words fail to have the desired effect, the tempter consoles himself with the hope that he will still overcome his enemy, saying, 'Sooner or later some hurtful or malicious or angry thought must arise in his mind; in that moment I shall be his master.' 'And from that hour,' adds the Jātaka chronicler, 'he followed him, on the watch for any failing, cleaving to him like a shadow, which follows the object from which it falls.'[1] Gautama rode a long distance that night, not stopping till he reached the bank of the river Anomā, beyond the Koliyan territory. There, taking off his ornaments, he gave them and the horse in charge to his charioteer, to take them back to Kapilavastu. Channa asked, indeed, to be allowed to stay with his master, that becoming an ascetic, he might continue to serve him; but Gautama would not

[1] Fausböll's Jātaka commentary, p. 63.

hear of it, saying, 'How will my father and my relations know what has become of me unless you go back and tell them?' Gautama then cut off his long hair, and exchanging clothes with a poor passer-by, sent home the dejected and sorrowing Channa, while he himself hurried on towards Rājagriha, to begin his new life as a homeless mendicant ascetic.

Rājagriha, the capital of Magadha, was the seat of Bimbisāra, one of the then most powerful princes in the eastern valley of the Ganges; and was situated in a pleasant valley, closely surrounded by five hills, the most northerly offshoot of the Vindhya mountains.[1] In the caves on these hill-sides, free from the dangers of more disturbed districts, and near enough to the town whence they procured their simple supplies, yet at the same time surrounded by the solitude of nature, several hermits had found it convenient to settle. Gautama attached himself, first, to one of these Brahman teachers, named Alārá, and, being dissatisfied with his system, afterwards to another named Udraka, learning under them all that Hindu philosophy had then to teach about this world or the next.

It may be noticed, in passing, that the question of the relations between Buddhism and the different systems of Hindu philosophy is as difficult as it is interesting. Six such systems are accounted orthodox among the Hindus; but the history of their rise and development has yet to be written. Only the fully-

[1] For a detailed description of the ruins at Rājagriha (modern Rajgir), see General Cunningham's 'Ancient Geography of India, Buddhist Period,' pp. 462–468. The ruins of the walls of the new citadel, built by Bimbisāra, are still traceable.

developed systems are now extant in their different sūtras or aphorisms: but though it is doubtful whether any of these were pre-Buddhistic or not, it is certain that, long before Gautama's time, the Brahmans had paid great attention to the deepest questions of ontology and ethics, and were divided into different schools, in one or other of which most of Gautama's metaphysical tenets had previously been taught. Such originality as can be claimed for him arises more from the importance which he attached to moral training above ritual, or metaphysics, or penance; and to the systematized form in which he presented ideas derived from those of various previous thinkers. Like all other leaders of thought, he was the creature of his time, and it must not be supposed that his philosophy was entirely of his own creation. One of the northern authorities gives long accounts of the discussions he held with Bhagavā, Alāra, and Udraka,[1] which are interesting as being probably founded on ancient tradition. Professor Monier Williams in his 'Indian Wisdom' has given an excellent popular sketch of the six systems just referred to,[2] and the most important authorities on the subject will be found mentioned there.

One of the most frequently inculcated tenets of the Brahmans was a belief in the efficacy of penance as a means of gaining superhuman power and insight; and when Gautama, after studying the systems of Alāra and Udraka, was still unsatisfied, he resolved to go apart, and see what progress he could himself make

[1] Beal, 'Romantic Legend,' pp. 152-177.
[2] Lectures, iii.-vi., pp. 48-126.

by this much-vaunted method. He withdrew accordingly into the jungles of Uruvela, near the present temple of Buddha Gayā,[1] and there for six years, attended by five faithful disciples, he gave himself up to the severest penance, until he was wasted away to a shadow by fasting and self-mortification. Such powerful self-control has always excited the wonder and admiration of weaker men, and we need not be surprised that his fame is said to have spread round about 'like the sound of a great bell hung in the canopy of the skies.'[2] If by these means he could have won that certitude, that peace of mind for which he longed, the gain might have been worth the cost. But the more he thought, the more he examined himself and denied himself, the more he felt himself a prey to a mental torture worse than any bodily suffering; a fear lest all his efforts should have been wasted, and that he should die, having gone wrong, and, after all his weary efforts, only failed.[3] At last one day, when walking slowly up and down, lost in thought, he suddenly staggered and fell to the ground. Some of the disciples thought he was actually dead; but he recovered, and, despairing of further profit from such penance, began again to take regular food, and gave up his self-mortification. Then, when he was most in need of sympathy, when his wavering faith might have been strengthened by the tender trust and re-

[1] Beal's 'Travels of Fa Hian,' p. 120.

[2] Bigandet, p. 49 (first edition); compare Jātaka, 67, 27.

[3] Gautama's doubts and disquietudes at this juncture are again represented as temptations of the visible Tempter, the Arch-enemy Māra.—Alabaster 'Wheel of the Law,' p. 140.

spect of faithful followers, his disciples forsook him, and went away to Benāres. To them it was an axiom that mental conquest lay through bodily suppression. In giving up his penance he had to give up also their esteem; and in his sore distress they left him to bear, alone, the bitterness of failure.

There now ensued a second struggle in Gautama's mind, described in both the southern and the northern accounts with all the wealth of poetic imagery of which the Indian mind is master. The crisis culminated on a day each event of which is surrounded in the Buddhist lives of their revered Teacher with the wildest legends, in which the very thoughts passing through the mind of Gautama appear in gorgeous descriptions as angels of darkness or of light. Unable to express the struggles of his soul in any other way, they represent him as sitting sublime, calm, and serene during violent attacks made upon him by a visible Tempter and his wicked angels, armed by all kinds of weapons; the greatness of the temptation being shadowed forth by the horrors of the convulsion of the powers of Nature. 'When the conflict began between the Saviour of the world and the Prince of Evil a thousand appalling meteors fell; clouds and darkness prevailed. Even this earth, with the oceans and mountains it contains, though it is unconscious, quaked like a conscious being—like a fond bride when forcibly torn from her bridegroom—like the festoons of a vine shaking under the blasts of a whirlwind. The ocean rose under the vibration of this earthquake; rivers flowed back towards their sources; peaks of lofty mountains, where countless trees had grown for ages, rolled crumbling to the earth; a fierce storm howled all around; the roar of the concussion became terrific; the very sun enveloped itself in awful darkness, and a host of headless spirits filled the air.'[1]

It may be questioned how far the later Buddhists have been able to realise the spiritual truth hidden under these material images; most of them have doubtless believed in a real material combat, and a

[1] Madhurattha Vilāsinī apud Turnour, J. B. A. S., vii. 812, 813; with which may be compared several passages of Milton's 'Paradise Regained,' though the Christian poet, as might be expected, uses much simpler images:—

. . . . And either tropic now
'Gan thunder, and both ends of heaven; the clouds
From many a horrid rift abortive pour'd
Fierce rain with lightning mix'd, water with fire
In ruin reconciled: nor slept the winds
Within their stony caves, but rush'd abroad
From the four hinges of the world, and fell
On the vex'd wilderness; whose tallest pines
Tho' rooted deep as high, and sturdiest oaks,
Bow'd their stiff necks, loaden with stormy blasts
Or torn up sheer. Ill wast thou shrouded then,
O patient Son of God, yet stood'st alone
Unshaken! nor yet staid the terror there;
Infernal ghosts and hellish furies round
Environ'd thee; some howl'd, some yell'd, some shriek'd,
Some bent at thee their fiery darts, while thou
Sat'st unappall'd in calm and sinless peace!

Par. Reg., bk. iv.

A curious point of resemblance between Milton and the Buddhist poets is, that the former makes 'Paradise' to have been 'regained' not on Calvary, but in the Wilderness; just as the Buddhists regard Gautama's mental struggle under the Bo-tree as the most important event in his career, and the act by which he regained salvation for mankind. Hence the Buddhists look upon the Bo-tree as most Christians have looked upon the Cross.

real material earthquake. But it is not in India alone that the attempt to compress ideas about the immaterial into words drawn from tangible things has failed, and has produced expressions which have hardened into false and inconsistent creeds. To us, now, these legends may appear childish or absurd, but they are not without a beauty of their own; and they have still a depth of meaning to those who strive to read between the lines of these, the first half-inarticulate efforts the Indian mind had made to describe the feelings of a strong man torn by contending passions. Comparing the different accounts of the events of that decisive day in the light of the past and future history of Gautama, the meaning sought to be conveyed by the exuberant imagery of the Buddhist writers seems, in its principal features, unmistakable.

Disenchanted and dissatisfied, Gautama had given up all that most men value, to seek peace in secluded study and self-denial. Failing to attain this object while learning the wisdom of others, and living the simple life of a student, he had devoted himself to that intense meditation and penance which all philosophers then said would raise men above the gods. Still unsatisfied, longing always for a certainty that seemed ever just beyond his grasp, he had added vigil to vigil, and penance to penance, until,—when to the wondering view of others, he had become more than a saint,—his indomitable resolution and faith had together suddenly and completely broken down. Then, when sympathy would have been most welcome, he found his friends falling away, and his disciples leaving him. Soon after, if not on the very day when his followers had gone, he wandered out towards the banks of the Nairanjara, receiving his morning meal from the hands of Sujātā, the daughter of a neighbouring villager, and sat himself down to eat it under the shade of a large tree (a *ficus religiosa*), to be known from that day as the sacred Bo-tree, or tree of wisdom.[1] There he remained through the long hours of that day, debating with himself what next to do. The philosophy he had trusted in seemed to be doubtful; the penance he had practised so long had brought no certainty, no peace; and all his old temptations came back upon him with renewed force. For years he had looked at all earthly good as vanity, worthless and transitory. Nay, more, he had thought that it contained within itself the seeds of evil, and must inevitably, sooner or later, bring forth its bitter fruit. But now to his wavering faith the sweet delights of home and love, the charms of wealth and power, began to show themselves in a different light, and to glow again with attractive colours. They were within his reach, he knew he would be welcomed back, and yet,—would there even then be satisfaction? Were all his labours to be

[1] This tree came to occupy much the same position among Buddhists as the cross among Christians. Worship was actually paid to it, and an offshoot from it is still growing on the spot where the Buddhist pilgrims found it, and where they believed the original tree had grown in the ancient temple at Bodh Gāyā, near Rajgir, built about 500 A.D., by the celebrated Amara Sinha. A branch of it planted at Anurādhapura in Ceylon, in the middle of the third century B.C., is still growing there—*the oldest historical tree in the world.* See below p. 237; and for plans and history of the temple of the Bo-tree at Bodh Gāyā, Cunningham's 'Archæological Reports,' vol. i. pp. 6 *et seq.*

lost? Was there *no* sure ground to stand on? Thus he agonised in his doubt from the early morning until sunset. But as the day ended the religious side of his nature had won the victory; his doubts had cleared away; he had become Buddha, that is, enlightened; he had grasped, as it seemed to him, the solution of the great mystery of sorrow, and had learnt at once its causes and its cure. He seemed to have gained the haven of peace, and *in the power over the human heart of inward culture, and of love to others*, to rest at last on a certitude that could never be shaken.

But his victory had not been won without a loss. The works of penance and self-mortification he had so long and so resolutely carried out had been tried in the fire and found wanting; from that day he not only claimed no merit on account of them, but took every opportunity of declaring that from such penances no advantage at all could be derived,—a renunciation greater, probably, to one in his position, than that which the Buddhists call the 'Great Renunciation.'

Gautama had now arrived at those conclusions regarding the nature of man, and of the world around him, at that psychological and moral system to which he in the main adhered during his long career. But, as before the apparent simplicity and power of this new system the efficacy of sacrifice and penance seemed to him to fade away into nothingness, so did Gautama feel more and more intensely the immensity of the distance which separated him from the beliefs of those about him. That feeling of utter loneliness which is often the lot of the leaders of men, especially in moments of high exaltation and insight, broke upon him with such force that it seemed to him impossible to go to his fellow-countrymen with a doctrine to them necessarily so strange, so even incomprehensible. How could men subject to the same temptations as those whose power he had just so keenly experienced, but without that earnestness and insight which he felt himself to possess,—how could such men grasp the reality of truths so fundamental and so far-reaching in fact, but so simple and so powerless in appearance, as those of his system of salvation—salvation merely by self-control and love, without any of the rites, any of the ceremonies, any of the charms, any of the priestly powers, any of the gods, in which men love to trust?

That such a thought should, under the circumstances, have occurred to him, is so very natural, that we need not be surprised at the account of his hesitation as given in the books. And the reason which they assign as the motive for his final determination is worthy of notice: it is said to have been love and pity for humanity,—the thought of mankind, otherwise, as it seemed to him, utterly doomed and lost,—which made Gautama resolve, at whatever hazard, to proclaim his doctrine to the world. To the pious Buddhist it is a constant source of joy and gratitude that 'the Buddha,' not then only, but in many former births, when emancipation from all the cares and troubles of life was already within his reach, should again and again, in mere love for man, have condescended to enter the world, and live amidst the sorrows inseparable from finite existence. To those who look upon Gautama in a less mystic light, as a man of mixed motives and desires, it will suggest itself that other considerations of a less lofty kind must have tended, half-unconsciously perhaps, in the same direction. For silence would be taken as a confession of failure; and, even apart from what had happened, there is always a sweetness in declaring the unknown, or being the bearer of good news. It is at least certain that Gautama, like Muhammad, had an intense belief in himself; a confidence that must have been peculiarly strong in that moment of clearness when he had seemed at last to stand face to face with the deep realities or rather unrealities of life; and his sense of isolation yielded soon before his consciousness of power, and his prophetic zeal.

At first, it is said, he intended to address himself to his old teachers, Alāra and Udraka, but finding that they were dead, he walked straight to Benāres, where his former disciples were then living. On the way he meets with an acquaintance named Upaka, and from him receives his first rebuff. The account of the conversation is only preserved to us in one of the less authentic biographies,[1] but is so striking that it is deserving of notice. The Brāhman surprised at Gautama's expression and carriage, asks him, 'Whence comes it that thy form is so perfect, thy countenance so lovely, thy appearance so peaceful? What system of religion is it that imparts to thee such joy and such peace?'

To this question Gautama replies, in verse, that he has overcome all worldly influences and ignorance, and sin, and desire.

Then the Brāhman asks whither he is going; and on hearing he was going to Benāres, asks him for

[1] In Beal's 'Romantic Legend,' from the Chinese, p. 245.

what purpose; to this the 'World-honoured' replies in the following verses:—

'I now desire to turn the wheel of the excellent Law.
For this purpose I am going to that city of Benāres
To give Light to those enshrouded in darkness,
And to open the gate of Immortality to men.'

To further questioning he then informs Upaka that having completely conquered all evil passion, and for ever got rid of the remnants of personal being, he desires by the light of his religious system to dispense light to all, even as a lamp enlightens all in the house.

On this the Brāhman, unable apparently to brook any longer such high-flown pretensions, says curtly, 'Venerable Gautama, your way lies yonder,' and turns away himself in the opposite direction.

Unfortunately we have not this episode in the Pāli, the Jātaka commentary merely mentioning that Gautama on his way to Benāres met Upaka, and announced to him his having become a Buddha;[1] and the account in Bigandet is very short.[2] But turning the wheel of the excellent Law means, I think, 'To found a kingdom of righteousness'; and the expression 'to open the gate of Immortality to men' being quite unbuddhistic, has probably arisen from a misunderstanding of the word *amata*, ambrosia, or nectar. This is a name applied to Nirvāna as being the heavenly drink of the wise (who are above the gods); it never means immortality, and could not grammatically have that sense. So that the striking parallel between the Chinese verses and 2 Tim. i. 10, falls to the ground.[3]

[1] Jātaka, 81, 24. [2] Life or Legend of Gautama, 108.
[3] Compare on turning the wheel below, p. 45, on 'Amata,' p. 111.

Nothing daunted, the new prophet goes on to Benāres, and in the cool of the evening enters the Deer-park, about three miles north of the city, where his five former disciples were then living.[1] They, seeing him coming, resolve not to recognize as a master one who has broken his vows, and to address him simply by his name; but, on the other hand, as he was of high caste descent, to offer him a mat to sit down upon. They respect him still, but a strong sense of duty prevents their receiving again as an authoritative teacher one whom they are forced to regard as fallen from orthodoxy. One of them only, the aged Kondanya, held aloof from this design; but Gautama noticed the change of manner in the others, and told them they were wrong to call him 'Venerable Gautama,' that they were still in the way of death where they must reap sorrow and disappointment, whereas he had found the way of salvation, which had so long remained hidden; and having become a Buddha, could show them also how to escape from the evils of life. They object, naturally enough, from a Hindu ascetic point of view, that he had failed before when he kept his body under, and how can his mind

[1] This place, now called Dhamek, was held by the Buddhists only less sacred than that where the holy Bo-tree grew. Asoka, in the third century B.C., built a memorial tower there, which was seen by the Chinese pilgrims, and the remains of which, and of numerous later buildings, still exist. A great deal has been written on the discoveries at Dhamek, the fullest description, with plans, facsimiles of the inscriptions, &c., being by General Cunningham, 'Archæological Reports,' 1862, vol. i. pp. 103–130. See also chapter xviii. of the Rev. M. A. Sherring's 'Sacred City of the Hindus,' pp. 230 *et seq.*

have won the victory now when he serves and yields to his body? Gautama replied by explaining the fundamental truths of his system, an exposition preserved in the *Dhammacakka-ppavattana Sutta*, the Sūtra of the Foundation of the Kingdom of Righteousness.

This expression is usually translated 'Turning the wheel of the Law,' which, while retaining the Buddhist figure of speech, fails to represent the idea the figure was meant to convey; the rendering in the text gives up the figure in order to retain the underlying meaning. The '*cakra*' (Pāli *cakka*) is no ordinary wheel; it is the sign of dominion; and a '*cakravarti*' is 'he who makes the wheels of his chariot roll unopposed over all the world'[1]—a universal monarch. *Dharma* (Pāli Dhamma) is not law, but that which underlies and includes the law,—a word often most difficult to translate, and best rendered here by truth or righteousness; whereas the word 'law' suggests ceremonial observances, outward rules, which it was precisely the object of Gautama's teaching to do away with. *Pravartana* (Pāli ppavattana) is 'setting in motion onwards,' the commencement of an action which is to continue. The whole phrase means, therefore, 'To set rolling the royal chariot-wheel of a universal empire of truth and righteousness'; but this would sound more grandiloquent to us than the original words can have done in the ears of Buddhists, to whom the allusion to the chakra was familiar through its connection with ancient Hindu mythology. As we cannot, therefore, make use of this figure without adding explanatory words which spoil its

[1] Böhtlingk-Roth in their Sanskrit Dictionary.

simplicity, it is necessary to choose another; and the one used above is at once exact and appropriate.

This Sūtra has been translated by Mr. Gogerly, and the latter accounts are poetical versions of the ancient tradition. The angels throng to hear the discourse until all the heavens are empty; and the sound of their approach is like the noise of a storm, till at the blast of the archangel's trumpet they become as still as a waveless sea. All nature is moved; the everlasting hills, on which the world is built, leap for joy, and bow themselves before the Teacher; while the powers of the air dispose all things as is most meet; gentle breezes sigh, and delicious flowers fill the air with their scent. 'The evening was like a lovely maiden; the stars were the pearls upon her neck, the dark clouds her braided hair, the deepening space her flowing robe. As a crown she had the heavens where the angels dwell; these three worlds were as her body; her eyes were the white lotus flowers, which open to the rising moon; and her voice was, as it were, the humming of the bees. To worship the Buddha, and hear the first preaching of the word, this lovely maiden came.' When Gautama spoke, though he spoke in Pāli, each one of the assembled hosts thought himself addressed in his own language, and so thought the different kinds of animals, great and small.[1] Only the Chinese life and

[1] Chiefly from the Sinhalese. Hardy, 'Manual of Buddhism,' 186. Compare Beal, 'Romantic Legend,' 244–254; Gya Tcher Rol Pa., ch. 26; Bigandet, p. 111; Jātaka, pp. 81, 82; Gogerly, 'Journal of the Ceylon Asiatic Society,' 1845, p. 24: 1865, pp. 118–122.

the Lalita Vistara gave any lengthened account of what was actually said, and they differ almost entirely, as might be expected, in the miraculous and poetical details; but they agree on the whole, as to the course of Gautama's argument, with the summary in two lines given by Spence Hardy, and with the account given by Gogerly from the Pitakas.

The discourse laid stress on the necessity of adhering to the 'Middle Path'; that is to say, in being free, on the one hand, from "devotion to the enervating pleasures of sense which are degrading, vulgar, sensual, vain, and profitless"; and on the other, from any trust in the efficacy of the mortifications practised by Hindu ascetics, "which are painful, vain, and useless."[1] This Middle Path was summed up in eight principles or parts (*angas*)[2] found in all schools of Buddhism:—

1. Right Belief.
2. Right Feelings.
3. Right Speech.
4. Right Actions.
5. Right Means of Livelihood.
6. Right Endeavour.
7. Right Memory.
8. Right Meditation.

The necessity of adhering to this 'path,' this middle course of a virtuous life, resulted from four

[1] The claim to be in the Middle Path, inferring or suggesting that all others are at one of two *extremes*, is a very common one; and among religious teachers naturally assumes the form of the belief that one's own sect alone is defending the centre of Truth against Superstition on the one side, and Worldliness or Infidelity on the other. The figure was a favourite one also with Gautama, and he uses it again (*teste* the Sanyutta Nikāya, as quoted by Gogerly, J. C. A. S., 1867, 125), when describing his view of Karma.

[2] See Gogerly, J. C. A. S., 1845, p. 24; Foucaux, 'Lalita Vistara,' 293; Burnouf, 'Lotus de la Bonne Loi,' 519.

fundamental truths, called 'the four Noble Truths,' as the path is called 'the Noble Eightfold Path.' The four truths are, Suffering, the Cause of suffering, the Cessation of suffering, the Path which leads to the cessation of suffering.

1. *Suffering or sorrow.* Birth causes sorrow; growth, decay, illness, death, all cause sorrow; separation from objects we love, hating what cannot be avoided, and craving for what cannot be obtained, cause sorrow; briefly, such states of mind as co-exist with the consciousness of individuality, with the sense of separate existence, are states of suffering and sorrow.

2. *The cause of suffering.* The action of the outside world on the senses excites a craving thirst for something to satisfy them, or a delight in the objects presenting themselves, either of which is accompanied by a lust of life. These are the causes of sorrow.

3. *The cessation of sorrow.* The complete conquest over and destruction of this eager thirst, this lust of life, is that by which sorrow ceases.

4. *The path leading to the cessation of sorrow* is the Noble Eightfold Path briefly summed up in the above description of a virtuous life.[1]

Lastly, the Buddha declared that he had arrived at these convictions, not by study of the Vedas, nor from the teachings of others, but by the light of reason and intuition alone.

It will be difficult for the reader to realize all the

[1] See below p. 108 for the different stages of this 'path.' For the Four Truths, compare 'Lalita Vistara,' Foucaux, p. 392, with the Vinaya Pitaka; Gogerly, J. C. A. S., 1845, 24, 25. All other accounts are derived from these. See also below, p. 106.

meaning that is carefully condensed into these short phrases; and, on the other hand, to avoid putting a Christian interpretation on these Buddhist expressions; but they will be further considered later on, and to attempt to deal with them now would interrupt too much the course of the narrative. Such classified statements of moral truth seem to us forced and artificial, but it must be remembered that they were addressed to Brāhmans skilled in the dialectics of the time, accustomed to put all their knowledge into short aphorisms to assist their memory, and quite free from that impatience which is so marked a characteristic of our modern modes of thought. To them time was no object, and they would sit under the trees listening with grave politeness, whilst their former teacher, earnest and dignified, laid down the principles of his system; and then doubtless at some length, and not without repetitions, explained and commentated upon them. It may even be open to question whether the completeness of the form and the manner of its presentation would not weigh more with them than the truth of the principles which were thus presented. When we also remember the relation which these men had long borne to him, and that they already held very strongly beliefs nearly allied to those parts of his doctrine that are most repugnant to us—the pessimist view of life, and the doctrine of transmigration—it is not difficult to believe that his persuasions were successful, and that, after a time of hesitation, his old disciples were the first to acknowledge Gautama in his new character. It was the aged Kondanya, ready for his release from life, who first openly gave in his adhesion; but the others also, after many talks with the Buddha, sometimes separately, sometimes together, soon accepted in its entirety his plan of salvation.[1]

[1] Hardy, 'Manual,' 187; and Turnour, J. B. A. S., vii. 815, only mention here the conversion of Kondanya, which all the accounts put first. Foucaux, p. 396, and Bigandet, 1st edit., p. 97, convert the other four on the same day; the Jātaka, p. 82, on the four subsequent days; and Beal 'Catena,' 134, during the succeeding three months. Beal 'Rom. Leg.,' 255, is doubtful, but allows some interval. Comp. also p. 186 below.

APPENDIX TO CHAPTER II.

GAUTAMA'S WIFE AND RELATIONS.

GAUTAMA is said to have been related to his wife and to several of his principal disciples in the manner appearing in the following table. It is taken chiefly from the 'Mahāvansa,' p. 9, where, after tracing the descent of Jayasena from the mythical first king among men, the author gives the list [on p. 52] of the immediate ancestors of Gautama and Yasodharā.[1]

The Southern Buddhists agree in stating that Gautama had only one wife; they give her different names, but mean the same person. She is called Yasodharā by Bigandet (24, 34, 124); and the same by Spence Hardy, who adds that she was the daughter of Suprabuddha (Manual of Buddhism, 146, 152, 206); but she is usually called simply Rāhula-mātā, the mother of Rāhula, in the oldest authorities (Jātaka, 54, 6; 58, 18; 90, 24; Turnour, J. B. A. S. vii. 804). The name of Buddhakaçana given by Turnour (loc. cit. 816), is a mere mistake for Subhadrakañcanā, and is there stated to be the same as Yasodharā.

[1] On the general question of the value of these genealogies, compare Sénart, 357, 369, 511; Köppen, 'Religion des Buddha,' 1, 76; Lassen, 'Ind. Alterth.,' vol. ii. app. ii.

The Chinese life gives three wives, Yasodharā (the mother of Rāhula), Gotamī, and Manoharā.[1] The Chinese editor significantly adds concerning the last, 'Some Doctors of the Law say that the attendants on Manoharā only knew her name, but never saw her presence,' and this evidently mythical person is never mentioned elsewhere. Gotamī is the name used only in one story (Beal, p. 96), which does not occur in any other authority, and the epithet would be applicable of course to every member of the Gautama clan, as Prajāpatī, for instance, is also called Gotamī. Gotamī is made the daughter of Daṇḍapāṇī, whilst Yasodharā, the only wife who appears throughout the book, is made the daughter of Mahānāma.

The Lalita Vistara speaks only of one wife Gopā, the daughter of Daṇḍapāṇī, and relates of her the stories which are related elsewhere of Yasodharā; but Foucaux in a note to p. 152, says that Gautama had three other wives, Yasodharā, Mrigajā or Gopā, and Utpalavarṇā. Of the last, he gives one detail which identifies her with Yasodharā, namely, that she and Prajāpati were the first Buddhist nuns.

Finally, Alexander Csoma, the great authority on Tibetan Buddhism, mentions three wives, and names them Gopā, Yasodharā, and Utpala Varnā,[2] but states elsewhere[3] that the first two are the same; and in another place that the name of the third is Mrigajā.[4]

All this seems to be explicable on a very natural hypothesis. The oldest accounts agree in giving to Gautama only one wife, whom they call 'the mother of Rāhula.' As the legends grew she was surrounded with every virtue and grace, and was spoken of as the Lotus-coloured, the Attractive, the Illustrious, and so on. Still later, these epithets were supposed to refer to different individuals; but the curious confusions in the Northern accounts in which they are mentioned, show that they can be traced back to the one wife of the older story.

---

[1] Beal's 'Romantic Legend,' p. 101, where the word is spelt Manodara, but explained 'who seizes the mind,' for which the Sanskrit can only be as given above.

[2] Asiatic 'Researches,' xx. p. 308, n. 21.

[3] 'Tibetan Grammar,' p. 162, note.

[4] 'As. Res.' xx. 290.

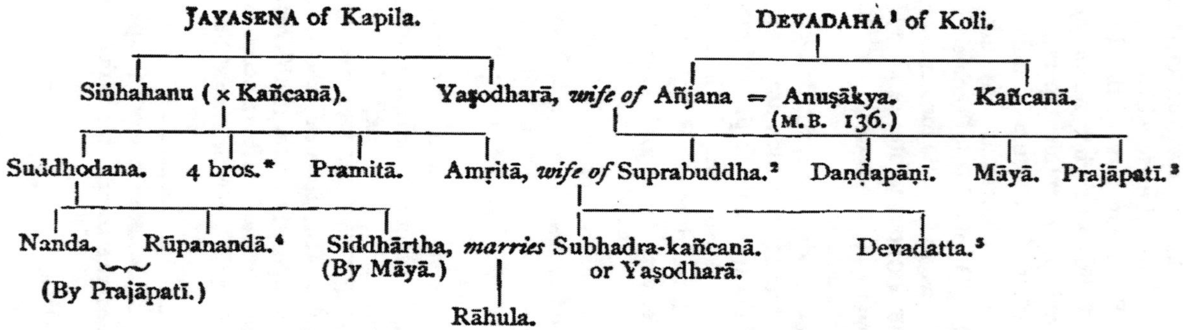

* 1. Ṣuklodana, whose sons were Devadatta and Ānanda.
2. Amṛitodana ,, Mahānāma and Anuruddha[6].
3. Dhotodana ,, Pho so and Pa thi[7].
4. Ghanitodana, only mentioned by name in the Mahāvansa Tīkā.

---

[1] This is also a name of the town of Koli. Hardy's 'Manual of Buddhism,' p. 136. Beal's 'Romantic Legend,' p. 47. Jātaka, 52, 10. Mahāvansa, loc. cit.: but Bigandet (pp. 20, 24,) calls it simply Dewah, and Schiefner (p. 7) restores it to Devadishṭā.

[2] The Northerns and Hardy in one place (p. 134), put Suprabuddha in the place of Anjana, and Daṇḍapāni in the place of Supra-buddha.

[3] She is also called Gotamī by the Northerns. Beal, R. L., p. 126. Foucaux, 'Gya Tcher Rol Pa,' p. 152 n. Burnouf, 'Lotus de la Bonne Loi,' 164, and in the Amāwatura in Hardy, p. 306. Compare Sénart, p. 339.

[4] Fausböll's 'Dhamma-pada,' p. 313.

[5] See also 'Manual of Buddhism,' p. 231. Yasa is called son of Suprabuddha, and Tishya son of Amita, by Beal, pp. 258 and 64.

[6] Hardy's 'Manual of Buddhism,' 227, gives Amritodana's wife's name as Sanda, and his daughter's as Rohini. Comp. Big. 173.

[7] These are the names given by Rémusat (Foe Koue Ki, p. 203). Beal, p. 64, calls Suklodana's sons, Bhatrika and Nandaka, and Anuruddha Aniruddha, and even at p. 379, Maniruddha. Compare Big. 174.

CHAPTER III.

LIFE OF GAUTAMA FROM THE COMMENCEMENT OF HIS PUBLIC MINISTRY TILL HIS DEATH.

GAUTAMA now remained for some time in the Migadaya wood,[1] teaching his new doctrines, quietly it is true and only to those who came to him, but in a manner which shows us at once how great was the gulf which divided him from the professional teachers of the time.[2] His was no mere scholastic system, involved like those of the Brāhmans in a mysterious obscurity; and even in that half-incomprehensible form offered to the consideration of only a few selected adepts. He joined to his gifts as a thinker a prophetic ardour and missionary zeal, which prompted him to popularize

[1] Gen. Cunningham, 'Arch. Reports,' I. p. 107, says, 'The Mrigadāwa' or "Deer Park," is represented by a fine wood, which still covers an area of about half a mile, and extends from the great tower of Dhamek on the north, to the Chaukundi mound on the south.'

[2] It may be interesting to notice how many of the modern leaders of metaphysical thought have similarly been private, non-professional men; the names, among others, of Spinoza, Descartes, Berkeley, Hobbes, Locke, Comte, Mill, and Spencer, will at once suggest themselves. It is true that among the professional men in Germany and Scotland there are many great names, but Leibnitz, Hume, and Schopenhauer are striking exceptions.

his doctrine, and to preach to all without exception, men and women, high and low, ignorant and learned alike.[1] Thus all of his first disciples were laymen, and two of the very first were women. The first convert was a rich young man named Yasa, who joined the small company of personal followers; the next were Yasa's father, mother, and wife, who, however, remained lay disciples. It was not till some time afterwards that Gautama established an order of female mendicants, the evils inseparable from which he estimated as very great; and though he held the life of a mendicant to be necessary to rapid progress towards deliverance from that 'thirst' which was the cause of all evil, yet he highly honoured the believing householder. A lay disciple, though not yet able or willing to cast off the ties of home or of business, might yet 'enter the paths,'[2] and, by a life of rectitude and kindness, ensure for himself in a future existence more favourable conditions for his growth in holiness. There is no magic in any outward act; every one's salvation consists of and depends entirely on a modification and growth in his own inner nature, to be brought about by his own self-control and diligence, and thus the earnest layman will advance further in 'the paths' than the mendicant who is wanting in self-control and energy. The subject will be further discussed below when we come to

[1] See on this point the admirable remarks of Bishop Bigandet, note 63, p. 117, which have suggested some of the above. Some of the details of Yasa's conversion (Hardy, 'Manual,' p. 187; Bigandet, 112–119, 2nd ed.; Beal, 'Romantic Leg.,' 258, 266) are evidently borrowed from the story of Gautama's own conversion.

[2] See below, pp. 108, 148.

treat more fully of the 'paths': it is sufficient to state here that Gautama's whole teaching resolved itself into a system of intellectual and moral self-culture, and that the fruitless cares and empty hopes of ordinary life were considered incompatible with the highest degree of this self-culture, while they would become distasteful to those who had reached in it even a lower stage.

Five months after the crisis under the Bo-tree, and three months after Gautama's arrival at the Migadāya wood, he called together all his disciples, who are represented to have numbered already sixty persons, and sent them in different directions to preach and teach, Yasa only remaining at Benāres, near his parents.[1]

The Burmese account puts on this occasion the following curious speech into Gautama's mouth:—'Beloved Rahans, I am free from the five great passions which, like an immense net, encompass men and *nats*[2]; you too, owing to the instructions you have received from me, enjoy the same glorious privilege. There is now incumbent on us a great duty, that of labouring effectually on behalf of men and *nats*, and procuring to them the invaluable blessing of the deliverance. To the end of securing more effectually the success of such an undertaking, let us part with each other and proceed in various and opposite directions, so that not two of us should follow up the same way. Go ye now, and preach the most excellent Law, expounding every point thereof,

[1] Jātaka, 82; Hardy, 'Manual,' 188; Bigandet, 122; Beal, 'Rom. Leg.,' 268.

[2] *i.e.* Angels.

and unfolding it with care and attention in all its bearings and particulars. Explain the beginning, the middle, and the end of the law, to all men without exception: let everything respecting it be made publicly known and brought to the broad daylight. Show, now, to men and nats the way leading to the practice of pure and meritorious works. You will meet, doubtless, with a great number of mortals not as yet hopelessly given up to their passions, and who will avail themselves of your preaching for re-conquering their hitherto forfeited liberty, and freeing themselves from the thraldom of passions. For my part, I will direct my course to the village of Sena, situate in the vicinity of the solitude of Uruwela.'

I have retained the quaint phraseology of Bishop Bigandet's translation, which will well represent the quaintness of the original. Rahans are mendicants, the five passions I presume to be those arising from the five senses; nats are angels; the most excellent Law is, doubtless, the Dharma, the Buddhist religion. Of course, these cannot have been the actual words spoken by Gautama. He cannot have thought his followers already perfect, and, whatever his opinions about supernatural beings (an interesting question we cannot here discuss), it is at least certain that they were inconsistent with the expressions put into his mouth. To the Burmese author they would seem quite natural, but whence did he derive the idea of the duty of proclaiming to all men alike the whole of 'the most excellent law,' living as he did in a country where the missionary spirit had long died out?[1] Not,

[1] Bigandet, p. 225, note.

certainly, from Hinduism; nor is any other source conceivable except a genuine survival of the spirit of early Buddhism.

Throughout his career, Gautama was in the habit of travelling about during most of the fine part of the year, teaching and preaching to the people; but during the four rainy months, from June to October, he remained in one place, devoting himself more particularly to the instruction of his declared followers. This custom has survived down to the present day in the Southern Church; but in a form which is a curious instance of the way in which the letter of such religious ordinances can be observed, and turned to real use, long after the reason of their original institution has ceased to operate. The wandering mendicants have become settled celibate parochial clergy; but every year, during those months which were the rainy season in Magadha in the time of Gautama, they leave their permanent homes; and, living in temporary huts, put up by the peasantry of some district who specially invite them, hold a series of public services, in which they read and explain the three Pitakas to all of any age or sex or caste who choose to listen. This period, called *was* (from the Sanskrit *varsha*, rain), is in Ceylon the finest part of the year; and as there are no regular religious services at any other time, the peasantry celebrate the reading of *bana* (or the Word) at *was* time as their great religious festival. They put up under the palm-trees a platform, roofed, but quite open at the sides, and ornamented with bright cloths and flowers; and round it they sit in the moonlight on the ground, and listen through the night with great satisfaction, if not with great intelligence, to the sacred words repeated by relays of shaven monks. The greatest favourite at these readings of *bana* is the 'Jātaka' book, which contains so many of the old fables and stories common to the Aryan peoples, sanctified now, and preserved by the leading hero in each, whether man, or fairy, or animal, being looked upon as an incarnation of the Buddha in one of his previous births. To these wonderful stories the simple peasantry, dressed in their best and brightest, listen all the night long with unaffected delight; chatting pleasantly now and again with their neighbours; and indulging all the while in the mild narcotic of the betal leaf, their stores of which (and of its never failing adjuncts, chunam, that is, white lime, and the areka nut), afford a constant occasion for acts of polite good fellowship. The first spirit of Buddhism may have passed away as completely as the old reason for *was*; neither hearers nor preachers may have that deep sense of evil in the world and in themselves, nor that high resolve to battle with and overcome it, which animated some of the early Buddhists; and they all think themselves to be earning 'merit' by their easy service. But there is at least at these festivals a genuine feeling of human kindness, in harmony alike with the teachings of Gautama, and with the gentle beauty of those moonlight scenes.[1]

The importance afterwards attached to the accession of Gautama's next convert is shown by the number of miraculous events which are said to have preceded it. Of these, the only possible historical

[1] Bigandet, p. 127; Hardy 'Manual,' 101; 'Eastern Monachism,' 232–237.

basis is that in the solitudes of Uruwela there were then three brothers named Kāṣyapa, fire worshippers and hermit philosophers, whose high reputation as teachers had attracted a considerable number of scholars; and that after Gautama had remained some time among them, the elder brother adopted his system, and at once took a principal place in the small body of believers. His brothers and their scholars followed his example, and the first set discourse preached by Gautama to his new disciples is preserved in the Pitakas under the title Āditta-pariyāya Sutta (Sermon on the Lessons to be drawn from Burning).

This Sutta affords an excellent example of the method so often adopted by Gautama of inculcating his new doctrines by putting a new meaning into the religious ceremonies of the time, or into the common occurrences of life. The new disciples, who had been worshippers of Agni, the sacred fire, were seated with Gautama on the Elephant Rock, near Gāyā, with the beautiful valley of Rājagriha stretched out before them, when a fire broke out in the jungle on the opposite hill.[1] Taking the fire as his text, the Teacher declared that so long as men remained in ignorance they were, as it were, consumed by a fire—by the excitement produced within them by the action of external things. These things acted upon them through the five senses and the heart (which Gautama regarded as a sixth organ of sense). The eye, for instance, perceives objects: from this

[1] For the site of the Elephant Rock, see Gandhahasti, at the foot of Map, Pl. iii., Cunningham's 'Archæological Reports,' vol. 1. On the sentiment comp. below, p. 155.

perception arises an inward sensation, producing pleasure or pain. Sensations produce this misery and joy, because they supply fuel as it were to the inward fires, concupiscence, anger, and ignorance, and the anxieties of birth, decay, and death. The same was declared to be the case with the sensations produced by each of the other senses. But those who follow the Buddha's scheme of inward self-control,—the four stages of the Path whose gate is purity and whose goal is love,—have become wise; the sensations from without no longer give fuel to the inward fire, since the fires of concupiscence, &c., have ceased to burn [1]; true disciples are thus free from that craving thirst which is the origin of evil; the wisdom they have acquired will lead them on, sooner or later, to perfection; they are delivered from the miseries which would result from another birth; and even in this birth they no longer need the guidance of such laws as those of caste and ceremonies and sacrifice, for they have already reached far beyond them!

One may well pause and wonder at finding such a sermon preached so early in the history of the world, —more than 400 years before the rise of Christianity,—and among a people who have long been thought peculiarly idolatrous and sensual; a sermon remarkable enough for what it says, but still more remarkable for what it leaves unsaid. Its meaning is perhaps scarcely clear without a knowledge of the

[1] In a passage from Jina Alankāra, given by Burnouf (Lotus, 332), the Buddha is described as 'that great man who, unaided, works out salvation for all the world; and extinguishes by the rainfall of the nectar of his teaching, the fires of passion, and sin, and error; of birth, old age, disease, and death; of pain, lamentation, grief, disappointment, and despair.'

'paths,' and of the 'senses,' but to explain them here would detain us too long, and the general spirit which it breathes is sufficiently unmistakable.

From Gāyā, Gautama and his new disciples walked on towards Rājagriha, then the capital of Bimbisāra, the most powerful chieftain in the eastern valley of the Ganges, whose kingdom of Magadha extended about 100 miles south from the river Ganges, and 100 miles east from the river Sona. Both Gautama and Kāṣyapa were well known in the town, and when the rāja came out to welcome the teachers, the crowd was uncertain which was the master and which the disciple. Gautama therefore asked Kāṣyapa why he had given up sacrificing to Agni. The latter saw the motive of the question, and replied that, while some took pleasure in sights and sounds and taste and sensual love, and others in sacrifice, he had perceived that all these alike were worthless, and had given up sacrifices whether great or small. Nirvāna was a state of peace unattainable by men under the guidance of sense and passion; a rest destructive of transmigration, birth, decay, and death: a happy state to be reached by inward growth alone.[1] Gautama is then said to have told the people a Jātaka story about Kāṣyapa's virtue in a former birth; and seeing how impressed they were, to have gone on to explain to them the four Noble Truths. At the end of this sermon the rāja professed himself an adherent of the new system; and the next day all the people in the place, excited by the conversion of Kāṣyapa and

[1] For the story of the conversion of Kāṣyapa, see Jātaka, p. 82; Bigandeṭ, 130–144; Beal, 'Romantic Legend,' 292–304; Hardy, 'Manual,' 185–191. Bigandet's note is especially valuable

Bimbisāra, crowded to the Yashṭivana grove, where Gautama had rested, to see him and hear what new thing he had to say; and when Gautama went towards midday to the city to the rāja's house to receive his daily meal, he was surrounded by an enthusiastic multitude. The rāja received him with great respect, and, saying that Yashṭivana was too far off, assigned to him as a residence a bamboo grove (*veḷuvana*) close by, which became celebrated as the place where Gautama spent many rainy seasons, and delivered many of his most complete discourses.[1]

There he stayed for two months, and during that time two ascetics, named Ṣāriputra and Moggallāna, afterwards conspicuous leaders in the new crusade, joined the Sangha or Society, as the little company of Buddhist mendicants was called. The high position which Gautama soon after assigned these new disciples created some ill-feeling among the older members of the Sangha, which Gautama, however, allayed by calling together his followers and addressing them at some length on the means requisite for Buddhist salvation, which he summed up in the celebrated verse.

'To cease from all sin,
To get virtue,
To cleanse one's own heart,—
This is the religion of the Buddhas.'

At the same time he laid down the first rules for the

[1] Curiously enough while Yashṭivana has been identified by General Cunningham ('Ancient Geography of India,' p. 461, and map xii.), the site of Veḷuvana has not yet been discovered: it must have occupied about the position where the ancient basements, marked K. K. K. and G. in Cunningham's map of Rājagriha (Pl. xiv. Reports, vol. i.), were found by him. See above, p. 33.

guidance of the society, the simple code being called 'Pātimokkha,' 'that which should be binding,' a word afterwards applied to a book containing a summary of the more complex system of laws, as it had been elaborated at the time of Gautama's death. This meeting of mendicants at which the Society was first, so to speak, incorporated, is known as the 'Sāvaka-sannipāta,' or assembly of the disciples.[1]

The enthusiasm of the people seems to have cooled down as rapidly as it arose, for we hear of no other conversions besides those of Ṣāriputra and Moggallāna, and their pupils; and the members of the society began even to complain to Gautama that, when they went out to beg their daily food, they were received with abuse and ridicule; on the ground that the new teaching would deprive households of their support, and depopulate and ruin the country. This they did not know how to answer, which is not surprising, for the charge was unfortunately true. The Brāhmans, indeed, held celibacy in high honour, but only in youth and old age; and the tāpasas or ascetics, so far from seeking imitators, added such penance to their celibacy as they hoped, rightly enough, would be unattainable by ordinary men; whereas the Buddhists painted in glowing colours the contrast between the miseries of life in the world, and the sweet calm of life in the Order, and wanted every one for his own sake to share at once in their salvation. Gautama's

[1] Jātaka, p. 85; Hardy, M. B., 198; Turnour, J. B. A. S., vii. 816. Hardy says that the verse above quoted (v. 183 of the Dhammapada), 'constitutes the discourse,' called Pātimokkha. Compare my 'Ancient Coins and Measures of Ceylon,' p. 5, and below p. 162.

answer, perhaps the best possible, does not dispute the charge, but simply reasserts that what the people called ruin he called good. He advised his followers to say that the Buddha was only trying to spread righteousness, as former Buddhas had done; that he used no weapons except persuasion; those whom he gained, he gained only by means of the truth, which he proclaimed for the benefit of all.

While the new teacher was laying the foundations of his order, and experiencing first the devotion and then the attacks of the multitude, his relations at Kapilavastu had not remained ignorant of the change in his life; and Suddhodana had sent to him asking him to visit his native city, that his now aged father might see him once more before he died. Gautama, accordingly started for Kapilavastu, and on his arrival there stopped, according to his custom, in a grove outside the town. There his father, uncles, and others came to see him; but the latter at least were by no means pleased with their mendicant clansman; and though it was the custom on such occasions to offer to provide ascetics with their daily food, they all left without having done so. The next day, therefore, Gautama set out, accompanied by his disciples, carrying his bowl to beg for a meal. As he came near the gate of the little town, he hesitated whether he should not go straight to the rāja's residence, but at last he determined to adhere to a rule of the Order, according to which a Buddhist mendicant should beg regularly from house to house. It soon reached the rāja's ears that his son was walking through the streets begging. Startled at such news, he rose up, and holding his outer robe together with his hand went out quickly, and hastening to the place where Gautama was, he said, 'Why, master, do you put us to shame? Why do you go begging for your food? Do you think it is not possible to provide food for so many mendicants?'

'Oh, Mahārāja,' was the reply, 'this is the custom of all our race.'

'But we are descended from an illustrious race of warriors. and not one of them has ever begged his bread.'

'You and your family,' answered Gautama, 'may claim descent from kings; my descent is from the prophets (Buddhas) of old, and they, begging their food, have always lived on alms. But, my father, when a man has found a hidden treasure, it is his duty first to present his father with the most precious of the jewels;' and he accordingly addressed his father on the cardinal tenet of his doctrine, his words being reported in the form of two verses given in the Dhamma-pada: —[1]

'Rise up! and loiter not!
Follow after a holy life!
Who follows virtue rests in bliss,
Both in this world and in the next.
Follow after a holy life!
Follow not after sin!
Who follows virtue rests in bliss,
Both in this world and in the next.'

Suddhodana made no reply to this, but simply taking his son's bowl, led him to his house, where the members of the family and the servants of the house-

[1] Verses 168, 169; and comp. p. 148 below.

hold came to do him honour, but Yasodharā did not come. 'If I am of any value in his eyes, he will himself come,' she had said; 'I can welcome him better here.' Gautama noticed her absence, and attended by two of his disciples, went to the place where she was; first warning his followers not to prevent her, should she try to embrace him, although no member of his Order might touch or be touched by a woman. When she saw him enter, a recluse in yellow robes with shaven head and shaven face, though she knew it would be so, she could not contain herself, and falling on the ground she held him by the feet, and burst into tears. Then remembering the impassable gulf between them, she rose and stood on one side. The rāja thought it necessary to apologize for her, telling Gautama how entirely she had continued to love him, refusing comforts which he denied himself, taking but one meal a day, and sleeping, not on a bed, but on a mat spread on the ground. The different accounts often tell us the thoughts of the Buddha on any particular occasion; here they are silent, stating only that he then told a Jātaka story, showing how great had been her virtue in a former birth. She became an earnest hearer of the new doctrines; and when, sometime afterwards, much against his will, Gautama was induced to establish an order of female mendicants, his widowed wife Yasodharā became one of the first of the Buddhist nuns.[1]

[1] For Gautama's journey to Kapilavastu, and interviews with his father and his wife, compare Jātaka, 87–90, with the commentary on Dhammapada, vv. 168, 169; Bigandet, 156–168; Spence Hardy, 'Manual,' 198–204; and Beal, pp. 360–364.

About a week afterwards, Yasodharā dressed Rāhula, her child and Gautama's, in his best, and told him to go to his father to ask for his inheritance. 'I know of no father, but the rāja,' said the boy, meaning Suddhodana; 'Who is my father?' Yasodharā holding him up to the window, pointed out to him the Buddha, and saying, 'That monk, whose appearance is so glorious, is your father, and he has great wealth, which we have not seen since the day when he left us; go to him and ask for your rights; say, "I am your son, and shall be the head of the clan, and shall want my inheritance. Give it to me."'[1] Rāhula went up to Gautama and said, without fear, and with much affection, 'Father, how happy I am to be near you.' Gautama said nothing, but presently having finished his meal, rose up to go to the Nigrodha grove, where he was staying. Rāhula followed him, asking for his inheritance. The Buddha was still silent, but as he did not stop his son's asking, so neither did his disciples interfere. When they reaced the Nigrodha grove, Gautama thought, 'This wealth that he is seeking from his father perishes in the using, and brings vexation with it: I will give him the sevenfold nobler wealth I acquired under the Bo-tree, and make him the heir of a spiritual inheritance.'[2] Then turning to Ṣāriputra, he told him to admit Rāhula into the Order, which was accordingly done.

[1] If this legend be founded on fact, it would seem to show that Yasodharā was of a grasping disposition, inconsistent with the lofty love for her prophet-husband, with which she is credited in the preceding episode; but the Jātaka there also suggests that she acted from pride, rather than from love.

[2] Jātaka, p. 91, lines 30–33.

When Suddhodana heard of this he was exceeding sorrowful; for Nanda, Gautama's half-brother, had already become a mendicant, so that his two sons were lost to him as far as all earthly hopes were concerned, and now his grandson was taken from him. He therefore went to the Buddha and asked him to establish a rule that no one should in future be admitted to the Order without the consent of his parents. Gautama granted this request, and after some more interviews with his father returned towards Rājagriha.

On his way he stayed for some time at Anūpiya, on the banks of the Anomā, in a mango grove, near the spot where he had sent Channa back on the eventful night of the 'Great Renunciation'; and whilst he was there the society received several important accessions, chiefly from his own clan, or from that of his relatives, the Koliyans. Among these Ānanda, Dewadatta, Upāli, and Anuruddha deserve especial mention. The first became the most intimate friend of his cousin, Gautama, as will especially appear in the account of the teacher's death. The second, also his cousin, became afterwards his rival and opponent, and is accordingly represented as a most wicked and depraved man.[1] The third, Upāli, was a barber by caste and occupation, whose deep religious feeling and great intellectual powers made him afterwards one of

[1] The Chinese account even says that Gautama refused to admit him to the Order, on the ground that his mind was not in a proper condition; telling him first to go home and bestow all his wealth in charity, so as to make himself fit to become a mendicant. Beal, p. 378; but the commentary on the Dhammapada, p. 139, confirms Hardy, p. 231, andBigandet, pp. 174, 175.

the most important leaders in the Order—a striking proof of the reality of the effect produced by Gautama's disregard of the supposed importance of caste. The last, Anuruddha, became the greatest master of Buddhist metaphysics.

After spending his second *was* at Rājagriha with his new disciples, Gautama visited Ṣrāvasti, on the river Rapti, a town about as far N.W. of Benāres as Rājagriha is E. of that place. Ṣrāvasti has been identified without a doubt by General Cuningham with the ruins of Sāhet-Māhet, in Oudh;[1] it was in Gautama's time one of the most important cities in the valley of the Ganges, and the capital of Prasenajit, King of Kosala. Gautama visited this place in acceptance of an invitation given him by a merchant, Anāthapiṇḍika, who had heard his preaching in Rājagriha, and who presented to the society a wood called Jetavana. There Gautama afterwards often resided, and many of the discourses and Jātaka stories are said to have been first spoken there.

The accounts of Buddha's life in the Jātaka commentary and that of the Chinese work translated by Mr. Beal come here to a close. From this time to a few days before his death we have only a few passages in the Pāli commentary on the Dhamma-pada, and certain tales recorded by Bigandet and Spence Hardy, which are probably derived from the above or other commentaries on the different utterances of the Buddha therein related. Those of these stories

[1] Ancient Geography of India, 407 *et seq.*

which can be arranged chronologically refer only to the next seventeen years of Gautama's ministry; the first *was* having been spent in Benāres, the two following at Rājagriha.

In the *4th year* Gautama admits the rope-dancer, Uggasena,[1] to the Order, and then, crossing the Ganges into Wesāli, lives for a time in the Mahāvana grove. Whilst there he hears of a quarrel between the Sākyas and the Koliyans about the water in the boundary river Kohāna, and, flying to Kapilavastu through the air, he reconciles the two clans, and then returns to Mahāvana, and prepares to spend the rainy season there.

5th year. In the middle of *was*, however, he hears of the illness of Suddhodana, and again returns to Kapilavastu, and is present at the death of his father, then ninety-seven years old, at sunrise of Saturday, the full-moon day of the month of August in the year of the Eetzana era, 107.[2] After comforting his relatives, and carrying out the cremation of the body with due ceremony, Gautama returns to the Kūṭāgāra Wihāra at Mahāvana. He is there followed by his father's widow, Prājāpatī, Yasodharā, and other Sākya and Kolyan ladies, who earnestly ask to be allowed to take the vows. He is very unwilling to admit them to the Order, but at last yields to the earnest advocacy of Ānanda, and lays down certain rules for female mendicants. He then retires to the hill Makula, at Kosambī, near Allahabād.

[1] Dhamma-pada, v. 348 is said to have been addressed on this occasion to Uggasena.

[2] Bigandet, p. 197.

6th year. After spending the rainy season at Makula, Gautama returns to Rājagriha, and whilst there admits Kshemā, the wife of Rājā Bimbisārā, to the Order. One of his disciples gaining a *patra*, or alms-bowl, by the display of miraculous powers, the Buddha had the patra broken to pieces, and forbids any miracles; but, on Bimbisāra telling him that the heretics think this arises from fear, he himself works some mighty miracles at Ṣrāvasti, at a place and time appointed; and then goes to heaven to reach the law to his mother, who had died seven days after his birth.[1]

7th year. He descends from heaven at Sankissa, and walks to Ṣrāvasti, to the Jetavana Wihāra. While there the orthodox teachers induce a woman named Chinchā to accuse him of a breach of chastity, but her deceit is exposed.[2]

8th year. The rainy season was spent at the rock Saṅsumāra, near Kapilavastu. Conversion of the father and mother of Nakula, and of the father and mother of Moggali. Gautama returns to Kosambī, near Allahabad.

9th year. Moggali stirs up enmity against Gautama, and Ānanda urges him to go elsewhere, but he refuses. A dissension then breaks out in the Order, and Gautama in vain exhorts the two parties to patience, union, and charity, and then sorrowfully leaves

[1] The Buddha is never said to have descended into hell, but there is a later legend among the northern Buddhists of Avalokiteswara (see p. 205) having done so. Compare Prof. Cowell in the "Journal of Philology," vol. vi. p. 222 *et seq.*

[2] Fausböll's Dhamma-pada, pp. 338–340.

his disciples and goes, alone, to the forest of Pārileyyaka.

10th year. There, in a hut built by the villagers, he spends his 10th rainy season. The refractory mendicants seek him out to ask pardon, are well received, and forgiven; Gautama addressing to them a kind of half-apology (with a sting in it) 'outsiders who knew not the littleness of all things might indeed quarrel, but they should have been wiser. He who has found prudent, sober, and wise companions, may walk happy, if he be considerate; but rather than be with the unwise let him walk alone, without sin, and with few wishes, like the lonely elephant.'[1] With the repentant disciples he returns to Ṣrāvasti, and thence goes on to Magadha.

11th year. In a village near Rājagriha, he converts the Brahman Bhāradwāja by the parable of the sower.[2] After spending the rainy season there, he returns to Kosala to a town called Satiabia.

12th year. Thence he goes to the neighbouring town of Weranja, where he spends the 12th rainy season.[3] After it is over, he undertakes the longest journey he had yet made, penetrating as far as Mantala (to the south?), returning *viâ* Benāres, and Vesāli, to Srāvasti in Kosala, preaching in all the places he visited. On his return he preached the Mahā Rāhula Sutta to his son Rāhula, then eighteen years old.

[1] Comp. Bigandet, 224, with the commentary on Dhammapada, vv. 328–330, and especially p. 105.

[2] The parable is given below, p. 134.

[3] Fausböll's Dhamma-pada, p. 275.

13th year. Gautama then went to Chāliya, where he spent the 13th rainy season, and then returned to Ṣrāvasti.

14th year. In this year Gautama ordained at the Jetavana Wihāra in Ṣrāvasti his son Rāhula, delivering on this occasion the Rāhula Sutta, of which a summary in verse has been translated by Sir Kumāra Swāmi in his Sutta Nipāta. He then travelled to Kapilavastu.

15th year. The 15th season was spent at the Nigrodha grove near that town. Gautama addressed to his cousin Mahānāma, who had succeeded Bhadraka, the successor of Suddhodana, in the headship of the Sākya clan, a discourse summarized by Bigandet (p. 230). Suprabuddha, the rāja of Koli, who was angry with Gautama for deserting his daughter, Yasodharā, curses him publicly, and is shortly afterwards swallowed up by the earth. The Buddha then returned to the Jetavana Wihāra, where he delivered a discourse on the superiority of righteousness (Dharma) to almsgiving in answer to four questions propounded by a Deva.[1]

16th year. Gautama next goes to Ālawī, where he converts a mythical monster who ate the children of the district; a story which in its present shape seems to include a sun myth.

17th year. During the 17th rainy season which he spent at Rājagriha, Gautama preaches a sermon on

[1] It is instructive to notice that these very questions (Big. 232) are in the Sutta Nipāta, p. 47 (comp. Hardy M. B. 265) put into the mouth of Ālawaka, whom Bigandet only mentions in the following year.

the occasion of the death of Sirimatī, a courtezan; and in the fine weather, returns through Srāvasti to Ālawī, preaching in all the places he passed through. At Ālawī he refuses to preach to a hungry man until he has been well fed.

18th year. The rainy season is again spent at Chāliya, near Ṣrāvasti, where the 13th had been spent; and while there, the teacher comforts a weaver who had accidentally killed his daughter. Gautama then returned to Rājagriha.

19th year. After spending the rainy season in the Weluvana Wihāra, Gautama travelled through Magadha preaching in all the villages. On one occasion, finding a deer caught in a snare, he releases it, and sitting down under a tree near by, becomes absorbed in meditation. The angry hunter tries to shoot him, but is restrained by a miracle, and the Buddha recovering from his trance, preaches to him and his family, who become lay disciples. Gautama then goes on to Ṣrāvasti.

20th year. There he spends the rainy season, and having been twice treated contemptuously by the mendicant who had carried his alms-bowl, he appoints Ānanda to be his constant companion. Then he goes to a forest near Chāliya, and succeeds in overcoming by kindness a famous robber, named Angulimāla, whom he persuades to become a mendicant.

As neither the Sinhalese nor the Burmese authors from whom Spence Hardy and Bigandet translate give any account of the sources from which they draw their information, it is not possible to say whether these details depend upon the authority of the three

Pitakas themselves, or only upon the commentary. The chronological order in which the stories are arranged is due to a later hand, and it is not unlikely that in the course of compilation discrepancies have been smoothed over, and lacunæ filled up. As the stories are full of legendary matter, of which we have not as yet the earliest forms before us, I have not given them at length; but the general picture they give of Gautama's mode of life is probably not inaccurate, and many of them may well have had some real foundation in fact. Had there been any desire to make the chronology complete, the remaining years of the life might easily have been filled up by other events which are now related without a time being fixed for them, especially as some of these are of great importance. Among them are the stories of certain women who devoted their lives and their substance to the new movement, notably one Wisākhā of Ṣrāvasti, who presented the society with a grove to the east of the town, and built there a Wihāra called the Pubbārāma, or Eastern Garden.[1]

Another event of the greatest importance in the history of the Order was the schism created by Gautama's cousin Dewadatta; who, having been offended with certain slights put upon him by the people of Kosāmbi, during one of the Buddha's visits to that place, had returned to Rājagriha, where he settled in a home built for him by the rāja Bimbisāra's son, Ajātaṣatru. Some years afterwards, Gautama came to Rājagriha to spend the rainy season in

[1] Big. 247; Hardy's Manual, 220, *et seq.*

the Veḷuvana Wihāra, and Dewadatta still professing himself a Buddhist, asked permission to found a new Order under his own leadership, the rules of which should be much more stringent than those adopted by Gautama. The refusal of this is said to have determined him to break with Buddhism altogether, and to found a new religion of his own; and when, soon after (in the 37th year of Buddha's mission),[1] Ajātaṣatru put to death his father, Bimbisāra, this act is said to have been instigated by Dewadatta, who hoped to profit by the change. Three times attempts were then made on the life of Gautama, and these failing, Dewadatta went with due solemnity to Veḷuvana, and formally called upon Gautama to insist on the stricter rules which he advocated. These were, that the mendicants should live in the open air, and not close to towns; should dress in cast-off rags; should always beg their food from door to door (that is never accept invitations, or food sent to the Wihāras); and should eat no meat. Gautama answered that his precepts could be kept in any place, that he had no objection to such members of the Order as wished to do so keeping stricter rules, but that they were not necessary, and could not be kept at all by the young or delicate; as to food, the members of the Order might eat whatever was customary in the countries where they were, so long as they ate without indulgence of the appetite. It was pos-

[1] Mahāvansa, p. 10; Bigandet, p. 249. Hardy, M.B., 193, says, 'he rendered assistance to Buddha during thirty-six years,' which comes to the same thing.

sible to become holy at the foot of a tree, or in a house; in cast-off clothes, or in clothes given by laymen; whilst abstaining from flesh, or whilst using it. To establish one uniform law would be a hindrance in the way of those who were seeking Nirvāna; and it was to show men the way to Nirvāna which was his sole aim. Dewadatta upon this returned to his own Wihāra, and founded a new and stricter Order, which gradually grew in numbers, and was openly supported by Ajātaṣatru. Dewadatta, however, did not live long, and Ajātaṣatru soon after became, in name at least, a supporter of the Buddha; though in the year before Gautama's death he not only took Ṣrāvasti, the head-quarters, as it were, of Buddhism, but totally destroyed Kapilavastu.[1]

While the accounts of Gautama's life since his first visit to Kapilavastu are only available at present in imperfect and fragmentary notices found in Hardy and Bigandet, confirmed by a few passages in the commentary on the Dhamma-pada, we have in the Pitakas themselves the Mahā-parinibbāna Sutta, a portion of which gives a detailed description of the events of the last three months before his death.[2]

[1] Compare the Commentary on Dhamma-pada, vv. 90, 162, 163, with Hardy, 315–329, Bigandet, 248–253, Burnouf, Lotus, 448, Beal's Fa Hian, 87. The relation in which Dewadatta stood to Gautama seems to have resembled, in some essential points, the relation in which the Judaizing Christians stood to St. Paul.

[2] See above p. 13; and comp. the Commentary on Sudassana Jātaka, Fausböll, p. 391.

Gautama spent the 44th rainy season after his Buddhahood in the Jetawana Wihāra at Ṣrāvasti, and then returned to the Vulture's Peak, a cave on the side of the loftiest of the five hills, overhanging the beautiful valley of Rājagriha.[1] Ajātaṣatru was then planning an attack on the confederation of the Wajjian clans, who occupied the plains on the northern shore of the Ganges, opposite to Magadha. Gautama declared that as long as they were united in their adherence to their ancient customs they would be able to retain their independence, and he took occasion to inculcate very earnestly on the mendicants, whom he assembled for that purpose, the absolute necessity of union, in obedience to the precepts and customs of the Order. It is, perhaps, needless to add that agreement on such a basis was found impossible. The history of Buddhism is the history of the struggles of so-called heretics against the continual additions made to the Rules and Beliefs of the Order by the majority who called themselves orthodox; and new sects of reformers are at this moment rising both in Siam and Ceylon.

The teacher then crossed the Ganges at a spot where, on the site of the modern city of Patna, Ajātaṣatru was then building a fort to keep the Wajjians in check,—the beginning of a town which soon began to rival Rājagriha, and afterwards became the capital of the enlarged kingdom of Magadha.

[1] Bigandet, 253. The site of the cave is given by Cunningham; 'Archæological Reports,' map xiv. Compare pp. 20, 21; and Julien's Hwen Thsang III. 20; Beal's Fa Hian, p. 114.

He went on to Ambapāli, where he became the guest of the leading courtesan of the place, to the great offence of the Wajjian nobles.[1] Thence he proceeded to Belu-gāmaka, where he spent the 45th rainy season, during which he was attacked by a severe and painful illness, and openly declared that he could not live long. After the season of *was* was over he went slowly through the villages of Wesāli, everywhere collecting the members of the Order, and exhorting them to adhere to his doctrine.

'O Mendicants! thoroughly learn, and practise, and perfect, and spread abroad the Law, thought out and revealed by me, in order that this religion of mine (literally, this purity) may last long, and be perpetuated for the good and happiness of the great multitudes, out of pity for the world, to the advantage and prosperity of gods and men.[2] . . . . Now, alas, O mendicants, in a little while the Tathāgata (he who is like others) will pass away. In three months from now the Tathāgata will die. My age is accomplished, my life is done; leaving you, I depart, having relied on myself alone. Be earnest, O mendicants, thoughtful, and holy! Steadfast in resolve, keep watch over your own hearts! Whosoever shall adhere unweariedly to this Law and Discipline,[3] he shall cross the ocean of life, and make an end of sorrow!'

[1] Childers's Parinibbāna Sutta, *loc. cit.* p. 69.

[2] Then followed an enumeration of the divisions of the Law. See below, p. 171.

[3] Dharma and Vinaya: perhaps older recensions of the present Pitakas are here referred to; but I think the words only signify generally the doctrines taught by the Buddha. Parinibbāna Sutta *loc. cit.* p. 227; and below pp. 18, 45, 82.

On reaching Pāvā he is entertained by a goldsmith of that place named Chunda (a man therefore of one of the lower castes), who prepares for him a meal of rice and young pork—and it may be noticed in passing how improbable it is that the story of the Buddha's death having been due to such a cause should be a mere invention. In the afternoon he started for Kusi-nagara, a town about 120 miles N.N.E. of Benāres, and about 80 miles due East of Kapila-vastu. About half-way between the two places flows the river Kukushṭā; before reaching it, however, he was obliged to rest, and being thirsty he asks Ānanda to bring him some water from the river. Thus refreshed he is able to bathe in the river, and resting many hours reaches in the evening a grove outside Kusinagara, where he rests for the last time.

At the river, feeling that he was dying, and afraid that Chunda should reproach himself or be reproached by others, he says to Ānanda, 'After I am gone tell Chunda that he will in a future birth receive very great reward; for, having eaten of the food he gave me, I am about to pass away. Say it was from my own mouth that you heard this. There are two gifts that will be blest above all others, that of Sujātā before I attained Buddhahood under the Bo-Tree, and this gift of Chunda's before I finally pass away.' While in the grove of trees he talked long and earnestly with Ānanda about his burial and about certain rules (mostly relating to intercourse with female disciples), to be observed by the Order after his death.

At the close of this conversation Ānanda broke

down, and went aside to weep—'I am not yet perfect, and my teacher is passing away: he who is so kind.' But Gautama missed him, and sending for him comforted him with the hope of Nirvāna, repeating what he had so often said about the impermanence of all things. 'O! Ānanda; do not let yourself be troubled, do not weep. Have I not told you that we must part from all we hold most dear and pleasant? No being soever born, or put together, can overcome the dissolution inherent in it; no such condition can exist. For a long time, Ānanda, you have been very near to me by kindness in act, and word, and thoughtfulness. You have always done well: persevere, and you too shall be quite free from this thirst of life, this chain of ignorance'; and, turning to the rest of the disciples he spoke to them at some length on the insight and kindness of Ānanda.[1]

As the night wore on, Subhadra, a Brahman philosopher of Kusanagara, came to ask some questions of the Buddha, but Ānanda, fearing that this might lead to a longer discussion than the sick teacher could bear, would not admit him. Gautama heard the sound of their talking, and asking what it was, told them to let Subhadra come. The latter began by asking whether the six great teachers [2] knew all things as they said they did, or whether they knew

Childers's Parinibbāna Sutta, *loc. cit.*, p. 244.

[2] By these are meant the six Brahman teachers, a sketch of whose systems is given in the Sāmañña-phala Sutta, Burnouf, Lotus, 449–498; with which compare Hardy, Manual 290–292. The Burmese corruptions of the Indian names are often curious,

some, or none. 'This is not the time for such discussions,' was the answer; 'listen and I will preach to you my law'; and Gautama went on to declare that salvation could not be found in any system which ignored the virtuous life, the eight stages of the Path of Holiness, which begins with purity and ends in love. By this discourse Subhadra is said to have been converted.

Soon after the dying teacher says to Ānanda, 'You may perhaps begin to think, "the word is ended now, our Teacher is gone": but you must not think so. After I am dead let the Law and the Rules of the Order, which I have taught, be a Teacher to you.'[1] He then gave instructions as to the mode in which the elder and younger members of the Order should address one another; and laid a penalty on one Channa, who spoke indiscriminately whatever occurred to him. Then addressing all the disciples, he called upon anyone who had any doubt or misgiving as to any matter of the law, or regarding the paths, or virtuous conduct, to ask him and he would resolve the doubt: 'lest they should afterwards regret not having asked when they had opportunity.' When Ānanda expressed his astonishment that none came forward in response to this appeal, Gautama said

but the most remarkable instance is that of these six names which arè given by Bigandet, at p.150, as Mekkali, Gow, Sala, Thindzi, Jani, and Ganti. The first name is in Pali Makkhali Gosāla, the last is Nigaṇṭha, son of Nātha; so that the syllables Thindzi Ja are all that is left in Burmese of the other four names !.

[1] Dharma and Vinaya, Parinibbāna Sutta, *loc. cit.*, p. 250. Compare the note above, p. 79.

that the very least of all those present who had once been converted (who had entered 'the paths') could not entirely fall, but was certain eventually to arrive at complete enlightenment.[1]

After another pause he said, 'Mendicants! I now impress it upon you, the parts and powers of man must be dissolved; work out your salvation with diligence!' These were the last words the Teacher spoke: shortly afterwards he became unconscious, and in that state passed away.[2]

In concluding this sketch of the early Buddhist accounts of the life of Gautama, I shall make no attempt to sum up his personal character[3]; such opinions as we may fairly allow ourselves to have on that subject will be more safely derived from the record of his teachings, than from the record of his life. But the foregoing account will be sufficient, I hope, to remove at least one misconception—the prevalent notion that Gautama was an enemy to Hinduism, and that his chief claim on the gratitude of his countrymen lies in his having destroyed a system of iniquity and oppression and fraud. This is not the case. Gautama was born, and brought up, and lived, and died a Hindu. Asoka, the most distinguished of the lay followers of Gautama, is now most often thought of as the philanthropic and righteous Buddhist Emperor. But he loved to

[1] Parinibbāna, Sutta, p. 251.

[2] On the date of this, see below, p. 212.

[3] See the remarks of the Rev. M. A. Sherring, 'Sacred City of the Hindus,' pp. 12, 13.

call himself, 'Asoka, the delight *of the gods*';[1] and though he was an earnest Buddhist, it would be more exact to call him a Hindu of the Buddhist sect. There was not much in the metaphysics and psychology of Gautama which cannot be found in one or other of the orthodox systems, and a great deal of his morality could be matched from earlier or later Hindu books. Such originality as Gautama possessed lay in the way in which he adopted, enlarged, ennobled, and systematized that which had already been well said by others; in the way in which he carried out to their logical conclusion principles of equity and justice already acknowledged by some of the most prominent Hindu thinkers. The difference between him and other teachers lay chiefly in his deep earnestness and in his broad public spirit of philanthropy. Even these differences are probably much more apparent now than they were then, and by no means deprived him of the support and sympathy of the best among the Brahmans. Many of his chief disciples, many of the most distinguished members of his Order, were Brahmans: he always classed them with the Buddhist mendicants as deserving of respect, and he used the name Brahmans as a term of honour for the Buddhist Arahats or saints.[2] Doubtless, his abolishing caste within the limits of his Order, and his declaring the

[1] His contemporary, the pious Buddhist king of Ceylon, also called himself by the same epithet, viz., *Devānam piya*. Compare the Rock Pāli inscription, published by me in the 'Indian Antiquary' for May, 1872.

[2] See below, p. 154.

road to Nirvāna to be as open to the lowest outcast as it was to the proudest of the 'twice born' occasioned no little discontent; while his contempt for ritualism, and his belief in the capacity of every man to work out here, in this life, his own salvation, seemed to the conservative party to be dangerous doctrines:—it is even true that in the long run the two systems were quite incompatible. But neither Gautama nor the great body of the Brahmans believed them probably to be so then. We hear of no persecutions till long after the time of Asoka, when Buddhism had become corrupt; and Buddhism grew and flourished within the fold of the orthodox belief. So far from showing how depraved and oppressive Hinduism was, it shows precisely the contrary: for none will deny that there is much that is beautiful and noble in Buddhism; and Buddhism was the child, the product of Hinduism. Gautama's whole training was Brahmanism; he probably deemed himself to be the most correct exponent of the spirit, as distinct from the letter of the ancient faith; and it can only be claimed for him that he was the greatest, and wisest, and best of the Hindus.

CHAPTER IV.

THE ESSENTIAL DOCTRINES OF BUDDHISM, THE SKANDHAS, TRISHNĀ, KARMA AND NIRVĀNA.

WITH regard to Gautama's teaching we have more reliable authority than we have with regard to his life. It is true that none of the books of the Three Pitakas can at present be satisfactorily traced back before the Council of Asoka, held at Patna about 250 B.C., that is to say, at least 130 years after the death of the teacher; but they undoubtedly contain a great deal of much older matter. And when it is recollected that Gautama Buddha did not leave behind him a number of deeply simple sayings, from which his followers subsequently built up a system or systems of their own, but had himself thoroughly elaborated his doctrine, partly as to details, after, but in its fundamental points even before, his mission began; that during his long career as teacher, he had ample time to repeat the principles and details of the system over and over again to his disciples, and to test their knowledge of it; and finally, that his leading disciples were, like himself, accustomed to the subtlest metaphysical distinctions, and trained to that wonderful command of memory which Indian ascetics then possessed; when these facts are recalled to mind, it will be seen that much more reliance may reasonably be placed upon the doctrinal parts of the Buddhist Scriptures, than upon correspondingly late records of other religions, or on the biographical parts of the Buddhist canon itself. It may be possible, hereafter, when the Pitakas shall have been published, to ascertain which parts of them are older than the rest, and whether they contain an older system hidden under a later one; at present it can only be said that of difference in age there is already sufficient evidence, but of growth or change in fundamental ideas none of any certainty,—except, indeed, as regards the person of Gautama himself.

Postponing, therefore, this last question for consideration later on, let us first endeavour to give a brief outline of the explanation which early Buddhism has to offer of the nature of man, and of his relation to the world around him.

Buddhism does not attempt to solve the problem of the primary origin of all things. 'When Mālunka asked the Buddha whether the existence of the world is eternal or not eternal, he made him no reply; but the reason of this was, that it was considered by the teacher as an inquiry that tended to no profit.'[1] Buddhism takes as its ultimate fact the existence of the material world and of conscious beings living within it; and it holds that everything is subject to the law of cause and effect, and that everything is constantly, though imperceptibly, changing. There is no place where this law does not operate; no heaven or hell, therefore, in the ordinary sense. There are worlds

[1] Spence Hardy's Manual of Buddhism, p. 375.

where angels live, whose existence is more or less material, according as their previous lives were more or less holy; but the angels die, and the worlds they inhabit pass away. There are places of torment where the evil actions of men or angels produce unhappy beings; but when the active power of the evil that produced them is exhausted, they will vanish, and the worlds they inhabit are not eternal. The whole kosmos—earth, and heavens, and hells—is always tending to renovation or destruction; is always in a course of change, a series of revolutions, or of cycles, of which the beginning and the end alike are unknowable and unknown. To this universal law of composition and dissolution, men and gods form no exception; the unity of forces which constitutes a sentient being must sooner or later be dissolved; and it is only through ignorance and delusion that such a being indulges in the dream that it is a separate and self-existent entity.

A watchman on a lofty tower sees a charioteer urging his horse along the plain: the driver thinks he is moving rapidly, and the horse in the pride of life seems to scorn the earth from which it thinks itself so separate; but to the watchman above, horse and chariot, and driver, seem to crawl along the ground, and to be as much a part of the earth as the horse's mane, waving in the wind, is a part of the horse itself. As a child grows up, its mind reflects as in a dim mirror the occurrences of the surrounding world; and practically, though unconsciously, it regards itself as the centre round which the universe turns. Gradually its circle widens somewhat, but the grown man never escapes from the delusion of self, and spends his life in a constant round of desires and cares, longing for objects which when attained, produce not happiness, but fresh desires and cares, —always engaged in the pursuit of some fancied good. For the majority of men these cares are mean, petty, and contemptible; but even those whose ambition urges them to higher aims, are equally seeking after vanity, and only laying themselves open to greater sorrows and more bitter disappointment.

Such teachings are by no means peculiar to Buddhism, and similar ideas lie at the foundation of earlier Indian philosophies. They are to be found, indeed, in other systems widely separated from these in time and place; and Buddhism in dealing with the truth which they contain, might have given a more decisive and more lasting utterance, if it had not also borrowed a belief in the curious doctrine of transmigration—a doctrine which seems to have arisen independently, if not simultaneously, in the valley of the Ganges and the valley of the Nile. The word transmigration has been used, however, in different times and at different places, for theories similar, indeed, but very different; and Buddhism in adopting the general idea from post-Vedic Brahmanism, so modified it as to originate, in fact, a new hypothesis.

The new belief, like the old one, related to life in past and future births, and contributed nothing to the removal, here, in this life, of the evils whose existence it was supposed to explain. To this end Buddhism teaches that there is a way, the 'noble eightfold path.' We shall endeavour therefore, first to make clear the

Buddhist metaphysical explanation of the origin of evil, and shall then discuss the Buddhist way of salvation.

The modification which Buddhism introduced into the idea of transmigration was necessitated by the early Buddhist theories of the nature of sentient beings; according to which, man consists of an assemblage of different properties or qualities, none of which corresponds to the Hindu or modern notion of soul. These are *material* qualities, *sensations*, abstract *ideas*, *tendencies* of mind, and mental *powers*,[1] and as the point is a matter of great importance for a right appreciation of Buddhist teaching, and the enumeration is not without interest for its own sake, a few words may be devoted to the details of each of these *Skandhas* or *Aggregates*.

1. The *Material* Properties or Attributes (Rūpa) are twenty-eight in number:—

Four elements; earth, water, fire, air.[2]
Five organs of sense; eye, ear, nose, tongue, body.
Five attributes of matter; form, sound, smell, taste, substance.[3]
Two distinctions of sex; male, female.
Three essential conditions; thought, vitality, space.
Two means of communication; gesture, speech
Seven qualities of living bodies; buoyancy, elas-

[1] See Childers's Pāli Dictionary, s. v. Rūpa, Vedanā, Saññā, Sankhārā, and Viññāna.

[2] According to Colebrooke, the Buddhists think that these elements of matter consist of atoms, and deem compound bodies to be conjoint primary atoms. Essays 1. 4. 6.

[3] In some lists this is omitted, and 'food' added later on. Visuddhi Magga apud Childers, s. v. Rūpa; and Alabaster, Wheel of the Law, p. 237.

ticity, power of adaptation, power of aggregation, duration, decay, change.

2. The Sensations (vedanā) are divided into six classes, according as they are received immediately by each of the five senses, or sixthly, by the mind (through memory); and further, into eighteen classes, as each of these six classes may be either agreeable, disagreeable, or indifferent.

3. The Abstract Ideas (saññā) are divided into six classes corresponding to the six classes of sensations; for instance, the ideas blue, a tree, are classed under sight; the idea sweetness, under taste, and so on.

4. The Tendencies or Potentialities (literally *confections*, sankhārā), are in fifty-two divisions, which are not, however, mutually exclusive. Some of these include, or are identical with, items in the previous classes; but whereas the previous groups are arranged as it were from an objective, this group is arranged as it were from a subjective point of view:—

1. Contact (Phassa).
2. The resulting sensation (Vedanā).
3. Abstract ideas, formed on sensation (Saññā).
4. Thought, the regrouping of ideas (Cetanā).
5. Reflection, turning these groups over and over (Manasikāra).
6. Memory (Sati).

7. Vitality (Jīvitindriya; also in Group 1).
8. Individuality (Ekaggatā).

9. Attention (Vitakka, which may cause contact No. 1).
10. Investigation (Vicāra; continued attention).
11. Effort (Vīriya, which assists all other faculties).
12. Steadfastness (Adhimokkha, continued effort).

13. Joy (Pīti).
14. Impulse (Chanda).
15. Indifference (Majjhattatā).

16, 17. Sleep and torpor (Thīna and Middha, the opposites of attention, No. 8; and of mind-lightness, No. 33).

18, 19. Stupidity and intelligence (Moha and Paññā).

20, 21. Covetousness and content (Lobha and Alobha).

22, 23. Fear and rashness (Ottappa and Anotappa).

24, 25. Shame and shamelessness (Hiri and Ahirika).

26, 27. Hatred and affection (Dosa and Adosa).

28–30. Doubt, faith, and delusion (Vicikicchā, Saddhā, Diṭṭhi).

31, 32. Repose of body or mind (Pasiddhi).

33, 34. Lightness, activity; of body or mind (Lahutā); also in Group 1.

35, 36. Softness; elasticity of body or mind (Mudutā); also in Group 1.

37, 38. Adaptability, pliancy; of body or mind (Kammaññatā); also in Group 1.

39, 40. Dexterity; of body or mind (Pāguññatā).

41, 42. Straightness; of body or mind (Ujjukatā)

43–45. Propriety; of speech, action, or life (Sammā).

46. Pity; sorrow for the sorrow of others (Karuṇā).
47. Gladness; rejoicing in the joy of others (Muditā).
48. Envy; sorrow at the joy of others (Issā).
49. Selfishness; dislike to share one's joy with others (Macchariyā).

50. Moroseness (Kukkucca)
51. Vanity (Uddhacca).
52. Pride (Māno).

5. Thought, Reason (Viññāna), is the last skandha, and is really an amplification from another point of view of the fourth of the last group (sankhārā) which is inherent in all the others. It is divided from the point of view of the merit or demerit resulting from different thoughts into eighty-nine classes; a division which throws no light on the Buddhist scheme of the constituent elements of being, and does not, therefore, concern us here.[1]

The above enumeration includes all the bodily and mental parts and powers of man, and neither any one of them, or any group of them, is permanent. 'The first group, *material qualities*, are like a mass of foam, that gradually forms, and then vanishes. The second group, the *sensations*, are like a bubble dancing on the face of the water. The third group, the *ideas*, are like the uncertain mirage that appears in the sunshine. The fourth group, the mental and moral *predispositions*, are like the plantain stalk, without firmness or solidity. And the last group, the *thoughts*, are like a spectre or magical illusion.'[2]

It is repeatedly and distinctly laid down in the Pitakas that none of these *Skandhas* or divisions of the qualities of sentient beings is the soul.[3] The body itself is constantly changing, and so of each of the

[1] The seat of viññāna is supposed to be the heart, mentioned in the 1st group. Gogerly, J. C. A. S., 1867, p. 122.

[2] From Spence Hardy's Manual, p. 424. He gives his authorities for the chapter at p. 399. Comp. below, p. 171.

[3] See the passages quoted by Gogerly in the Journal of the Ceylon Asiatic Society, 1867, 118, 121. Such Northern Buddhist books as are known say exactly the same: see Burnouf's quotations, Intr. 507, 510.

other divisions, which are only functions of the living body, produced by the contact of external objects with the bodily organs. Man is never the same for two consecutive moments, and there is within him no abiding principle whatever.

So important is this doctrine, and so difficult is it for a mind impregnated with Christian ideas to recognize it fully and freely as a fundamental tenet of the widely-adopted religion of Gautama, that I must ask attention to the following passages and authorities. The first is from the Sutta Pitaka, and is also found in a Northern Buddhist work from which Burnouf drew a great deal of his information.[1] Gautama is there reported to have said :—

"Mendicants, in whatever way the different teachers (Samanas and Brāhmanas) regard the soul, they think it is the five skandhas, or one of the five. Thus, mendicants, the unlearned, unconverted man—who does not associate either with the converted or the holy, or understand their law, or live according to it,—such a man regards the soul either as identical with, or as possessing, or as containing, or as residing in the material properties (rūpa), or as identical with, or as possessing, or as containing, or as residing in sensation (vedanā)," and so on of each of the other three skandhas (ideas, propensities, and mind). "By regarding soul in one of these twenty ways,

[1] The Abhidharma Kosha Vyākhyā : part is quoted by Burnouf, Introduction à l'histoire du Buddhisme Indien, p. 263, n. 2. The original Pāli is in the 5th Sutta of the Khandha Vagga, of the Sañyutta Nikāya in the Sutta Pitaka, quoted by Alwis, Buddhist Nirvāna, p. 71. Compare Dhp., p. 420.

he gets the idea 'I am.' Then there are the five organs of sense, and mind, and qualities, and ignorance. From sensation (produced by contact and ignorance), the sensual unlearned man derives the notions 'I am.' 'This I, exists,' 'I shall be,' 'I shall not be,' 'I shall or shall not have material qualities,' 'I shall or shall not have, or shall be neither with nor without, ideas.' But now, mendicants, the learned disciple of the converted, having the same five organs of sense, has got rid of ignorance and acquired wisdom; and therefore (by reason of the absence of ignorance, and the rise of wisdom) the ideas 'I am' (&c., as above) do not occur to him."

This belief in self or soul is regarded so distinctly as a heresy that two well-known words in Buddhist terminology have been coined on purpose to stigmatise it. The first of these is *sakkāyadiṭṭhi*, the 'heresy of individuality,' the name given to this belief as one of the three primary delusions (the others being doubt, and belief in the efficacy of rites and ceremonies) which must be abandoned at the very first stage of the Buddhist path of holiness.[1] The other is *attavāda*, 'the doctrine of soul or self,' which is the name given to it as a part of the chain of causes which lead to the origin of evil. It is there classed —with sensuality, heresy (as to eternity and annihilation), and belief in the efficacy of rites and ceremonies—as one of the four upādānas, which are the immediate cause of birth, decay, death, sorrow, lamentation, pain, grief, and despair.

[1] On these delusions, called sañyojanas, see p. 108.

Another proof of the prominence of this doctrine of the non-existence of the soul is the fact that the Brahmans, who have misunderstood many less important or less clearly-expressed tenets of Buddhism, recognise this as one of its distinctive features.[1]

It is expressed in a more popular manner in the Milinda Prashnaya, or Questions of Menander, a Sinhalese translation of a very ancient Pali work of the same name, professing to elucidate that system of Buddhism which was taught about the commencement of our era by Nāgarjuna or Nāgasena, the founder of the Madhyamika school of Northern Buddhism. The book is a series of conversations between the Greek king, Menander, of Sagala, in the Punjāb, and Nāgasena, and at the very beginning of the series is placed the following dialogue :—

The king said, 'How is your reverence known? What is your name?'

Nāgasena replied, 'I am called Nāgasena by my parents, the priests, and others. But Nāgasena is not a separate entity.'

To this the king objected, very much as a modern Christian might, that in that case there could be no virtue, nor vice; no reward, nor retribution (in other words, no 'sanction'). He then mentioned one after another all the parts of the body, and mind, and the *Skandhas* just described, and asked of each whether it was Nāgasena. All these questions were answered in the negative. 'Then,' said the king, 'I do not see Nāgasena. Nāgasena is a sound without meaning. You have spoken an untruth. There is no Nāgasena.'

[1] See Colebrooke's Essays 1, 417, of Prof. Cowell's edition.

The mendicant asked, 'Did your majesty come here on foot, or in a chariot?'

'In a chariot,' was the answer.

'What is a chariot?' asked Nāgasena. 'Is the ornamental cover the chariot? Are the wheels, the spokes of the wheels, or the reins, the chariot? Are all these parts together (in a heap) the chariot? If you leave these out, does there remain anything which is the chariot?'

To all this the king said, 'No.'

'Then I see no chariot, it is only a sound, a name. In saying that you came in a chariot you have uttered an untruth. I appeal to the nobles, and ask them if it be proper that the great king of all Jambudwīpa should utter an untruth?'

Rather neat, doubtless, and not undeserved, but the king is not convinced. 'No untruth have I uttered, venerable monk. The cover, wheels, seat, and other parts all united or combined (chariot-wise) form the chariot. They are the usual signs by which that, which is called a chariot, is known.'

'And just so,' said Nāgasena, 'in the case of man'; and he quoted the words of the Teacher, where he had said, 'As the various parts of a chariot form, when united, the chariot, so the five Skandhas, when united in one body, form a being, a living existence.'

Whatever we may think of the argument it is at least clear that a soul is just as much and just as little acknowledged in man as a separate substance is acknowledged in a chariot. It shows also that this doctrine is not drawn from Buddhism by implication, but must have been clearly and consciously held, with some apprehension, more or less correct, of the possible objections to it.

This will, however, appear still more clearly from a curious passage in the Brahmajāla Sutta.[1] To quote the whole of it would be impossible, but, in short, Gautama discusses sixty-two different kinds of wrong belief; among which are those held by men who think 'The soul and the world are eternal; there is no newly-existing substance; but these remain as a mountain peak unshaken, immovable. Living beings pass away, they transmigrate; they die and are born; but these continue, as being eternal.' After showing how the unfounded belief in the eternal existence of God or gods arose, Gautama goes on to discuss the question of the soul; and points out thirty-two beliefs concerning it, which he declares to be wrong. These are, shortly, as follows:—'Upon what principle, or on what account, do these mendicants and Brahmans hold the doctrine of future existence? They teach that the soul is material, or is immaterial, or is both, or neither; that it is finite, or infinite, or both, or neither; that it will have one or many modes of consciousness; that its perceptions will be few or boundless; that it will be in a state of joy or of misery, or of neither.'[2] These are the sixteen heresies teaching a *conscious* existence after death. Then there are eight heresies teaching that the soul,

[1] In the Dīgha Nikāya of the Sutta Pitaka, translated by Gogerly, in the 'Journal of the Ceylon Asiatic Society,' 1846.

[2] There is an omission somewhere, as we have only fifteen views actually stated. I think it is here, and we ought to add, 'or of mixed joy and misery.'

material or immaterial, or both or neither, finite or infinite, or both or neither, has an *unconscious* existence after death. And, finally, eight others which teach that the soul, in the same eight ways, exists after death in a state of being, *neither* conscious *nor* unconscious.' 'Mendicants,' concludes the sermon, 'that which binds the Teacher to existence (viz. taṇhā, thirst) is cut off; but his body still remains. While his body shall remain he will be seen by gods and men, but after the termination of life, upon the dissolution of the body, neither gods nor men will see him.'

Would it be possible in a more complete and categorical manner to deny that there is any soul—anything, of any kind, which continues to exist, in any manner, after death?

But Gautama had not been able to give up the belief in transmigration. He, like some other seekers after truth who are at the same time deeply religious, had gradually formed his belief—not by working up from the simple to the complex, from the well known to the less known, and pausing humbly where uncertainty begins—but by gradually rejecting those parts of his earliest creed which could be proved (to his mind) to be inconsistent with what he held to be actual fact. In such cases every surrender causes a wrench; each standpoint is defended more strongly than the last; and the ultimate belief is not necessarily *more true* than those which have been abandoned; but only *less easily proved false.*

It is natural, moreover, for the mind to resist the longest the disproof of those hypotheses which satisfy it most completely by the explanation they afford of otherwise inexplicable mysteries. Now the doctrine of transmigration, in either the Brahmanical or the Buddhist form, is not capable of disproof; while it affords an explanation, quite complete to those who can believe it, of the apparent anomalies and wrongs in the distribution here of happiness or woe. A child, for instance, is blind; this is owing to his eye-vanity, lust of the eye, in a former birth: but he has also unusual powers of hearing; this is because he loved, in a former birth, to listen to the preaching of the Law. The explanation can always be exact, for it is scarcely more than a repetition of the point to be explained; it may always fit the facts, for it is derived from them; and it cannot be disproved, for it lies in a sphere beyond the reach of human inquiry.

It is probable that the idea of transmigration first originated in that curious trick of the memory, by which we sometimes feel so sure that sensations we are experiencing have been experienced by us before, and yet we know not how or when.[1]

However this may be, the belief was retained in Buddhism as providing a moral cause for the suffering condition of men in this birth; and as Buddhism does not acknowledge a soul, it has to find the link of connection, the bridge between one life and another, somewhere else. In order to do this, and thus save the moral cause, it resorts to the desperate ex-

[1] Several interesting instances of this are given by scientific psychologists. See the cases quoted by Dr. Carpenter, 'Mental Physiology,' pp. 430, *et seq.*, and Sir B. Brodie, 'Psychological Inquiries,' second series, p. 55.

pedient of a mystery—one of the four acknowledged mysteries in Buddhism (which are also the four points in which it is most certainly wrong)[1]—the doctrine namely of '*karma*.' This is the doctrine that, as soon as a sentient being (man, animal, or angel) dies, a new being is produced in a more or less painful and material state of existence, according to the 'karma,' the desert or merit, of the being who had died. The cause which produces the new being is 'trishṇā,' thirst, or 'upādāna,' grasping; which are expressions for nearly similar states of mind, and will be explained further on. Sensations originate in the contact of the organs of sense with the exterior world; from sensation springs a desire to satisfy a felt want, a yearning, a thirst (trishṇā); from trishṇā results a grasping after objects to satisfy that desire (upādāna); that 'grasping state of mind[2] causes the new being' (not, of course, a new soul, but a new set of skandhas, a new body with mental tendencies and capabilities). The 'karma' of the previous set of skandhas, or sentient being, then determines the locality, nature, and future of the *new* set of skandhas, of the new sentient being.

The reader will now be prepared to agree with the Buddhist dogma, that this is an incomprehensible

[1] These are—1. The effects of *karma*. 2. The supernatural powers attained by *iddhi*. 3. The size, age, and first cause of the *kosmos* (*loka*). 4. The omniscience, &c., of *the Buddha*.

[2] It is divided into four classes: sensuality (kāma), delusion (about the soul, uccheda-vāda and sassata-vāda), ritualism (sīlabbata), and the delusion of self (attavāda). (Alabaster, 'Wheel of the Law,' 239.) These are like the straws which a drowning man catches at. On Trishṇā comp. below p. 106.

mystery. It has been also the most stable doctrine of Buddhism; the one which, in all the different systems developed out of the original teaching of the Pitakas, has been most universally accepted, and has had the greatest practical effect on the lives of its believers.

Though, however, the mode of action of *karma* is an incomprehensible mystery (not as the Buddhist thinks, because the Teacher said so, but simply because the force itself is a nonexistent fiction of the brain), it is possible to throw some light on the hypothesis, and even to find the foundation of truth on which it rests; the same truth which lies at the bottom of the widely prevalent beliefs in fate and predestination. I do not intend to say that fate and *karma* are the same; the difference is very obvious. Fate is unmoral (neither moral nor immoral), and is an interruption to the law that effects are due to causes; the doctrine of *karma* finds a *moral cause* for the effects it seeks to explain. But both depend on a perception of the fact that happiness and misery in this life are apportioned with an utter disregard of the moral qualities of men according to the current notions of good and bad.

When the innocent is oppressed, and his persecutor prospers in the world, the sufferer, if he believed in fate, would think, 'This was preordained, I must submit'; and he would try to rectify the balance of justice by assuming a *result*, beyond what he sees, in the darkness of the *future;* if he believed in *karma*, he would think, 'This is my own doing, I must bear no malice,' and would try to rectify the balance of justice by assuming a *cause*, beyond what he sees, in the darkness of the *past*.

Karma, from a Buddhist point of view, avoids the superstitious extreme, on the one hand, of those who believe in the separate existence of some entity called the soul; and the irreligious extreme, on the other, of those who do not believe in moral justice and retribution. Buddhism claims to have looked through the word soul for the fact it purports to cover; and to have found no fact at all, but only one or other of twenty[1] different delusions which blind the eyes of men. Nevertheless, Buddhism is convinced that if a man reaps sorrow, disappointment, pain, he himself, and no other, must at some time have sown folly, error, sin; and if not in this life, then in some former birth. Where then, in the latter case, is the identity between him who sows and him who reaps? *In that which alone remains* when a man dies, and the constituent parts of the sentient being are dissolved; in the result, namely, of his action, speech, and thought, in his good or evil *karma* (literally his 'doing'), which *does not* die.

We are familiar with the doctrine, 'Whatever a man soweth that shall he also reap'; and can therefore enter into the Buddhist feeling, that whatever a man reaps, that he must also have sown; we are familiar with the doctrine of the indestructibility of force, and can therefore understand the Buddhist dogma (however it may contravene our Christian notions), that no exterior power can destroy the fruit

[1] See above, p. 94.

of a man's deeds, that they must work out their full effect to the pleasant or the bitter end. But the peculiarity of Buddhism lies in this, that the result of what a man is or does is held, not to be dissipated, as it were, into many separate streams, but to be concentrated together in the formation of one new sentient being,—new, that is, in its constituent parts and powers, but the same in its essence, its being, its doing, its *karma*.

As one generation dies and gives way to another—the heir of the consequences of all its virtues and all its vices, the exact result of pre-existing causes; so each individual in the long chain of life inherits all, of good or evil, which all its predecessors have done or been; and takes up the struggle towards enlightenment precisely there, where they have left it. But it is never conscious (except in a few rare instances, when it has risen above the possibility of pleasure and of pain) of what its predecessors were, or of what its successors shall be. And so the true Buddhist saint does not mar the purity of his self-denial by lusting after a positive happiness, which he, himself, shall enjoy hereafter. His consciousness will cease to feel, but his virtue will live and work out its full effect in the decrease of the sum of the misery of sentient beings.

Most forms of Paganism, past and present, teach men to seek for some sort of happiness here. Most other forms of belief say that this is folly, but the faithful and the holy shall find happiness hereafter, in a better world beyond. Buddhism maintains that the one hope is as hollow as the other; that the consciousness of self is a delusion; that the organized being, sentient existence, since it is not infinite, is bound up inextricably with ignorance, and therefore with sin, and therefore with sorrow. 'Drop then this petty foolish longing for personal happiness,' Buddhism would say! 'Here it comes of ignorance, and leads to sin, which leads to sorrow; and there the conditions of existence are the same, and each new birth will leave you ignorant and finite still. There is nothing eternal; the very kosmos itself is passing away; nothing is, everything becomes; and all that you see and feel, bodily or mentally, of yourself will pass away like everything else; there will only remain the accumulated result of all your actions, words, and thoughts. Be pure then, and kind, not lazy in thought. Be awake, shake off your delusions, and enter resolutely on the 'Path' which will lead you away from these restless, tossing waves of the ocean of life; and take you to the calm City of Peace, to the Joy and Rest of Nirvāna!'

Strange is it and instructive that all this should have seemed not unattractive these 2,300 years and more to many despairing and earnest hearts—that they should have trusted themselves to the so seeming stately bridge which Buddhism has tried to build over the river of the mysteries and sorrows of life. They have been charmed and awed perhaps by the delicate or noble beauty of some of the several stones of which the arch is built; they have seen that the whole rests on a more or less solid foundation of fact; that on one side of the keystone is the necessity of justice, on the other the law of causality. But they have failed to see that the very keystone itself, the link between one life and another, is a mere word—this wonderful hypothesis, this airy nothing, this imaginary cause beyond the reach of reason—the individualized and individualizing force of Karma.[1]

The Paths of Holiness.

We have seen that in the first explanation which Gautama gave of his system he laid down the 'four Noble Truths' concerning Sorrow, its Cause, its Suppression, and the Path leading to its extinction.

Briefly explained, these four Truths come to this:[2]

1. That (those events which are distinctive of individual existence, such as) birth, the five Skandhas, decay, disease, death, and (those which bring forcibly into mind the sense of separate existence, such as) contact with disagreeable objects, separation from pleasant ones, unfulfilled desire of possession,—are precisely those states which are full of suffering or sorrow.

2. The kind of craving excitement, which follows on sensation, and causes the delusion of self and the lust of life—creating either delight in the objects that present themselves, or an eager desire to supply a felt want—this eager yearning thirst (Trishṇā, Pāli taṇhā)

[1] Individualized, in so far as the result of a man's actions is concentrated in the formation of a second sentient being; individualizing, in so far as it is the force by which different beings become one individual. In other respects the force of karma is real enough.

[2] The authorities are quoted above, p. 48.

growing into sensuality, desire of future life, or love of the present world, is the origin of all suffering.[1]

3. Sorrow and suffering will be overcome, extinguished, if this 'thirst' be quenched, this lust of life destroyed. "He who overcomes this contemptible thirst (difficult to be conquered in this world), sufferings fall off from him, like water drops from a lotus leaf."[2]

4. To accomplish this end there is only one way,—the 'Noble Path' of a virtuous and thoughtful life: "Enter on this Path and make an end of sorrow: verily the Path has been preached by me, who have found out how to quench the darts of grief. You yourselves must make the effort: the Buddhas are only preachers: the thoughtful who enter the Path are freed from the bondage of the deceiver, Māra.'[3] And this means of salvation is not a mere vague admonition to 'be good'; it is worked out into detail, expressed in the Eight Divisions and Four Stages.

[1] As taṇhā may be produced by sensations received through either of the five senses, or through the memory, it is said to be six-fold; and as each of these may grow in the three ways mentioned in the text, it is eighteen-fold; and by further dividing each of these into two (outward and inward), it is thirty-six-fold; and, again, by dividing each of these into three (past, present, and future), we have, finally, 108 different kinds of 'thirst.' 'And thus the little taṇhā becomes a hydra-headed monster possessed of one hundred and eight modes of inflicting suffering on humanity,' (Vijesinha Mudaliar, in Childers's Pali Dictionary, under the word taṇhā.) 'The man whom this contemptible thirst—that poison in the world—overcomes, that man's sorrows grow, like the bīrana-weed when it is spreading,' 'Dhammapada,' verse 335).

[2] 'Dhammapada,' verse 336, and compare vv. 342, 354. Compare v. 285, below, p. 128.

[3] Ibid., verses 275, 276.

The Eight Divisions as already mentioned (p. 48) are as follows :—

1. Right views.
2. Right feelings.
3. Right words.
4. Right behaviour.
5. Right mode of livelihood.
6. Right exertion.
7. Right memory.
8. Right meditation and tranquillity.

The four Paths or Stages of the Path are[1] :—

1. The 'entering upon the stream,' *Conversion;* which follows on, (1) companionship with the good, (2) hearing of the law, (3) enlightened reflection, or (4) the practice of virtue. The unconverted man is unwise, under the influence of sin, enmity, and impurity; but if by one or more of the means just mentioned he has arrived at a perception of the 'four Noble Truths,' he has become converted, and has entered the first Path. While in this path he becomes free successively, (1) from the delusion of self, (2) from doubt as to the Buddha and his doctrines, and (3) from the belief in the efficacy of rites and ceremonies. 'Better than universal empire in this world, better than going to heaven, better than lordship over all worlds is (this three-fold) fruit of the first Path.'[2]

2. *The path of those who will only return once to this world.*—The converted man free from doubt and the delusions of self and ritualism, succeeds in this path in reducing to a minimum, lust, hatred and delusion.

3. *The path of those who will never return to this world:* in which the last remnants of (4) sensuality and

[1] See Parinibbāna Sutta in the J. R. A. S., vol. vii. part i., p. 67, and Hardy's 'Eastern Monachism,' 288.

[2] 'Dhammapada,' verse 178.

(5) malevolence, being destroyed, not the least low desire for oneself, or wrong feeling towards others can arise in the heart.

4. *The path of the Holy Ones*, more exactly, worthy ones, *Arahats:* in which the saint becomes free from (6, 7) desire for material, or immaterial, existence; from (8, 9, 10) pride and self-righteousness, and ignorance.

He is now free from all sin; he sees and values all things in this life at their true value; evil desires of all kinds being rooted up from his mind, he only experiences right desires for himself, and tender pity and regard and exalted spiritual love for others. "As a mother, even at the risk of her own life, protects her son, her only son: so let there be goodwill without measure among all beings. Let goodwill without measure prevail in the whole world, above, below, around, unstinted, unmixed with any feeling of differing or opposing interests. If a man remain steadfastly in this state of mind all the while he is awake, whether he be standing, walking, sitting, or lying down, then is come to pass the saying "Even in this world holiness has been found."[1]

The ten sins or evil states of mind thus conquered in the course of the four paths are the ten Sangyojanas or Fetters,[2] which with their Pāli names are:—

1. Delusion of self (Sakkāya-diṭṭhi).

[1] 'Metta Sutta,' from Childers's text, J. R. A. S., 1869, describing the state of the Arahats.

[2] With numbers 1, 2, 5, 8, 9, compare numbers 28, 30, 26, 51, 52, of the Sanskāras: above, p. 92. On No. 1 see also p. 95; and on all the Fetters Dhp. v. 221. *Bandzhana* at Dhp. 345, 346, is quite different.

2. Doubt (Vicikicchā).
3. Dependence on rites (Sīlabbata-parāmāsa).[1]
4. Sensuality, bodily passions (Kāma).
5. Hatred, ill-feeling (Patigha).
6. Love of life on earth (Rūparāga).
7. Desire for life in heaven (Arūparāga).
8. Pride (Māno).
9. Self-righteousness (Uddhacca).
10. Ignorance (Avijjā).

When the first five fetters are completely broken, the converted Buddhist has become an Arahat, and has entered the fourth path; when the other five are broken, he has become Asekha, and thus put an end to all delusion and to all sorrow.

One might fill pages with the awe-struck and ecstatic praise which is lavished in Buddhist writings on this condition of mind, the Fruit of the fourth Path, the state of an Arahat, of a man made perfect according to the Buddhist faith. But all that could be said can be included in one pregnant phrase—THIS IS NIRVĀNA.

"To him who has finished the Path, and passed beyond sorrow, who has freed himself on all sides, and thrown away every fetter, there is no more fever of grief." "He whose senses have become tranquil, like a horse well broken-in by the driver; who is free from pride and the lust of the flesh, and the lust of existence, and the defilement of ignorance—him even the gods envy. Such a one whose conduct is right, remains like the broad earth, unvexed; like the pillar

[1] Compare the first few lines of p. 24. Modern Buddhists class Christianity under this Fetter. Alabaster, 'Wheel of the Law,' p. 237.

of the city gate, unmoved; like a pellucid lake, unruffled. For such there are no more births. Tranquil is the mind, tranquil the words and deeds of him who is thus tranquillized, and made free by wisdom."[1]

"They who, by steadfast mind have become exempt from evil desire, and well trained in the teachings of Gautama; they, having obtained the fruit of the fourth Path, and immersed themselves in that ambrosia, have received without price, and are in the enjoyment of Nirvāna. Their old karma is exhausted, no new karma is being produced; their hearts are free from the longing after future life; the cause of their existence being destroyed, and no new yearnings springing up within them, they the wise, are extinguished like this lamp."[2] "That mendicant conducts himself well, who has conquered (sin) by means of holiness, from whose eyes the veil of error has been removed, who is well-trained in religion; and, who, free from yearning, and skilled in the knowledge, has attained unto Nirvāna."[3]

What then is Nirvāna, which means simply going out, extinction; it being quite clear, from what has gone before, that this cannot be the extinction of a soul? *It is the extinction of that sinful, grasping condition of mind and heart, which would otherwise, according to the great mystery of Karma, be the cause of*

[1] 'Dhammapada,' verses 90, 94–96.

[2] 'Ratana Sutta,' 7, 14. Of Amata, it should be noted that when it was first used of Nirvāna, it had acquired the sense of ambrosia, and always alludes to it. Thus we have the Lake of Ambrosia, Fausboll's 'Jātaka,' v. 25, and 'Sweet food and heavenly drink' at Rat Sutta, v. 4. See also below pp. 60, 184.

[3] 'Sammāparibbājanīya Sutta,' 14.

renewed individual existence. That extinction is to be brought about by, and runs parallel with, the growth of the opposite condition of mind and heart; and it is complete when that opposite condition is reached. Nirvāna is therefore the same thing as a *sinless, calm state of mind;* and if translated at all, may best, perhaps, be rendered 'holiness'—holiness, that is, in the Buddhist sense, *perfect peace, goodness, and wisdom.*

To attempt translations of such pregnant terms is however always dangerous, as the new word—part of a new language which is the outcome of a different tone of thought—while it may denote the same or nearly the same idea, usually calls up together with it very different ones. This is the case here; our word holiness would often suggest the ideas of love to, and awe in the felt presence of, a personal creator—ideas inconsistent with Buddhist holiness. On the other hand, Nirvāna implies the ideas of intellectual energy, and of the cessation of individual existence; of which the former is not essential to, and the latter is quite unconnected with, our idea of holiness. Holiness and Nirvāna, in other words, may represent states of mind not greatly different; but these are due to different causes, and end in different results; and in using the words, it is impossible to confine one's thought to the thing expressed, so as not also to think of its origin and its effect.

It is better, therefore, to retain the word Nirvāna as the name of the Buddhist *summum bonum,* which is a blissful holy state, a moral condition, a modification of personal character; and we should allow the word to remind us, as it did the early Buddhists, both of the 'Path' which leads to the extinction of sin, and also of the break in the transfer of Karma, which the extinction of sin will bring about. That this must be the effect of Nirvāna is plain ; for that state of mind which in Nirvāna is extinct (upādāna, klesa, trishā) is precisely that which will, according to the great mystery of Buddhism, lead at death to the formation of a new individual, to whom the Karma of the dissolved or dead one will be transferred.[1] That new individual would consist of certain bodily and mental qualities or tendencies, enumerated, as already explained, in the five Skandhas or aggregates. A comprehensive name of all the five is *upādi*, a word derived (in allusion to the name of their cause, upādāna), from upādā, to grasp, either with the hand or the mind. Now, when a Buddhist has become an Arahat, when he has reached Nirvāna, the fruit of the fourth Path, he has extinguished upādāna, and klesa (*i.e.* sin), but he is still alive; the upādi, the Skandhas, his body with all its powers, that is to say, the fruit of his former sin, remain. These, however, are impermanent, they will soon pass away; there will then be nothing left to bring about the rise of a new set of skandhas, of a new individual; and the Arahat will be no longer alive or existent in any sense at all; he will have reached Parinibbāna, complete extinction, or Nir-upādi-sesa-nibbāna-dhātu,[2] extinction so com-

[1] See above, p. 101.

[2] Parinibbāna Sutta, J. R. A. S., vol. viii. p. 238. In contradistinction, Nirvāna is called sa-upādi-sesa-nibbāna ('Vangīsa Sutta,' verse 14). Comp. Julien's Hiouen Thsang II. 58.

plete that the upādi, the five skandhas, survive no longer—that is, in one word, Death.

The life of man, to use a constantly recurring Buddhist simile or parable, is like the flame of an Indian lamp, a metal or earthenware saucer in which a cotton wick is laid in oil. One life is derived from another, as one flame is lit at another; it is not the same flame, but without the other it would not have been. As flame cannot exist without oil, so life, individual existence, depends on the cleaving to low and earthly things, the sin of the heart. If there is no oil in the lamp, it will go out, though not until the oil which the wick has drawn up, is exhausted: and then no new flame can be lighted there. And so the parts and powers of the sinless man will be dissolved, and no new being will be born to sorrow. The wise will pass away, will go out like the flame of a lamp, and their Karma will be individualized no longer.[1]

Stars, long ago extinct, may be still visible to us by the light they emitted before they ceased to burn; but the rapidly vanishing effect of a no longer active cause will soon cease to strike upon our senses; and where the light was, will be darkness. So the living, moving body of the perfect man is visible still, though its cause has ceased to act: but it will soon decay, and die, and pass away; and as no new body will be formed, where life was, will be nothing.

Death, utter death, with no new life to follow, is then a result of, but it is not Nirvāna. The Buddhist heaven is not death, and it is not on death but on

[1] Compare Ratana Sutta, v. 14, quoted above, p. 111, and the parable of the Tree, below, p. 137.

a virtuous life here and now, that the Pitakas lavish those terms of ecstatic description which they apply to Nirvāna, as the fruit of the fourth Path or Arahatship.

Thus of the Dhamma-pada Professor Max Müller, who was the first to point out the fact, says,[1] "If we look in the Dhamma-pada at every passage where Nirvāna is mentioned, there is not one which would require that its meaning should be annihilation, while most, if not all, would become perfectly unintelligible if we assigned to the word Nirvāna" that signification.

The same thing may be said of such other parts of the Pitakas as are accessible to us in published texts. Thus the commentator on the Jātakas quotes some verses from the Buddhavansa, or History of the Buddhas, which is one of the books of the Second Pitaka. In those verses we have (*inter alia*) an argument based on the logical assumption that if a positive exists, its negative must also exist; if there is heat, there must be cold; and so on. In one of these pairs we find existence opposed, not to Nirvāna, but to non-existence; whilst, in another, the three fires (of lust, hatred, and delusion) are opposed to Nirvāna.[2] It follows, I think, that to the mind of the composer of the Buddhavansa, Nirvāna meant not the extinction, the negation, of being, but the extinction, the absence, of the three fires of passion. To quote here *all* the passages in the Pitakas in which the word Nirvāna occurs would be tedious, but they will be found in the appendix to this chapter, together

[1] 'Buddhaghosha's Parables,' p. xli.

[2] Fausböll, Jātaka text, p. 14.

with the most important passages from the Ceylon fifth-century commentators, and from other later books, both Sanskrit and Pāli. From those passages it would seem that the word was used in its original sense only, even as late as the time of Buddhagosha; after that time we occasionally (but very seldom, and only when the context makes the modification clear) find Nirvāna used where we should expect anupādisesanibbāna or parinibbāna,—just as bow is actually used for rainbow, where 'in the heaven,' or some such expression, is in the context; and it is conceivable that 'phrase' might come to be used for 'paraphrase.' In these cases the general sense of the context has the same force as the qualifying prefix, or prefixed word, would otherwise have had; and so far from this usage being a proof that Nirvāna, without the qualifying prefix, meant the same as Parinirvāna, it is very striking that such a use of the word should not occur in books even much earlier than those in which it is actually found.

So little is known of the books of the Northern Buddhist canon, that it is difficult to discover their doctrine on any controverted point; but so far as it is possible to judge, they confirm that use of the word Nirvāna which we find in the Pitakas. In the Lalita Vistara the word occurs in a few passages, in none of which the sense of annihilation is necessary, and in all of which I take Nirvāna to mean the same as the Pāli Nibbāna.[1] The Tibetan rendering of the word is a long phrase, meaning, according to Burnouf,

[1] Foucaux, pp. 106, 235, 262, 290, 340, 364-8, 391. Burnouf, 'Lotus,' 404.

'the state of him who is delivered from sorrow,' or, 'the state in which one finds oneself when one is so delivered' (*affranchi*).[1] This is confirmed by Mr. Beal's comprehensive and valuable work on Chinese Buddhism, where the Chinese version of the Sanskrit Parinirvāna Sūtra has the following passages:—"Nirvāna is just so. In the midst of sorrow there is no Nirvāna, and in Nirvāna there is no sorrow." "I" (Gautama) "devote myself wholly to moral culture, so as to arrive at the highest condition of moral rest (the highest Nirvāna)."[2]

And so again, in the verse quoted from the Prātimoksha.[3]

'The Heart, scrupulously avoiding all idle dissipation,
Diligently applying itself to the Holy Law of Buddha,
Letting go all lust, and consequent disappointment,
Fixed and unchangeable, enters on Nirvāna.'

If we can trust these translations through the Chinese,—and I think we may, as far as our purpose requires,—the early Sanskrit texts of the Northern Buddhists, like the Pāli texts of the Pitakas, look upon Nirvāna as a moral condition, to be reached here, in this world, and in this life.

In the later Sanskrit books the notices of Nirvāna are so meagre that no conclusion can be drawn as to the views of their authors; but it is clear that they use Parinirvāṇa and Anupadhiṣesha Nirvāṇa-dhātu in the sense of death with no life to follow.[4]

[1] 'Introduction à l'histoire du Buddhisme Indien,' p. 19.

[2] 'Catena of Buddhist Scriptures from the Chinese,' 174, 183. Compare 247, 250, 263, 283.

[3] *Ibid.*, p. 159.

[4] Nirvāna is mentioned at pages 114, 116, 118, 120, of the

The reader will not, I trust, think that the few pages devoted to the discussion of the meaning of Nirvāna have been, nevertheless, too many. It has seemed to me of the first importance to make my views on this point quite clear, and I have attempted to state them as shortly as possible, consistently with clearness. For controversy there has been no space, and even had there been, I should have avoided it. It only remains for me to express my obligations to others. No one has written a work on Buddhism without touching on this great question; each one has thrown some light upon it, and if my view of it be correct, has had foundation for his explanation of the term; but thanks are especially due to Professor Max Müller and Professor Childers. These distinguished scholars alone have sought to define the meaning of the word by a strict comparison of the passages in which it had been found to occur.[1] I have followed their method, and though in my conclusion I have ventured to differ somewhat from them, it seems to me to derive its chief confirmation

'Lotus de la bonne Loi.' Where Burnouf has *Nirvāna complet*, the original has, I presume, Parinirvāṇa. Compare the quotations from the Avadāna Ṣataka and Panca-krama, at pp. 78, 83, 590, 591, of the 'Introduction.' Upadhi-ṣesha is a blunder of the Sanskrit Buddhist writers for the Pāli upādi-sesa. See Childers's Dict. s. v. It was re-introduced into Ceylon in the 12th century, and is found in Parākrama Bāhu's inscription at the Gal Wihāre in Pulastipura.

[1] Professor Max Müller discusses the passage in the 'Dhammapada' (Nos. 1–11 below); Professor Childers added those in the 'Khuddaka Pāṭha' (Nos. 12–14 and 16 below).

from the fact that it reconciles and depends upon both of theirs.[1]

[1] The argument in this chapter is taken from an article by the present writer in the 'Contemporary Review' for Jan., 1877. On Nirvāna, besides the passages quoted above and in the notes, see *Gogerly*, 'Journal of the Royal Asiatic Society,' Ceylon Branch, 1867-1870, part I., p. 130; *the Rev. G. Scott*, *ibid.* p. 89; *Spence Hardy's* 'Eastern Monachism,' pp. 280–309, and 'Legends and Theories of the Buddhists,' pp. 169–174; *Bigandet*, 'Legend of Guadama,' 143, 320–323; *Burnouf*, Introduction, pp. 516–522, 'Lotus' 519; *James d'Alwis*, 'Buddhist Nirvāna' (a pamphlet full of information, which has been too little read); *Wassilief*, 'Der Buddhismus,' pp. 84, 93–101, *Köppen*, 'Die Religion des Buddha,' i. pp. 306-309; *Alabaster*, 'Wheel of the Law,' p. xxxvii. *et seq.* and 165; *Rémusat*, 'Foe Koue Ki,' pp. 80, 156; *Sir Coomāra Swāmy*, 'Sutta Nipāta,' xxiv.; *Max Müller*, 'Chips,' i. 247-250, 280-290; and *Childers'* Dict., under Nibbānaṁ, Parinibbānaṁ, and Upādiseso. A number of references to other writers will be found in *Obry's* 'Du Nirvāna Bouddhique,' Paris, 1863.

APPENDIX TO CHAPTER IV.

PASSAGES IN THE PUBLISHED PARTS OF THE PITAKAS IN WHICH THE WORD NIBBĀNA (PĀLI FOR NIRVĀNA) OCCURS.

1. *Dhamma-pada*, *v.* 23.—These wise people (speaking of Arahats) meditative, persevering, ever full of strength, attain to Nirvāna, the highest bliss.

2. *Dhp. v.* 32.—The mendicant who delights in diligence, and looks with terror on sloth, cannot fall away,—he is in the very presence of Nirvāna.

3. *Dhp. v.* 134.—If thou keepest thyself as silent as a broken gong, thou hast attained Nirvāna; no angry clamour is found in thee. (The preceding verse condemns harsh speaking.)

4. *Dhp. v.* 184.—The Buddhas declare the best self-mortification to be patience, long-suffering; the best (thing of all) to be Nirvāna; for he is no (true) monk who strikes, no (true) mendicant who insults others.

5. *Dhp. vv.* 202, 203.—There is no fire like lust, there is no sin like hate, there is no misery like the Skandhas, there is no happiness like peace. Hunger is the worst disease, the Sanskāras the worst suffering: knowing this as it really is, is Nirvāna, the highest bliss.[1]

6. *Dhp. v.* 226.—Those who are ever on the watch, who study day and night, whose heart is set on Nirvāna, their sinfulness dies away (literally, their Āsavas[2] go to an end).

---

[1] On the Skandhas and Sanskāras see above, pp. 89–90. 'Hunger' surely alludes to taṇhā (thirst).

[2] The Āsavas are 4; sensual pleasure, lust after life, delusion (about the soul), and ignorance (of the four 'Noble Truths'). Burnouf, 'Lotus,' 823, says they are three, and omits delusion; but this is probably a slip, for his authority is the Parinibbāna Sutta; and the text itself (Childers's ed. J. R. A. S., 1876, pp. 228–230, &c.) gives the same four as Hardy, Manual, 496, E. M., 290. Anāsava is a synonym for the Arahat, who has entered the fourth Path.

7. *Dhp. v.* 283.—Cut down lust, not a tree; from lust springs fear: having cut down with (all) its undergrowth (vanatha), the forest of lust (vana) become Nir-vāna'd, (dis-lusted, free from yearning,) oh! mendicants.[1]

8. *Dhp. v.* 285.—Cut off the love of self, as (you might) an autumn lotus with your hand—devote yourself to the 'Path' of peace alone, (for) by the Blessed One, Nirvāna has been revealed.[2]

9. *Dhp. v.* 289.—The wise man, restrained according to the Precepts,[3] seeing the force of this truth, should at once clear the 'Path' leading to Nirvāna.

10. *Dhp. v.* 369.—Bail out, O! mendicant, this boat;[4] when bailed out it will go quickly: when you have cut off lust and hatred, thou shalt go to Nirvāna.

11. *Dhp. v.* 372.—There is no meditation (Dhyāna),[5] without wisdom, no wisdom without Dhyāna; he who has both wisdom and Dhyāna, is in the presence of Nirvāna.

12. *Mangala Sutta, v.* 11.—Temperance and chastity, to discern the Noble Truths, to experience Nirvāna, that is the greatest blessing.

---

[1] This curious pun is repeated at v. 344, almost exactly in the same form. As there is a doubt about the reading, however, I do not quote the latter verse.

[2] The idea, perhaps, is that though Gautama revealed the 'Noble eight-fold Path' leading to Nirvāna, yet only personal exertion can bring one to it. Compare v. 276, quoted above, p. 107.

[3] The Precepts (Sīlas) are the ten commandments (Hardy, E. M., 23). See below p. 141.

[4] At Kāma Sutta, v. 6, the same figure is used. I take the water as the Āsavas; the water-logged boat to be the sinful man; the sea to be Sansāra, transmigration; and Nirvāna to be the island, the other shore, having reached which one is safe from being tossed about again in future births, the waves of the ocean of transmigration. Compare Nāvā Sutta, 4 (below, p. 155).

[5] The four Dhyānas are four stages of religious meditation, whereby the believer's mind is gradually purged from all earthly emotions, while the body falls into trance. See Childers's Dict. *s. v.* Jhānaṁ, and below, p. 176.

13. *Ratana Sutta, v.* 12.—(Beautiful) as groves and thickets covered with blossoms in the first hot month of summer (the Buddha), preached for the good of all his glorious Law, which leads to Nirvāna.

14. *Nidhikaṇḍa Sutta, v.* 13.—All earthly glory, and heavenly joy, and the gain of Nirvāna, can be procured by this treasure, (charity, piety, and self-control).

15. The passage quoted above, p. 118, from the *Buddhavansa.* 'And as where heat is, there is also cold; so where the threefold fire (of lust, hatred, and ignorance) is, there Nirvāna must be sought.'

16. Lastly, the passage quoted from the Mahā Vagga of the first Pitaka, by Gogerly, 'on Buddhism,' p. 6. 'This is a matter hard to understand, the suppression of all the Sanskāras, the forsaking of all sin, the destruction of yearning (taṇhā), the absence of lust, the cessation (of sorrow), Nirvāna.'

The above are *all* the passages in which Nirvāna is mentioned in published texts from the Pitakas. It would be possible to strengthen the case by quoting all those passages in which the moral condition called, in those just quoted, Nirvāna, is expressed by some other figure. Such are the Heavenly Drink (by which the wise are nourished), the Tranquil State, the Unshaken Condition (alluding to the 'final perseverance' theory), Cessation (of sorrow), Absence (of sin, the four Āsavas), Destruction (of taṇhā), and other expressions. It would also be possible to strengthen the case by quoting all passages mentioning Parinibbāna, which is also something that takes place here on earth, viz. the 'going out,' the death, of an Arahat, of a man without the Āsavas, of one who has attained Nirvāna. "Some people are reborn as men; evil doers in hell; the well-conducted go to heaven, but the arahats go out altogether" ('Parinibbanti Anāsavā,' Dhp., v. 126). But I will only mention the important fact that in the Pāli Parinibbāna Sūtta, giving a long account of Gautama's death, the word Nibbāna standing alone in its ethical or figurative sense, does not once occur.[1]

[1] It occurs once in its literal sense (like the going out of a lamp, pajjotass' eva nibbānaṁ, J. R. A. S., 1876, viii. 252).

The passages in the later books in which the word Nibbāna occurs are as follows :—

'Pātimokkha,' pp. 3, 4, 5.

'Jina Alankāra,' *apud* Burnouf, 'Lotus,' pp. 332, 516, 545, 831. Compare 376.

'Rasavāhini,' p. 29.

'Mahāvansa,' p. 22, and also ch. xxx. (J. R. A. S. 1874), verse 30.

'Dhamma-pada Commentary,' the passages referring to the quoted verses, and compare pp. 118, 282.

'Jātaka' (Commentary), pp. 4, 14, 61, 393, 401. Compare Vimutti, pp. 77, 78, 80. Also Ten. Jāt., 91.

'Madurattha' Vilāsini J. Bengal A. S. vii. 796-797.

The word Nirvāna occurs in 'Saddharma Puṇḍarīka,' Burnouf's translation, pp. 11, 45, 63, 69, 73, 76, 77, 80, 88, 108, 109, 120.

'Saddharma Lankāvatara,' *apud* Burnouf, Introduction, &c. 516, 520.

'Avadāna Ṣataka,' *ibid*, 509.

CHAPTER V.

THE GENERAL MORAL PRECEPTS OF BUDDHISM.

In the last chapter an attempt has been made to put into clear and distinct language the principles of the intricate and obscure system of Buddhist metaphysics. The task has been no easy one; not only on account of the inherent difficulty of the subject, but because of the confusion arising from the utter strangeness of ideas, which are nevertheless expressed in words capable of being used in a Christian sense. Our present object, to give a sketch of Buddhist morality, will be more easily attained.

In the Buddhist age the humility of confessed ignorance was as yet impossible. To use a Buddhist expression, there was an upādāna, or grasping state of mind, which was the standing cause of a 'delusion'—the grasping, the lust, namely, after certainty, after absolute knowledge. From this upādāna the Buddha never freed himself, and it produced in him the 'delusion' of the great theory of Karma. To free himself and the world from the supposed effects of this non-existent hypothetical cause, he thought he had discovered a 'Path' which he called 'Noble,' an epithet it most assuredly deserves. Never in the whole history of the world has the bare and barren tree of metaphysical inquiry put forth, where one would least expect it, a more lovely flower—the flower that grew into the Fruit which gave the nectar of Nirvāna. The Fruit of the fourth Path was not, indeed, for ordinary hands to pluck, for it was first necessary to extinguish much evil in the heart by the cultivation of the opposite virtue. Though laymen could attain Nirvāna, we are told of only one or two instances of their having done so;[1] and though it was more possible for members of the Buddhist order of mendicants, we only hear, *after* the time of Gautama, of one or two who did so. No one now hears of such an occurrence; but the Buddhist hopes to enter, even though he will not reach the end of, the paths in this life; and if he once enters them, he is certain in some future existence, perhaps under less material conditions, to arrive at the goal of salvation, at the calm and rest of Nirvāna.

There are, accordingly, many directions of a much more general, and less metaphysical nature than those we have been discussing; precepts applicable to all men, not only to those who have devoted themselves to the religious life. Such, for instance, are the precepts laid down in the now well-known

Buddhist Beatitudes.

A deva speaks—

1. Many angels and men
Have held various things blessings,
When they were yearning for happiness.
Do thou declare to us the chief good.

---

[1] At p. 64 of the Jātaka Commentary, it is stated that Suddhodana, Gautama's father, reached Arahatship on his deathbed. At p. 308 of the commentary on the Dhamma-pada Santati, a prime minister, attains Nirvāna. Comp. Hardy, E. M. 14.

Gautama answers—

2. Not to serve the foolish,
But to serve the wise;
To honour those worthy of honour:
This is the greatest blessing.

3. To dwell in a pleasant land,
Good works done in a former birth,
Right desires in the heart:
This is the greatest blessing.

4. Much insight and education,
Self-control and pleasant speech,
And whatever word be well-spoken:
This is the greatest blessing.

5. To support father and mother,
To cherish wife and child,
To follow a peaceful calling:
This is the greatest blessing.

6. To bestow alms and live righteously,[1]
To give help to kindred,
Deeds which cannot be blamed:
These are the greatest blessing.

7. To abhor, and cease from sin,
Abstinence from strong drink,
Not to be weary in well-doing,
These are the greatest blessing.

8. Reverence and lowliness,
Contentment and gratitude,
The hearing of the Law at due seasons,
This is the greatest blessing.

9. To be long-suffering and meek,
To associate with the tranquil (*i.e.* Buddhist monks),
Religious talk at due seasons,
This is the greatest blessing.

---

[1] Quoted in the 'Dhamma-pada' Commentary, p. 317, as having been a well-known verse in the time of Gautama!

10. Self-restraint and purity,
The knowledge of the Noble Truths,
The realization of Nirvāna,
This is the greatest blessing.

11. Beneath the stroke of life's changes,
The mind that shaketh not,
Without grief or passion, and secure,
This is the greatest blessing.

12. On every side are invincible
They who do acts like these,
On every side they walk in safety,
And theirs is the greatest blessing.[1]

Again, the Nidhikaṇḍa Sutta (Treasure Chapter), after saying that what men call treasure, when laid up in a deep pit, profits nothing, and may easily be lost, goes on—

The (real) treasure is that laid up by man or woman
Through charity and piety, temperance and self-control,
In the sacred shrine, or the Buddhist church,
In individual man, in the stranger and sojourner,
In his father, and mother, and elder brother.
The treasure thus hid is secure, and passes not away;
Though he leave the fleeting riches of this world, this a man takes with him—
A treasure that no wrong of others, and no thief, can steal.
Let the wise man do good deeds—the treasure that follows of itself.'

Bald and literal translations like the above lose, of course, all the rhythm and beauty of the Pāli

---

[1] 'Mangala Sutta.' The text in Childers's 'Khuddaka Pāṭha.' Translated from the Pāli by the editor, *loc. cit.*, by Sir Coomāra Swamy, in his 'Sutta Nipāta,' p. 72; and by the Rev. J. Gogerly, in the 'Ceylon Friend' for June, 1839. Translated from the Burmese by Bigandet, p. 115, note 62.

verses, but it has been thought a less evil to convey a wrong impression of the grace of the original, than to convey a wrong impression of its thought.[1]

Of the same general nature, appealing to all men, are the following extracts from the Dhamma-pada or 'Scripture verses,' a collection common to both schools of Buddhism, though the Chinese collection is somewhat larger than the Pāli.[2]

5. For never in this world does hatred cease by hatred;
Hatred ceases by love; this is always its nature.

13. As rain breaks in upon an ill-thatched hut,
So passion breaks in upon the untrained mind.

26. The foolish follow after vanity; deluded men!
While the wise guards earnestness as his richest treasure.

27. Follow not after vanity, nor familiarity with the delight of lust,
For the earnest and the thoughtful obtain ample joy.

28. When by earnestness he has put an end to vanity,
And has climbed the terraced heights of wisdom,
The wise looks down upon the fools;
Serene he looks upon the toiling crowd,
As one standing on a hill looks down
On those who stand upon the plain.[3]

---

[1] In the last extract the idea is simply that good deeds done in one birth will be the very thing that will determine the material and spiritual lot of the individual in the next birth,—of another individual, from our point of view; of the same, according to the Buddhist theory. Passages like these have naturally been understood by Europeans to refer to a soul passing from a temporary state to an eternal one; but such an idea was never present to the mind of a Buddhist reading them. Compare Dhp., v. 176, quoted below, p. 130.

[2] Beal's 'Buddhist Tripitaka, as known in China and Japan,' p. 113.

[3] Childers's Dict., Preface, p. xiv. He there compares Lucretius, lib. ii. 7–14.

29. Earnest among the heedless;
Wide awake among the sleepers;
The wise makes progress, leaving those behind
As the swift steed the horse who has no strength.

35. It is good to tame the mind,
Difficult to hold in, and flighty;
Rushing where'er it listeth;
A tamed mind is the bringer of bliss.

42. Whatever an enemy may do to an enemy,
Or an angry man to an angry man,
A mind intent on what is wrong
Works evil worse.

49. As the bee—injuring not
The flower, its colour, or scent—
Flies away, taking the nectar;
So let the wise man dwell upon the earth.[1]

50. Not where others fail, or do or leave undone,
The wise should notice what himself has done or left undone.

52. Like a beautiful flower full of colour, without scent,
The fine words of him who does not act accordingly are fruitless.
Like a beautiful flower full of colour and full of scent,
The fine words of him who acts accordingly are full of fruit.

61. As long as the sin bears no fruit,
The fool, he thinks it honey;
But when the sin ripens,
Then, indeed, he goes down into sorrow.

103. One may conquer a thousand thousand men in battle,
But he who conquers himself alone is the greatest victor.

121. Let no man think lightly of sin, saying in his heart, 'It cannot overtake me.'

---

[1] Comp. 'Sigālovāda Sutta,' in 'Sept Suttas Pālis,' p. 305.

As the waterpot fills by even drops of water falling,
The fool gets full of sin, ever gathering little by little.

146. How is there laughter? How is there joy?
While the fire of passion, and hatred, and ignorance is always burning,
Ye, surrounded by darkness,
Why seek ye not a light?

159. Let a man make himself what he preaches to others;
The well-subdued may subdue others; one's self, indeed, is hard to tame.

172. He who formerly was heedless, and afterwards becomes earnest,
Lights up this world, like the moon escaped from a cloud.

176. The man who has transgressed one law, and (speaks) lies,
And scoffs at the next world, there is no evil he will not do.

197. Let us live happily, then, not hating those who hate us!
Let us live free from hatred among men who hate!

198. Let us live happily, then, free from ailments among the ailing!
Let us dwell free from afflictions among men who are sick at heart!

199. Let us live happily, then, free from care among the busy!
Let us dwell free from yearning among men who are anxious!

200. Let us live happily, then, though we call nothing our own!
We shall become like the bright gods who feed on happiness!

201. Victory breeds hatred, for the conquered is ill at ease.
The tranquil live well at ease, careless of victory and defeat.

222. He who holds back rising anger as (one might) a rolling chariot,
Him, indeed, I call a driver: others only hold the reins.

223. Let a man overcome anger by kindness, evil by good;
Let him conquer the stingy by a gift, the liar by truth.[1]

---

[1] This verse occurs also in the 'Mahābhārata,' v. 1518.

224. Let him speak the truth; let him not yield to anger;
Let him give when asked, even from the little he has!
By these three things he will enter the presence of the gods.

292. What ought to be done is neglected; what ought not to be done is done.
Those who are proud and slothful their āsavas (delusions) increase.[1]

354. The gift of the Law exceeds all gifts,
The sweetness of the Law exceeds all sweetness;
The delight of the Law exceeds all delight;
The extinction of thirst overcomes all grief.

Vasala Sutta, 27:—

Not by birth does one become low caste,
Not by birth does one become a Brahman;
By his actions alone one becomes low caste,
By his actions alone one becomes a Brahman.[2]

Āmagandha Sutta, 7, 11.—"Anger, drunkenness, obstinacy, bigotry, deception, envy, self-praise, disparaging others, high-mindedness, evil communications, these constitute uncleanness; not verily the eating of flesh.

"Neither abstinence from fish or flesh, nor going naked, nor shaving the head, nor matted hair, nor dirt, nor a rough garment, nor sacrifices to Agni (fire), will cleanse a man not free from delusions.

"Reading the Vedas, making offerings to priests, or sacrifices to the gods, self-mortifications by heat or cold, and many such-like penances performed for the sake of immortality, these do not cleanse the man not free from delusions."

[1] On the Āsavas, see above, p. 120.

[2] The same idea occurs in the 'Mahābhārata,' iii. 14,075, 17,392. See Dr. Muir, in the 'Indian Antiquary,' Nov. 1876, p. 312; and compare Köppen, i. 129.

Kinsīla Sutta, 5.—"Live ye freed from lasciviousness, firm-minded, abandoning inordinate laughter; not recounting worthless stories of kings and others; not lamenting, fretting, deceiving; without hypocrisy, greediness, malice, harshness, and rusty ignorance."

Uṭṭhāna Sutta, 1, 4.—"Rise! sit up! what advantage is there in your sleeping? To men ailing, pierced by the darts of sorrow, what sleep indeed can there be? Sloth is defilement, to be ever heedless is defilement! By earnestness and wisdom root out your darts of sorrow!"

It would be very interesting to know to whom we owe the actual composition of these and similar verses. They purport to be the real words spoken, or answers given by Gautama on certain specified occasions, on which it is gravely reported that he uttered such and such a stanza. It is believed that they occur in the midst of prose throughout the Pitakas, and the Dhamma-pada is confessedly merely a collection of such verses culled from the other scriptures. On the other hand, in later Buddhist books in modern languages the stories are often found without the verses. These stories are always very instructive, as showing the way in which Buddhism looks at human affairs, and some of them are not without charm when read merely as tales. One of these is the story of Kisāgotamī, given by Captain Rogers in his translation from the Burmese of some of these stories.[1]

[1] 'Buddhaghosha's Parables,' chap. x.—There are three verses of the 'Dhamma-pada' said to have been spoken about a Kisāgotamī, but they are all quite inapplicable to this story (vv. 114, 287, 395).

Parable of the Mustard-seed.

Kisāgotamī is the name of a young girl, whose marriage with the only son of a wealthy man was brought about in true fairly-tale fashion. She had one child, but when the beautiful boy could run alone, it died. The young girl in her love for it carried the dead child clasped to her bosom, and went from house to house of her pitying friends asking them to give her medicine for it. But a Buddhist mendicant, thinking 'She does not understand,' said to her, 'My good girl, I myself have no such medicine as you ask for, but I think I know of one who has.' 'O tell me who that is,' said Kisāgotamī. 'The Buddha can give you medicine; go to him,' was the answer. She went to Gautama, and doing homage to him, said, 'Lord and master, do you know any medicine that will be good for my child?' 'Yes, I know of some,' said the Teacher. Now it was the custom for patients or their friends to provide the herbs which the doctors required, so she asked what herbs he would want. 'I want some mustard-seed,' he said; and when the poor girl eagerly promised to bring some of so common a drug, he added, 'You must get it from some house where no son, or husband, or parent, or slave has died.' 'Very good,' she said, and went to ask for it, still carrying her dead child with her. The people said, 'Here is mustard seed, take it'; but when she asked, 'In my friend's house has any son died, or a husband, or a parent or slave?' they answered, 'Lady!

what is this that you say; the living are few, but the dead are many.' Then she went to other houses, but one said, 'I have lost a son'; another, 'We have lost our parents'; another, 'I have lost my slave.' At last, not being able to find a single house where no one had died, her mind began to clear, and summoning up resolution, she left the dead body of her child in a forest, and returning to the Buddha paid him homage. He said to her, 'Have you the mustard-seed?' 'My Lord,' she replied, 'I have not; the people tell me that the living are few, but the dead are many.' Then he talked to her on that essential part of his system—the impermanency of all things, till her doubts were cleared away, and, accepting her lot, she became a disciple and entered the first Path.

The Parable of the Sower.

In another of these stories, which is before us in three versions, from the Pāli, Sinhalese, and Burmese respectively,[1] we find the processes of agriculture worked out into an elaborate allegory. A wealthy Brahman, named Bhāradvāja, was holding his harvest-home when the Teacher comes and stands by with his bowl. Some of the people went up and paid him reverence, but the Brahman was angry, and said,

[1] Sir Coomāra Swamy's 'Sutta Nipāta,' 'Kasi Bhāradvāja Sutta,' p. 20–23; Hardy, 'Manual of Buddhism,' 214–216; and Bigandet, 'Life of Guadama,' 226, 227. The allegory in each differs in such essential points from the others that it is a pity we have not the Pitaka text. I have followed chiefly the version in 'Sutta Nipāta.' The occasion of this discourse will be found above, p. 72.

'Sramana (*i.e.* mendicant), I plough and sow, and having ploughed and sown, I eat; it would be better if you were in like manner to plough and sow, and then you would have food to eat.'

'O! Brahman,' was the answer, 'I too plough and sow, and having ploughed and sown, I eat.'

'You say you are a husbandman; but we see no signs of it,' said the Brahman. 'Where are your bullocks, and the seed, and the plough?'

Then the Teacher answered, 'Faith is the seed I sow, and good works are as the rain that fertilizes it; wisdom and modesty are the parts of the plough, and my mind is the guiding rein. I lay hold of the handle of the Law; earnestness is the goad I use; and diligence is my draught ox. Thus this ploughing is ploughed, destroying the weeds of delusion. The harvest that it yields is the ambrosia fruit of Nirvāna, and by this ploughing all sorrow ends.'

Buddhist Similes.

Parables similar to the above are constantly referred to in the verses of the 'Dhamma-pada,' and are used indeed as standing similes or poetical figures, so well known that there is no need to mention the thing signified, but only to suggest it. Agriculture naturally plays a great part in these parables. Thus *gifts* are looked upon as *seed* which should be sown in the field of humanity, and especially in that part of the field where there are fewest weeds, that is in the field of the Order where the weeds of hate, and passion, and vanity, and yearning have been destroyed. The crop in this case will be Kusala, meritorious Karma which will produce great re[illegible] in some future birth.[1] This is a parable w[illegible] the yellow-robed members of the Order would not willingly let die; and it has become a received truth that the Karma resulting from good or bad deeds is more efficacious both for good or bad, according to the spiritual advancement of those who were affected by the corresponding acts. One of the worst weeds to have in rice-fields is the *bīrana-grass*, whose roots go very deep into the ground, the smallest piece of root left in the ground propagating itself very rapidly. It is therefore most difficult to get rid of, and springs up again when the industrious peasant thinks he has quite got rid of it. This is a standing figure of Trishṇā, the yearning grasping state of mind, to have extinguished which, is to have reached Nirvāna.[2]

Another allegory is that of the *flood* (ogha), which comes down suddenly and carries off the careless sleeper; against which the wise must constantly be on the watch until he is safe on some bank or island which no flood can reach. The flood is of four kinds,—lust, sin, transmigration, and delusion; and the Arahat who has reached the island of Nirvāna is called Oghatiṇṇa, safe from the floods.[3]

Transmigration itself is also constantly called the *ocean:* its ever-tossing waves are births; the foam at

[1] The sequence of ideas, Gal. vi. 6–8, is curiously similar, but not the same. Comp. 'Dhp.,' pp. 356–359; Bigandet, p. 211; Beal, 'Catena,' 194.

[2] 'Dhp.,' verse 335. See the second 'Noble Truth,' p. 106.

[3] 'Dhp.,' verses 25, 47, 251, 287, 370; and 'Buddhaghosha,' at p. 432.

the crest of the waves is this perishable body; the other shore is Nirvāna; having reached which, one does not again enter the great ocean of Sang-sāra.[1]

Again the five Skandhas, the bodily and mental properties and tendencies, are like a *tree*. The tree produces a seed, a fruit, from which will spring another tree; but if the tree be cut off at the root, it will be visible a little while only whilst it decays, and will not produce any further seed.

Again, Trishṇā, the yearning thirst, is compared to a *creeper* which grows like a parasite on the sāla trees, and eventually destroys that on which it was nourished.[2]

A very large number of these similes or parables will be found in those passages quoted from Milinda Prashnaya by Spence Hardy, in his 'Manual of Buddhism'; and it is evident that the early Buddhists regarded such allegories, when they fitted well into any argument, as not only useful to make clear the speaker's meaning, but also of great value in proving the truth of what he said.

Dhammika Sutta.

The duties of a lay disciple are distinctly and clearly laid down in the latter part of the 'Dhammika Sutta,' of which the following verses are quoted from Sir Coomara Swāmy's translation.[3] Gautama himself

[1] Comp. pp. 92, 167. [2] 'Dhp.,' 162, 334, 340.

[3] 'Sutta Nipāta,' ch. 107. I have allowed myself a few alterations, such as 'mendicant' for 'priest,' in v. 18, and in v. 19, according to the commentary on 'Dhp.,' v. 405.

is supposed to be speaking; and has already described the duties of a mendicant, which will be considered separately below (p. 156):—

18. 'Now I tell you of the life which a householder should lead, of the manner in which a disciple should conduct himself well. Such duties as are peculiar to the mendicants cannot be fulfilled by one who has a family.

19. 'Are there any, strong-minded or feeble-minded, who have refrained from oppressing all beings? Neither should any one (of such men) *destroy any life at all*, or sanction the acts of those who do so.

20. 'A disciple then knowing (the law) should refrain from *stealing anything* at any place; should not cause another to steal anything, should not consent to the acts of those who steal anything, should avoid every kind of theft.

21. 'A wise man should avoid married life as if it were a burning pit of live coals. One who is not able to live in a state of celibacy *should not commit adultery*.

22. 'When one is come to a royal assembly or gathering,[1] he should *not tell lies* to any one, or cause any to tell lies, or consent to the acts of those who tell lies; he should avoid every kind of untruth.

23. 'The householder who delights in the law should not indulge *in intoxicating drinks*, should not cause others to drink, should not sanction the acts of those who drink, knowing that it results in insanity.

24. 'The ignorant commit sins in consequence of

[1] That is, at any official inquiry; so that the command here given is not to bear false witness.

drunkenness, and also make others drink. You should avoid this: it is the cause of demerit, insanity, and ignorance—though it be pleasing to the ignorant.

25. *The Eight Precepts.*

1. 'One should not destroy life.
2. 'One should not take that which is not given.
3. 'One should not tell lies.
4. 'One should not become a drinker of intoxicating liquors.
5. 'One should refrain from unlawful sexual intercourse—an ignoble thing.
6. 'One should not eat unseasonable food at nights.[1]
7. 'One should not wear garlands or use perfumes.[1]
8. 'One should sleep on a mat spread on the ground.[1]

'Such, they say,[2] is the eight-fold sacred formula declared by Buddha, who came amongst us to put an end to sorrows.

26. 'Moreover, being of a pious mind, one should observe Uposatha (keep Sabbath) on the 14th, 15th, and 8th day of the lunar fortnight, and Pāti-hārika pakkha (Lent) should also be duly observed.

27. 'In the next place, a wise man who has kept the Sabbath (Uposatha) should in the morning, being of a pious mind, and taking constant delight in so doing,

[1] On these three commands see below, pp. 140, 160.

[2] From this expression it seems that, while verses 18–24 are put into Buddha's own mouth, the rest of the verses are supposed to be spoken by some one else. The order of the commandments in v. 25 is also different from that of the preceding verses.

provide the members of the order with food and drink according to his ability.

28. 'He should maintain his father and mother in a just manner, and should practise a just trade; the householder observing this with diligence reaches the self-shining gods.'[1]

With regard to these commandments, the first five, placed above in the mouth of Gautama himself, require no commentary. They are called the five commandments, *par excellence* (pancha-sīla; Sinhalese, pan-sil), and are binding on every Buddhist.

The other three are not obligatory; but the pious layman is recommended to take the vow of the eight precepts (aṭṭhangasīla, in Sinhalese aṭa-sil). This he may do for any length of time, or for his whole life; and during the time he is under the vow, he should (at least according to Spence Hardy's Manual, p. 488), live apart from his family. But whether the vow has been taken or not, it is considered irreligious to break any of the eight precepts on Sabbath days; and it is, or was, considered especially meritorious to take the vows during the periods of 'extra Lent,' referred to in v. 26.

The Uposatha days are the four days in the lunar month when the moon is full, or new, or halfway between the two. Uposatha is, therefore, a weekly festival, and may well be rendered Sabbath. The numbers given in v. 26 must be understood as the 14th day from the new moon (*i.e.* full-moon day);

[1] It would be a curious fact if this should be the only commandment with promise; but, perhaps, the 'this' refers to all that has been said.

and the 15th day from the full moon (*i.e.* new-moon day); and the 8th day from each of these. The corresponding Sanskrit word is upavasatha, the fast-day previous to the offering of the intoxicating soma, connected with the worship of the moon. Instead of worshipping the moon, the Buddhists were to keep the fast-day by special observance of the moral precepts; one of many instances in which Gautama spiritualized existing words and customs. To place reliance on any sacrificial rite, or have anything to do with the intoxicating soma, would have been quite unbuddhistic. Modern Buddhists have now the same week as we have; and the days are similarly named, after the sun, moon, and five anciently known planets; Monday being Moonday, and so on. But this they derived from the Greek astronomers, probably as late as the sixth century of our era.

The Pātihārika-pakkha, or 'extra fortnights,' is an epithet of three distinct periods. 1. The three months of *Was*, or Lent, which have been explained above (p. 57). 2. The month succeeding Lent, called Chīvara māsa, or Robe-month, because it is then customary to provide mendicants, who require them, with new sets of robes. 3. The first half of the Robe-month; and it is to this third period that the term more particularly applies. During these periods, the observance of the eight precepts (aṭa-sil) is more common than at other periods.

These eight precepts (p. 139), together with two others—viz. 9, to abstain from dancing, music, singing, and stage plays; and, 10, to abstain from the use of gold and silver—are the *ten commandments*

(*Dasa-sīla*) binding on the mendicants. It is curious that the former of these two, in other parts of the Pitakas,[1] is not No. 9, but No. 7; so that it is one of the eight precepts, while the precept concerning beds (which usually runs not to use a high or large bed) is excluded from the eight. Where the Pitakas contradict themselves, it is perhaps presumptuous to attempt to decide between them; but the above poetical list from the 'Dhammika Sutta,' seems to be less reasonable, as it is also less well supported by authority than the usually received order.

The Ten Sins.

Besides the above division of moral duties into the five obligatory and three permissive precepts, there is another division into ten sins, which are:[2]—

Three of the body.
- Taking life.
- Theft (taking what has not been given).
- Unlawful sexual intercourse.

Four of speech.
- Lying.
- Slander (includes 'saying here what one hears there').
- Abuse (swearing).
- Vain conversation.

[1] For instance, in the 'Vinaya Pitaka,' as quoted in the 'Kammavācā' (edit. Dickson, p. 8; see also below, p. 160), and in the 'Khuddaka Paṭha' (edit. Childers, p. 3).

[2] Hardy, 'Manual of Buddhism,' p. 460. Compare the Sanskrit 'Sūtra of the 42 Sayings;' Beal, 'Catena,' p. 192.

Three of the mind.

Covetousness.

Malice.

Scepticism.

Each of these is explained at some length; but the explanations are mostly those which would occur to any moralist on those points. Scepticism, however, is applied to a particular class only, those who roundly deny everything, this world and the next, the Buddha and the law, the effect of moral causes, birth, transmigration, and existence, here or hereafter.

The favourite prose Sūtra or chapter, on the duties of every-day life, is one that is common to both the Northern and Southern schools of Buddhism, and known as

The Sigālowāda Sutta.[1]

The Teacher was staying at the bambu grove near Rājagriha; and going out as usual to beg, sees the householder Sigāla bowing down, with streaming hair, and wet garments, and clasped hands, to the four quarters of the heaven, and the nadir, and the zenith. On the Teacher asking the reason why, Sigāla says that he does this, 'honouring, reverencing, and holding sacred the words of his father.' Then the Teacher, knowing that this was done to avert evil from

[1] Translated from the Pali, by Gogerly, 'Journal of the Roy. As. Soc.,' Ceylon Branch, 1847, and by Childers, 'Contemporary Review,' Feb. 1876. Compare the Rev. S. Beal's Report on 'The Buddhist Tripitaka known in China and Japan,' p. 112. The text in Grimblot's 'Sept Suttas Pālis.'

the six directions, points out to him that the best way to guard the six quarters is by good deeds to men around him,—to his parents as the east,[1] his Teachers as the south, his wife and children as the west, his friends and relatives as the north, men devoted to the religious life (whether Brahmans or Buddhist mendicants) as the zenith, and his slaves and dependents as the nadir. Then in an orderly arrangement, evidently intended to assist the memory, after some general precepts and a description of true friendship, the chief duties men owe to one another are thus enumerated under the above six heads :—

1. *Parents and Children.*

Parents should—

1. Restrain their children from vice.
2. Train them in virtue.
3. Have them taught arts or sciences.
4. Provide them with suitable wives or husbands.
5. Give them their inheritance.

The child should say—

1. I will support them who supported me.
2. I will perform family duties incumbent on them.
3. I will guard their property.
4. I will make myself worthy to be their heir.
5. When they are gone, I will honour their memory

[1] Turning to the East is a very ancient Buddhist practice. Beal's Fa Hiam, 87, 178, 189. Burnouf, 'Lotus,' 451.

2. *Pupils and Teachers.*

The pupil should honour his teachers—

1. By rising in their presence.
2. By ministering to them.
3. By obeying them.
4. By supplying their wants.
5. By attention to instruction.

The teacher should show his affection to his pupils—

1. By training them in all that is good.
2. By teaching them to hold knowledge fast.
3. By instruction in science and lore.
4. By speaking well of them to their friends and companions.
5. By guarding them from danger.

3. *Husband and Wife.*

The husband should cherish his wife—

1. By treating her with respect.
2. By treating her with kindness.
3. By being faithful to her.
4. By causing her to be honoured by others.
5. By giving her suitable ornaments and clothes.

The wife should show her affection for her husband.

1. She orders her household aright.
2. She is hospitable to kinsmen and friends.
3. She is a chaste wife.
4. She is a thrifty housekeeper.
5. She shows skill and diligence in all she has to do.

4. *Friends and Companions.*

The honourable man should minister to his friends—

1. By giving presents.
2. By courteous speech.
3. By promoting their interest.
4. By treating them as his equals.[1]
5. By sharing with them his prosperity.

They should show their attachment to him—

1. By watching over him when he is off his guard.
2. By guarding his property when he is careless.
3. By offering him a refuge in danger.
4. By adhering to him in misfortune.
5. By showing kindness to his family.

5. *Masters and Servants.*

The master should provide for the welfare of his dependants—

1. By apportioning work to them according to their strength.
2. By supplying suitable food and wages.
3. By tending them in sickness.
4. By sharing with them unusual delicacies.
5. By now and then granting them holidays.

They should show their attachment to him as follows :—

1. They rise before him.

[1] This is Gogerly's rendering. Childers has 'By doing to them as he would be done by.' Compare Max Müller's note to 'Dhp.,' verse 129.

2. They retire later to rest.
3. They are content with what is given them.
4. They work cheerfully and thoroughly.
5. They speak well of him (or perhaps properly to him).

6. *Laymen and those devoted to Religion.*

The honourable man ministers to mendicants and Brahmans—

1. By affection in act.
2. By affection in words.
3. By affection in thoughts.
4. By giving them a ready welcome.
5. By supplying their temporal wants.

They should show their affection to him—

1. By dissuading him from vice.
2. By exhorting him to virtue.
3. By feeling kindly towards him.
4. By instructing him in religion.
5. By clearing up his doubts.
6. By pointing the way to heaven.

The whole is then summed up in a few general phrases, such as 'By thus acting the six quarters are each preserved in peace and free from danger.' 'He who worships *these* six quarters will be competent to the duties of a householder, and shall be exalted.' 'Liberality, courtesy, kindliness, and unselfishness—these are to the world what the linchpin is to the rolling chariot.' Sigāla then acknowledges himself converted, and becomes an upāsaka (a lay disciple).

Many of the ideas in the 'Sigālovāda Sutta' are only suitable to a state of society which we, in this anxious time of social struggle, have for ever left behind; but we can, at least, realize how happy would have been the village or the clan on the banks of the Ganges, where the people were full of the kindly spirit of fellow-feeling, the noble spirit of justice, which breathes through these naïve and simple sayings.

Before closing this slight sketch of the general principles of Buddhist morality, it should be pointed out that these precepts are apart from, and run (as far as they go) parallel to, those of the 'Noble Path.' One might obey many, if not most, of them without entering the Paths at all; and obedience to many of them is considered a necessary preliminary[1] to that pilgrimage, which leads to the 'heavenly land of the Arahats,' to the 'Lake of Ambrosia which washes away all sin,' to the 'glad City of Peace,' Nirvāna. By observing these outward commandments, the character will be ennobled and purified; much misfortune will be avoided, much social honour will be gained in this world; and in the next birth a happy entrance will be secured to some less material existence in those heavenly mansions where the bright gods feed on joy. But even good men will not thus escape from the troubled ocean of transmigration; when their good Karma shall be exhausted, they will fall again to a

[1] In this sense the ordinary morality is called Ādi-brahmacariya, while the righteousness of the Paths is Magga-brahmacariya.

lower life. The happiness of the gods themselves,—men or animals or plants,[1] perhaps, in some former birth,—is temporary, and marred by the consciousness that it soon must end. But the very gods envy the blessed state of those who, here on earth, escaped from the floods of passion, have gained the fruit of the Noble Path, and have become cleansed from all defilement, free for ever from all delusion and all sorrow, in that Rest which cannot be shaken,—Nirvāna, which can never be lost.

Thus it was that while most of the superstition and folly which had encrusted the ancient faith was repudiated or ignored, its beauty, and poetry, and truth were first ennobled and spiritualized,[2] and then made subservient to that life of self-control, and wisdom, and universal charity, which Gautama declared to be the highest aim and the highest happiness of man.

[1] Mahā Nidāna Sutta; Grimblot, 'Sept Sutta Pālis,' p. 245.

[2] *E.g.* Fire-worship (above, pp. 59, 155); Soma-worship (above, p. 141); the worship of the six directions (above, p. 144); Caste (Vasala Sutta, quoted p. 131). Ceremonial Bathing (Childers under Nahātaka). So the seven worldly treasures of the Cakravartī become in Buddhism seven virtues (*Ariyadhanāni*). Unclean food is spiritualised into wrong actions in the Āmagandha Sutta, above, p. 131.

CHAPTER VI.

THE SANGHA, THE BUDDHIST ORDER OF MENDICANTS.

It will seem strange to many that a religion which ignores the existence of God, and denies the existence of the soul, should be the very religion which has found most acceptance among men. They should consider that Buddhism has never been the only belief of the mass of its adherents, who have always also revered the powers of nature under the veil of astrology, or devil-worship, or witchcraft, or the belief in tantras and charms. One school of Buddhists has also developed a mythology of its own, and a sect of this school had even gone so far in the tenth or eleventh century as to evolve (not, perhaps, without Christian influence) a personal First Cause out of Buddhist metaphysics. The Northern school still condemns this sect as heretical, and the Southern Buddhists would condemn the whole mythology; but the purest adherent of the old Asoka Buddhism would believe firmly in Karma, which, from one point of view, has much analogy with soul; and, from another, is a name given to the moral power working in the universe.

It is probable, however, that the absence or presence of any particular belief had less to do with the spread of Buddhism than the organization of its

Order. Had the Buddha merely taught philosophy, he might have had as small a following as Comte. It is true that Gautama's power over the people arose in great measure from the glow of his practical philanthropy, which did not shrink in the struggle with the abuses most peculiar to his time; it is true that the equalizing tendencies of his teaching must have been attractive to the masses, from whose hands it struck off the manacles of caste; it is true also that his psychology and his ethics became a religion as soon as they had been addressed, not to a school only, but to the world. But there is no reason to believe that Gautama was conscious of this, or that he intended, either at the beginning or the end of his career, to be the founder of a new religion. He seems to have hoped that the new wine would go into the old bottles, by all men, Brahmans included, being gradually won over to his, the only orthodox form of the ancient creed. However the question of the historical succession or connection between the different systems of Hindu philosophy be ultimately settled—whether any of them, as we now possess them, were pre-Buddhistic or not—they afford at least sufficient evidence that beliefs, very inconsistent with the practical creed of the masses, met with little opposition if they were taught only in schools of philosophy; and Buddhist morality was not calculated to excite anger, or envy, or alarm. But the very means which Gautama adopted to extend and give practical effect to his teaching, while giving it temporary success, led to its ultimate expulsion from India. It was his Society rather than his

Doctrine—the Sangha rather than the Dharma, which first insured for his religion its great vitality and its rapid spread, and which afterwards excited the hostility of the Brahmans.

It was a logical conclusion from the views of life held by Gautama, that any rapid progress in spiritual life was only compatible with an ascetic life, in which all such contact with the world as would tend to create earthly excitement and desires should be reduced as much as possible; and accordingly, from the first he not only adopted such a mode of life for himself, but urged it on his more earnest disciples. He contemplated no such division between clergy and laity as obtains in Christian countries, and constantly maintained that there was no positive merit in outward acts of self-denial or penance; but holding that family connections and the possession of wealth or power were likely to prolong that mistaken estimate of the value of things, that yearning thirst, that clinging to life, which were the origin of evil, he taught that to forsake the world was a necessary step towards the attainment of spiritual freedom.

Little by little, as occasion arose, he laid down rules for the guidance of those who thus devoted themselves to the higher life; and insensibly as he did so, the Society became more and more like one of the monkish orders which sprang up afterwards in the West. But not even now has the Order become a priesthood: its members lay claim indeed, often with little ground, to superior wisdom and sanctity, but not to any spiritual powers; and its doors are always open, alike to those who wish to enter, and to those who wish to leave it. In a system which acknowledged no Creator, the monks could never become the only efficient intercessors between man and his Maker; their help was not required to avert by their prayers the anger of gods whose deity was temporary, and who had no power over men; and since salvation was held to be and to depend upon a radical change in man's nature, brought about by his own self-denial and his own earnestness, the monks could never obtain control over the keys of heaven and hell.

When successive kings and chiefs were allowed to endow the Society, not indeed with gold or silver, but with the 'necessaries' of the monkish life (including lands and houses), it gradually ceased in great measure to be the school of virtue and the most favourable sphere of intellectual progress, and became thronged with the worthless and the idle; but in the time of its founder it was undoubtedly purer, and contained few beside those who, in their better moments, longed, under his guidance, to train themselves in Buddhist wisdom and virtue.

In attempting a sketch of the rules under which they lived, we shall first, as in the chapter on lay morality, quote some general precepts from the Pitakas, and then descend to more minute particulars.

Dhp. v. 9. He who, himself not stainless,
Would wrap the yellow-stained robe around him,
He, devoid of self-control and honesty,
Is unworthy of the yellow robe.

10. But he who, cleansed from stains,
Is well grounded in the Precepts,

And full of honesty and self-restraint,
'Tis he who's worthy of the yellow robe.

362. The restrained in hand, restrained in foot,
Restrained in speech, the best of the self-controlled;
He whose delight is inward, who is tranquil,
And happy when alone—him they call mendicant.

363. The mendicant who controls his tongue, speaking wisely, and is not puffed up,
Who throws light on worldly and on heavenly things—
His word is sweet.

366. The mendicant who, though receiving little,
Thinks not his alms are less than he deserves,
Him the very gods will magnify,
Whose life is pure, who is not slothful.

368. That mendicant whose life is love,
Whose joy the teachings of the Buddha,
He will enter the tranquil lot,
Nirvāna's bliss, where the Sanskāras end.

374. As soon as ever he comprehends
The origin and end of the Skandhas,
He then receives joy and gladness,
That ambrosia of the wise (*i.e.* Nirvāna).

376. Let his livelihood be kindliness,
His conduct righteousness,
Then in the fulness of gladness,
He will make an end of grief.

377. As the Vassikā plant casts down its withered blossoms,
So cast out utterly, O mendicants, ill-will and lust.

---

[1] On the robes, see below, p. 165. On the precepts see above, p. 139. The two verses are full of puns, 'stain' being kasāva, while the reddish-yellow of the robe is kāsāva. 'Is worthy' is arahati, which is meant to suggest Arahats.

389. Do no violence to a Brahman,[1]
But neither let *him* fly at his aggressor.
Woe to him who strikes a Brahman!
More woe to him who strikes the striker!

392. He who has understood the Law
Revealed by the Omniscient One,
Let him worship that continually,
As the Brahman does the sacrificial fire.

393. Not by platted hair or family does a man become a Brahman,
In whom is truth and righteousness is joy and Brahmanship.

394. What is the use of platted hair, O fool!
What of a garment of skins?
Your low yearnings are within you!
And the outside thou makest clean.[2]

399. He who, though he has committed no offence,
Endures reproaches, bonds and stripes—
And out of much endurance
Makes for himself a mighty army—
He it is I call a Brahman.

Hiri Sutta, 5.—'Drinking of the water of a life of seclusion, of the water of the subjection of his passions, drinking also of the pleasant beverage called the perception of the truth, he becomes free from excitement and sin.'

Nāvā Sutta, 4.—'When a man has fallen into an overflowing river, whose waters are unfathomable and

[1] The idea underlying this and the following verses is that the Arahat is the true Brahman. See above, p. 84.

[2] Nec tonsura facit monachum, nec horrida vestis,
Sed virtus animi, perpetuusque vigor.

Max Müller translates the third line 'Within thee there is ravening,' with allusion to Matt. xxiii. 27, Luke xi. 39; and the analogy is indeed curiously exact. I retain the expression I have used in Chapter IV.

flow swiftly down, how can he in the torrent, and carried with it, cause others to escape'?[1]

Muni Sutta, 15.—'He who maintains a wife, and is at the head of a household; and that other who lives righteously, possessing nothing, these are not equals. The head of the house lives unrestrained, and brings about the destruction of men; but the wise and restrained is a protection to all living beings.'

Dhammacariya Sutta, 3.—'A mendicant who is fond of disputes, is walled in by ignorance, and understands neither religion nor the law of Gautama.

5. 'Such a mendicant going first to hell, will flit thence from womb to womb, from darkness to darkness, meeting everywhere affliction!'

Sammā-paribbājanīya Sutta, 2.—'That mendicant does right to whom omens, meteors, dreams, and signs are things abolished; he is free from all their evils.

8. 'That mendicant does right who is not found thinking "People should salute me"; who, though cursed by the world, yet cherishes no ill-will towards it.

13. 'That mendicant does right who is tranquil, and has completed his course, who sees truth as it really is, but is not partial when there are persons of different faith (to be dealt with), who with firm mind overcomes ill-will and covetousness—which injure men.'

The above passages will exemplify the general spirit which ought to animate the Buddhist mendi-

[1] See above, p. 136.

cant. The following summary mentions certain curious particulars, and should be compared with the summary given above (from the same Sutta) of a layman's duties.

Dhammika Sutta.

10. 'Hear me, O priests! and I will declare the sin-destroying law—all ye bear it in heart!

'The sage seeking after good should practise the Iriyāpatha suited to the Order (*i.e.*, should always carry himself with propriety and dignity).

11. 'A mendicant should not go to the village for food at unseasonable times; let him not go in the night time. As temptations cling to the mendicant doing so, the wise go not out at unseasonable times.

12. 'Form, sound, taste, smell, touch, these intoxicate beings;[1] cut off the yearning which is inherent in them. A mendicant should take his noonday meal in time.

13. 'A mendicant having received in right time his meal, returning alone, should sit in private, reflecting within himself; he should not spread out his mind; his mind should be well controlled.[2]

14. 'Should he speak with a follower of the Buddha or another mendicant, he should speak of the excellent Law, and not backbite or speak ill of another.

15. 'Some fortify themselves for controversy. We praise not those small-minded persons. Temptations from this source and that are made to cling to them,

[1] By causing *vedanā*, sensation, which causes *trishṇā*, thirst. See above, pp. 101, 106.

[2] Compare 'Dhamma-pada,' v. 35, above, p. 129.

and they certainly send their minds very far away when they engage in controversy.

16. 'One who follows the Buddha, in seeking for food, lodging, bed, seats, and water for cleaning robes or personal ablutions, should attend to the Law as preached by the Buddha.

17. 'And therefore he should not be careful about these things, food, bed, seats, clean robes, and water, like a water-drop which adheres not to the lotus-leaf.'[1]

Admission to the Order.

For admittance to the Society no other credentials were at first required than the mere wish of the applicant; afterwards as occasion arose,[2] a few necessary conditions were imposed. The applicant was obliged to state that he was free from contagious disease, consumption, and fits; that he was neither a slave nor a debtor, nor a soldier; that is, that he was *sui juris*, and that he had obtained the consent of his parents. At first, also, the candidate was admitted without any ceremony, merely having his head shaved, putting on the orange-coloured robes peculiar to the Order, and leading an ascetic life. Afterwards a simple ceremony was adopted, probably identical with that now in use in Ceylon, an excellent account of which has been given

[1] This is a standing metaphor. Compare 'Khagga-visāna Sutta,' v. 17, and 'Dhp.,' v. 401, where the Arahat is to be as unpolluted by low desires as the lotus-leaf untouched by water. At 'Dhp.' v. 336, quoted above, p. 107, the application is somewhat different.

[2] The instance of Rāhula will be found above, p. 65.

by Gogerly, in the 'Journal of the Ceylon Asiatic Society' for 1852, and by Mr. Dickson, in the 'Journal of the Royal Asiatic Society' for 1873.[1] At first, also, there is no mention of any distinction within the ranks of the Society; but the preparatory rank of novice was very early introduced, and later on, in some countries, as the religion became more and more corrupted, the Order became more and more subdivided, until, in Tibet, in the twelfth century, we find a complete episcopal hierarchy.

The ordination service just referred to as now held in Ceylon in accordance with the Pitakas, is briefly as follows:—

The layman who wishes for entrance to the Order must be at least eight years old before obtaining the noviciate, and at least twenty before receiving full ordination. On the day appointed, a chapter is held of not less than ten monks, the president being of at least ten years' standing. The monks forming the chapter sit on mats in two rows facing each other, the president being at the head of one row. The candidate, in lay dress, but carrying the three yellow robes of a mendicant, is introduced by his proposer (always a monk), makes salām to the president, and offers him a small present as a token of respect. He then three times asks for admission as a novice. 'Have pity on me, lord, take these robes, and let me be ordained, that I may escape from sorrow, and

[1] Gogerly's account is from the Mahā Vagga of the Vinaya Pitaka; Mr. Dickson's, from an ancient manual of unknown date, called the 'Kammavācā,' which keeps closely to the 'Pitaka' texts.

experience Nirvāna.' The president then takes the bundle of robes and ties them round the candidate's neck, repeating meanwhile a formula of meditation on the perishable nature of the human body. The candidate then retires and changes his dress, repeating the while a formula to the effect that though he wears robes he does so only out of modesty, and as a protection from heat, cold, &c. When he reappears clad as a mendicant, he kneels before the president, and repeats after him three times two well-known Buddhist formulas. The first of these is that called the Three Refuges.

'I go for refuge to the Buddha.
I go for refuge to the Law.
I go for refuge to the Order.'

The other is called the Ten Precepts,[1] which are as follows:—

1. 'I take the vow not to destroy life.
2. 'I take the vow not to steal.'
3. 'I take the vow to abstain from impurity.'
4. 'I take the vow not to lie.'
5. 'I take the vow to abstain from intoxicating drinks, which hinder progress and virtue.'
6. 'I take the vow not to eat at forbidden times.'
7. 'I take the vow to abstain from dancing, singing, music, and stage plays.'
8. 'I take the vow not to use garlands, scents, unguents, or ornaments.
9. 'I take the vow not to use a high or broad bed.'
10. 'I take the vow not to receive gold or silver.'

[1] See also above, p. 139.

The candidate then rises, pays respect to the president, and retires *a novice*. Here, for the noviciate, the ceremony ends.

A novice applying for full admission has to put off the robes, and again, as a layman, to go through the above forms. The candidate now returns, again makes his salām to the president, and gives his present, and three times respectfully asks him to become his 'superior.' This, the full signification of which will be noticed presently, being granted, the candidate retires to the end of the hall, where his begging-bowl is fastened round his neck. His proposer then goes down and leads him up again, placing him before the president, whilst another monk from the chapter rises and stands by the candidate, who is thus placed between two monks, who proceed to act as it were as examiners. Having been taken apart, he tells them his name and that of his superior; that he is provided with the alms-bowl and the robes; that he has none of the disqualifying diseases; that he is a male twenty years old, and *sui juris*, and that he has the consent of his parents. The examiners then report to the chapter the satisfactory result of their inquiries, and, on leave granted, the candidate, coming forward again, and kneeling, asks three times for ordination. 'Mendicants, I ask the chapter for admission; have pity on me, and lift me up.' The examiners then repeat the examination in the hearing of the chapter, and three times ask the chapter if any one objects to the candidate's admission. No one objecting, they bow to the president, and say, 'M. has been admitted by the

Society, N. being his superior. The chapter agrees to this, and therefore is silent. So we understand.'

This ends the ordination of that candidate, and after the same form has been observed with each of the other candidates, one of the chapter reads a short summary of the regulations of the Order, and the service is over.

The new member of the Order is supposed to reside at first in the same monastery with his superior; the latter advising and instructing him, and acting towards him, in sickness and in health, as among laymen a father would to a son; he, in return, treating his superior with the respect due to a father, and acting towards him as his personal attendant. In fact, however, this is not always carried out, the new monk living at some other place; but wherever that may be, a similar relation naturally springs up between the older and younger members of the Sangha.

The most usual names applied in the sacred books to the senior members of the Order are Sramaṇa and Bhikshu, and to the novices Sāmaṇera. The first, from which the third is derived, means one who exerts himself, controls himself; the second means simply a beggar. Self-conquest and poverty, these were to be the distinguishing characteristics of the 'sons of Ṣākya'; but it was not left to them to decide for themselves how far this self-suppression and abstinence were to be carried; the Teacher gave a number of rules and directions which have been handed down to us more or less correctly in the Vinaya, the second part of the Buddhist canon, and which are summed up in the Pātimokkha. This ancient summary for the use of the mendicants was not included in the canon, but its latest date cannot be much later than the great council of Asoka, about B.C. 250.[1] It is regarded with much reverence by the monks, from its having from time immemorial been ordered to be read twice monthly in every monastery. An excellent edition of it was published by Mr. Dickson in the 'Journal of the Royal Asiatic Society,' 1874; and Mr. Beal has given us a translation of it through the Chinese, in his 'Catena of Buddhist Scriptures,' page 204 *et seq.*

The rules it contains may roughly be divided into two divisions,—those which are obligatory on all, and those which are not enforced, but recommended to such as wish to work out their own salvation to a point further than that attainable by the ordinary rules. Both divisions will be found summarized under the following heads :—

Food.

No monk can eat solid food except between sunrise and noon, and total abstinence from intoxicating drinks is obligatory. The usual mode of obtaining food is for the monk to take his begging-bowl, a brown earthenware vessel, in shape nearly like a soup-tureen without its cover,[2] and holding it in his hands, to beg straight from house to house. He is to say nothing, but simply stand outside the hut, the doors and

[1] See my remarks on this point in 'Ancient Coins and Measures of Ceylon,' p. 5 (Part IV. of Mr. Thomas's 'International Numismata Orientalia'): and above, p. 8, n.

[2] This is the modern shape. General Cunningham 'Bhilsa Topes,' p. 69, thinks the ancient form was different.

windows of which in hot countries will usually be large and open. If anything is put into his bowl, he utters a pious wish on behalf of the giver, and passes on; if nothing is given, he passes on in silence, and thus begs straight on without going to the houses of the rich or luxurious rather than to those of the poor and thrifty.[1] As the food of all classes consisted almost exclusively of some form of curry, the mixture was not so very incongruous. When enough had been given, the monk retired to his home to eat it, thinking the while of the impermanence and worthlessness of the body which was thus nourished, and of the processes through which the food would have to pass. To quote a Buddhist idea in the quaint words of Herbert: 'Take thy meat, think it dust, then eat a bit, and say with all Earth to earth I commit.' From the first it was permitted to a wealthy or pious layman to invite one or more monks to take their midday meal at his house; and this was frequently done, especially on full-moon days; it was also allowed to the laity on special occasions to bring food to the monastery. But the practice of the Order possessing rice-fields, letting them out to be cultivated on condition of receiving a share of the produce, and then having their meals cooked at home by some lay follower, is of modern growth.

For the stricter devotees further vows are mentioned of abstinence from animal food; of eating the whole meal without rising; of refusing all invitations and all food brought to them; of eating everything in the bowl without leaving or rejecting anything, and

[1] See 'Metta Sutta,' v. 2; 'Khaggavisāna Sutta,' v. 31.

so on; but it is doubtful whether they are ever observed now: and they were formerly taken only for a time, and very rarely even so.

Residence.

Gautama considered a lonely life in the forest to be the most conducive to self-conquest; but as he himself, after having lived apart from the world, spent his life from the commencement of his prophetic career among men, so from the first the lonely life was adopted only by the most earnest, and that only for a time; the majority of the monks lived in companies in groves or gardens, and very soon the piety of laymen provided for them suitable monasteries, several of which were built even in the lifetime of Buddha.

During the fine weather the monks often travelled from place to place as their Teacher did; but during the rainy season they settled in one spot, in or near a town:[1] and near the ancient cities of India have lately been discovered extensive ruins on the site of the monasteries mentioned in the Pāli books. On the other hand, there have been found numerous rock caves, many of which, especially in Ceylon, were evidently meant for solitary hermits, and often bear inscriptions in the old Pāli alphabet brought by Asoka's son, Mahinda, to Ceylon in the third century B.C.[2]

Clothing.

As regards clothing, the monks were to be habited in cloths of no value, put together from cast-off rags;

[1] On this custom, as now observed, see above, p. 57.

[2] I have published a specimen of these in the 'Indian Antiquary' for May, 1872.

but here again, the practice of Buddha himself, and that followed by the large majority of the brethren, was to dress in simple robes of dull orange-colour, first torn to pieces and then sowed together again, so as to deprive them of commercial value. They formed two under garments, and one loose robe to cover the whole of the body, except the right shoulder. All three are simply lengths of cotton cloth; the two under ones, the *antara-vāsaka* and the *sanghāṭi*, being wrapt round the middle of the body, and round the thighs and legs, respectively; and the upper one, the *uttarāsanga*, being first wrapt round the legs, and then drawn over the left shoulder. The colour was probably at first chosen as the one regarded with most contempt, being nearly the same as that of very old rags of the common white cotton cloth, and because clothes of that colour were of no value at all for ordinary purposes; but the orange-coloured robes, from their very peculiarity as a sign of the members of the Sangha, soon became looked upon as an honour, and craved as such; so that the Dhamma-pada, as we have seen, has to give a warning that those who are not free from sin (kasāva), are not worthy of the orange colour (kāsāva).[1] In Buddhist countries men's ordinary dress was merely a cloth wrapt round the loins, whereas the monks are to cover the whole body, and are not permitted at any time to lay their robes aside. To do so would be to lay aside their membership of the Order; 'to put on,' or 'to put off, the robes,' being current expressions for joining or leaving the Society. Of course, no ornaments are allowed, and even the

[1] See the verse quoted above, p. 153; Dhp. v. 9.

natural ornament of hair is not permitted; complete tonsure being obligatory on all. No monk should possess more than one change of robes, and minute rules in detail are laid down to guard against any brother, even by indirect methods, taking any steps to procure himself new robes—to provide them spontaneously is the duty and privilege of the laity.

Chastity, Poverty, Obedience.

It is scarcely necessary to state that sexual intercourse, theft, and murder, entail upon the culprit irrevocable expulsion from the Order. On the vow of poverty, a few words ought to be said. In his individual right no monk is to possess more than the following eight articles:—1, 2, 3,—the three robes mentioned above; 4. a girdle for the loins; 5. an alms-bowl; 6. a razor; 7. a needle; 8. a water-strainer, through which he is to strain all he drinks, not only to remove impurities, but also, and chiefly, to prevent the accidental destruction of any living creatures. It is to be a cubit square, and to be carefully kept in serviceable repair.

This individual vow of poverty has, however, been swallowed up by the permission given to the community to possess not only books and other personal property, but even lands and houses. Gautama himself is related to have received such gifts on behalf of the Sangha, which, at the time of its expulsion from India, must have rivalled in wealth the most powerful orders of the Middle Ages; and in Buddhist countries at the present day the church is often as wealthy as it is among ourselves.

Otherwise, however, the individual vows have, in

Burma, Siam, and Ceylon been pretty well observed, and water-drinking celibates, who take only one meal a day, and dress in a simple uniform, could never indulge in unbounded personal luxury. The members of the Order are secured from want; some of them enjoy the fascinating power of wealth, so completely contrary to all the principles of their religion, and to the precepts laid down by their Teacher, for the attainment of spiritual progress; they are often lazy, and not seldom avaricious. But in the Southern Church, at least, they are not, as a body, disgraced by gluttony or drunkenness, and have never given way to the weak vanity of dress, or of the pomp and pride of ritual. There is no place in the Buddhist scheme for churches; the offering of flowers before the sacred tree or image of the Buddha takes the place of worship. Buddhism does not acknowledge the efficacy of prayers, and in the warm countries where Buddhists live, the occasional reading of the law, or preaching of the word, in public, can take place best in the open air, by moonlight, under a simple roof of trees or palms.

The vow of *obedience* was never taken by the Buddhist monks or nuns, and in this may be noticed a fundamental difference between them and the members of monastic orders in the West: mental culture, not mental death, was the aim set before the Buddhist ascetic by the founder of his Order. Each one is to conquer self by himself; and the observance of no ceremony, the belief in no creed, will avail him who fails in obtaining this complete mastery over himself. Outward respect and courtesy to his superiors is exacted from the novice; but his own salvation and his usefulness as a teacher depend on his self-culture; he is to obey not his brother but the Law; his superior has no supernatural gifts of wisdom or of absolution, and by himself must the ascetic stand or fall.

A few simple rules of discipline are laid down: but the highest punishment is to compel the fallen brother to retract his vows, and return to the world, which he has not sufficient self-control to reject. Twice a month, when the rules of the Order are read, a monk who has broken them is to confess his crime: if it be slight, some slight penance is laid upon him, to sweep the courtyard of the wihāra or sprinkle dust round the sacred Bo-tree; but no inquisitorial questions are to be put to any one. Charges may be brought against a monk for breach of the ordinances laid down in the Pitakas, and must then be examined into by a chapter; but no one can change or add to the existing law, or claim obedience from any novice, however young.

Daily Life of the Mendicants.

The daily life of the novice should, according to a manual called 'Dina Chariyāwa,'[1] be about as follows. He shall rise before daylight and wash; then sweep the wihāra or 'residence,'—as the clean little hut where the mendicant lives is called,—then sweep round the Bo-tree, fetch the drinking water for the day, filter it, and place it ready for use. Retiring to a solitary place, he shall then meditate on the regula-

[1] Mr. Beal has analysed a corresponding work of later Northern Buddhism ('Catena,' p. 239 *et seq.*), and it is instructive to notice how much the moral standard has been lowered in the lapse of time. Comp. Hardy, E. M. 24-28; and Big., p. 190.

tions. Then he shall offer flowers before the sacred dāgaba—the solid dome-shaped shrine in which relics of the Buddha are buried—or before the Bo-tree; thinking of the great virtues of the Teacher and of his own faults. Soon after, taking the begging-bowl, he is to follow his superior in his daily round for food, and on their return is to bring water for his feet and place the alms-bowl before him. After the meal is over, he is to wash the alms-bowl; then again to worship Buddha, and meditate on kindness and affection. About an hour afterwards he is to begin his studies from the books, or copy one of them, asking his superior about passages he does not understand. At sunset he is again to sweep the sacred places, and, lighting a lamp, to listen to the teaching of his superior, and repeat such passages from the canon as he has learnt. If he finds he has committed any fault he is to tell his superior; he is to be content with such things as he has; and keeping under his senses, to grow in grace without haughtiness of body, speech, or mind.

The superiors, relieved by the novices from any manual labour, were expected to devote themselves all the more earnestly to intellectual culture and meditation.

There are five principal kinds of meditation, which in Buddhism takes the place of prayer. The first is called 'Metta-bhāvanā,' or meditation on LOVE, in which the monk thinks of all beings and longs for happiness for each. Firstly, thinking how happy he himself could be if free from all sorrow, anger, and evil desire, he is then to wish for the same happiness for others, and lastly to long for the welfare of his foes. Remembering their good actions only, and that in some former birth his enemy may have been his father or his friend, he must endeavour in all earnestness and truth to desire for him all the good he would seek for himself.

The second meditation is 'Karunā-bhāvanā' or meditation on PITY, in which the mendicant is to think of all beings in distress, to realize as far as he can their unhappy state and thus awaken the sentiment of pity and sorrows over the sorrows of others.

The third meditation is Muditā-bhāvanā, or the meditation on JOY, the converse of the last, in which he is to think of the gladness and prosperity of others, and to rejoice in their joy.

The fourth is Asubha-bhāvanā, the meditation on IMPURITY, in which the mendicant thinks of the vileness of the body, and of the horrors of disease and corruption; how it passes away like the foam of the sea,[1] and how by the continued repetition of birth and death mortals become subject to continual sorrow.

The fifth is Upekshā-bhāvanā, the meditation on SERENITY, wherein the mendicant thinks of all things that worldly men hold good or bad; power and oppression, love and hate, riches and want, fame and contempt, youth and beauty, decrepitude and disease, and regards them all with fixed indifference, with utter calmness and serenity of mind.[2]

Summary of the Duty of the Order.

When Gautama, just before his death, took his last

[1] Compare the passage quoted at p. 93, and also p. 133.

[2] Hardy, 'Eastern Monachism,' p. 243.

formal farewell of the assembled Order at the Kūṭāgāra Hall, he is said to have charged them as follows: 'Oh, mendicants! thoroughly learn, and practise, and perfect, and spread abroad the law thought out and revealed by me, in order that this religion of mine (literally this purity) may last long, and be perpetuated for the good and happiness of the great multitudes, out of pity for the world, to the advantage and prosperity of gods and men. What is that law? It is the four earnest Meditations, the four great Efforts, the four roads to Iddhi, the five moral Powers, the seven kinds of Wisdom, and the Noble Eightfold Path.'[1]

It will be of great interest to determine more exactly what it was upon which Gautama is believed, in that last and solemn moment, to have laid stress, as the summary at once of his religion, and of the duty of the mendicants of his Order. To be made quite clear and intelligible, each one of the items would require, perhaps, as much space as we have devoted above to the fundamental ideas of Buddhist metaphysics; but the general spirit, at least, will be apparent from the following short descriptions.

The four Earnest Meditations (*Sati-paṭṭhānā*) are meditations—

1. On the impurity of the body.
2. On the evils which arise from sensation.
3. On the impermanence of ideas.
4. On the conditions of existence.

The four Great Efforts (*Sammappadhānā*) are the effort or exertion—

[1] 'Parimbbāna Sutta,' p. 226, 227. See above, p. 79.

1. To prevent sinfulness arising.
2. To put away sinful states which have arisen.
3. To produce goodness not previously existing.
4. To increase goodness when it does exist.

The four Roads to Saintship (*Iddhipādā*) are four means by which saintship (*Iddhi*, on which see below, p. 174) is obtained.

1. The will to acquire it.
2. The necessary exertion.
3. The necessary preparation of the heart.
4. Investigation.

The five Moral Powers (*Balāni*), also called mental organs (Indriyāni), are—

1. Faith; 2. Energy; 3. Recollection; 4. Contemplation; 5. Intuition.

The Seven Kinds of Wisdom (*Bodhi-angā*) are the second, third, and fourth of the last set, and also Investigation of Scripture, Joy, Repose, and Serenity.

The Noble Eightfold Path has been explained above in Chapter IV. These, and a few other similar technical terms formed as it were the Church Catechism of early Buddhism, and the numerical arrangement was adopted merely to assist the memory. Some of these aggregates were as well known, and their names called up as distinct ideas to the Buddhists, as the words Ten Commandments, or Four Gospels, or Five Senses, do to us. Of other enumerations doubtless, though the names were familiar enough, and called up a general idea, the details were known only to the more learned, very much as the Nine Muses or the Three Graces in England now.

Mystic Trance.

There remains to be considered one very obscure, but very instructive side of Buddhist teaching, viz., the belief that it was possible by intense self-absorption and mystic meditation to attain to a condition of trance, in which the ordinary conditions of material existence were suspended, and by which ten certain specific supernatural powers, called Iddhi, were acquired. So far as I am aware, no instance is recorded of any one, not either a member of the Order or a Brahman ascetic, acquiring these powers. A Buddha always possessed them; whether Arahats, *as such*, could work the particular miracles in question, and whether, of mendicants, only Arahats,[1] or only Asekhas,[1] could do so is at present not clear. They adhere, however, to the Karma, so that a person who has practised mystic ecstasy, or been very wise or very virtuous in one birth, may have extraordinary (supernatural) good fortune or powers in the next. This throws, perhaps, some light on the origin of the belief. Ordinary Karma was held sufficient to produce ordinary continuous states; but when some quite unexpected and extraordinary piece of good luck happened to some one who had evidently done nothing to deserve it, some quite extraordinary religious exaltation in the last birth was postulated to explain it. Thus, we are told of a child who was left

[1] Arahats are those who have entered the Fourth Path, and are clear from the first five Fetters. Asekhas are those who have finished the Fourth Path and are free from *all* the Fetters (see above, p. 109).

by mistake, alone, on a dark night, outside the city gate in a cart. During the night he saw many devils and ghosts come out of the shut gate of the city on the way to the cemeteries to procure nourishment; but they did the child no harm.[1] To him and the friends who heard of it these creatures of darkness were very real beings indeed; the child's delivery from such fearful enemies was clearly a miracle; but clearly, also, he had in this life acquired no miraculous powers. As every good or evil event in life has a moral cause in the former actions of the same individual, it was clear, therefore, that the child must have acquired some extraordinary goodness or wisdom in a former birth, of which this extraordinary good fortune was the result. It would be difficult to point out where else the orthodox Buddhist could find his *deus ex machinâ* for the solution of such knotty points; but no example of Iddhi has yet been found in the Pitakas themselves, and the Iddhipādas referred to in the above passage from the Parinibbāna Sutta[2] may have nothing miraculous about them after all.[3]

The state of trance by which these powers were apparently acquired is called in Pāli Jhāna, in Sanskrit Dhyāna, of which there are four stages. It is only by the completion of the fourth Jhāna that Iddhi is acquired, and the four are thus described in identical terms in northern and southern texts :—

'The first Jhāna is a state of joy and gladness born of seclusion, full of reflection and investigation,

[1] Hardy, 'Manual,' p. 502.
[2] Above, p. 173.
[3] Compare Burnouf, 'Lotus,' pp. 310–12; and 818-24.

the mendicant having separated himself from all sensuality and all sin.

'The second Jhāna is a state of joy and gladness born of deep tranquillity, without reflection or investigation, these being suppressed; it is the tranquillization of thought, the predominance of intuition.

'In the third Jhāna the mendicant is patient by gladness and the destruction of passion, joyful and conscious, aware in his body of that delight which the Arahats announce, patient, recollecting, glad.

'The fourth Jhāna is purity of equanimity and recollection, without sorrow and without joy, by the destruction of previous gladness and grief, by the rejection of joy, and the rejection of sorrow.'[1]

In the first Jhāna the mendicant, holy, pure, and alone, applies his mind to some deep subject of religious thought; reasoning upon it, investigating it. Gradually his mind becomes clear, reasoning vanishes, intuition has been reached—this is the second Jhāna. Then the consciousness of the subject thought of vanishes, and a state of trance, but conscious trance, is reached, wherein the whole body is lifted up with ecstasy—this is the third Jhāna. This felt ecstasy, however, soon passes away, and there is only left a kind of dream, a memory, without ecstasy, or joy or sorrow. So at least I understand this difficult and very ancient passage, which seems to me to be describing a state which has actually been reached; not a mere imaginary thing, but a matter of fact; a con-

[1] The Pāli text is in Childers's Dict. *s. v.* Jhāna; the Sanskrit text in 'Lalita Vistara,' chap. xxii., at the commencement, Calcutta ed., 439; and compare chap. xi.

dition possible then, and possible now; a kind of self-induced mesmeric trance.[1]

Buddhism, it thus appears, has not been able to escape from the natural result of the wonder with which abnormal nervous states have always been regarded during the infancy of science. It has mistaken the temporary cessation of the outward signs of life for an actual victory of mind over matter, and has regarded the loss of mental power as the highest form of mental activity. But it must be added, to its credit, that the most ancient Buddhism despises dreams and visions; and that the doctrine of Jhāna is of small practical importance compared with the doctrine of the Noble Eightfold Path.

[1] For an actual instance of Indian ascetics, having voluntarily entered into a lasting trance resembling the hybernation of bears and other animals, see Dr. Carpenter's interesting paper (in the 'Contemporary Review' for December, 1873), entitled 'The Psychology of Belief.' Instances of Jhāna and Samādhi are found, 'Jat.,' p. 75; 'Mahāvansa,' pp. 90, 262. A description how to attain it is given in Beal's 'Catena,' 269, *et seq.* Burnouf describes the four Jhānas in the 'Lotus,' pp. 801, *et seq.* The Pāli authority is *Sāmañña-phala Sutta* in Grimblot's 'Sept Suttas Pāli's,' pp. 139, *et seq.* In the *Parinibbāna Sutta* in Childers's separate edition, p. 61, it is stated that Gautama attained them when on his death-bed. Comp. Gogerly, 'Jour. Ceylon As. Soc.,' 1846, p. 14; and below, p. 204.

CHAPTER VII.

DEVELOPMENTS IN DOCTRINE.

I. *The Legend of the Buddha.*

THE supposed immovability of the institutions and beliefs of the East has become almost a proverb; but as our knowledge of the East increases, the proverb will be likely to fall into disuse. There have been times, not far remote, when the rate of progress in India or China has been so slow, that, compared with the progress in England or America, it has seemed as nothing; but there have been times when Eastern Asia has moved faster than Europe. Except in a much more limited sense than the expression is usually meant to convey, 'the immovability of the East' is a delusion. As well might the Japanese talk of the unchangeable customs and beliefs of Russia or of Spain.

Though but little is known of the religious and political history of India in the centuries immediately following the death of Gautama, enough is known to make it certain that this period was full of movement, both inside and outside of the Buddhist church. Outside that church the ideas and beliefs of Brahmanical Hindus were being modified by Buddhism; while inside the church Buddhism itself was being profoundly altered both by the reaction which must immediately have set in against the high standard of Gautama's morality, and by the growth of the legends which sprang up rapidly regarding his personal history. These latter changes are sufficiently evident from the books of the Pitakas themselves; but it is very difficult, if not impossible, at present to come to any definite conclusion as to what change took place in Buddhist doctrine, apart from the beliefs regarding the person of the Buddha, previous to the date of the recension of the Pitakas which we now possess.

Thus of the doctrine of the Buddhas it is impossible to say how early, before the settlement of the Pitakas in their present form, that doctrine arose; for it contains no internal evidence sufficient to show that it could not have existed, as is represented, in the time of Gautama himself, and have formed part of his actual teaching: and yet it is not so necessarily implied in, or closely connected with, the most important and original parts of his scheme of salvation as to exclude the possibility of its having arisen, or been largely developed, after his death.

In the Pāli and Sanskrit texts the word Buddha is always used as a title, not as a name. The historical Buddha, the Gautama of this little work, is represented to have taught that he was only one of a long series of Buddhas, who appear at intervals in the world, and who all teach the same system. After the death of each Buddha his religion flourishes for a time, and then decays, till it is at last completely forgotten, and wickedness and violence rule over the earth. Gradually then the world improves; until at last a new Buddha appears who again preaches the lost *Dharma* or Truth. The names of twenty-four of these Buddhas who appeared previous to Gautama have been handed down to us; and when, after 5,000 years shall have elapsed since his re-discovery of the Truth under the Bo Tree, the religion of Gautama shall be forgotten, a new Buddha will again open the door of Nirvāna to men, his name being *Maitreya Buddha*, the Buddha of kindness. The *Buddhavansa* or 'History of the Buddhas,' the last book of the *Khuddaka Nikāya* in the second Pitaka, gives the lives of all the previous Buddhas before commencing its account of Gautama himself; and the Pāli commentary on the Jātakas gives certain details regarding each of the twenty-four.[1]

It is sufficiently evident that nearly all these details are merely imitated from the corresponding details of the legend of Gautama; and it is, to say the least, very doubtful whether the tradition of these legendary teachers has preserved for us any grains of historical fact. If not, the list is probably later than the time of Gautama, for while it is scarcely likely that he should have deliberately invented these names, it may well have seemed to later Buddhists very edifying to give such lists, and very reasonable to include in them the names held in highest honour by the Brahmans themselves. In the *Sutta Pitaka*, one of the books of the second Pitaka, we have actually some sayings attributed to Kāṣyapa

[1] Fausböll's 'Jātaka,' pp. 2–44. Compare Turnour's 'Mahāvansa,' p. 1, and Spence Hardy's 'Manual of Buddhism,' pp. 49 *et seq.*

Buddha, the last of the twenty-four; but the passage in question, the *Āmagandha Sutta*, is quite in the manner and spirit of all the teaching ascribed to Gautama himself. In it, it is declared that it is not the eating of unclean food (*Āmagandha*) which defiles a man, but rather evil deeds, and the practice of evil habits; the argument being strikingly similar to that of the well known passages in the Gospels enunciating the same principle.[1] This putting of new wine into old bottles, this spiritualising, but still making use of an existing belief seems to me to be quite characteristic of Gautama's teaching;[2] and though nearly all Oriental reformers adopt, more or less frequently, the same method, they seldom carry it so far as he seems to have done. Yet, in the fourth century A.D., there was certainly near to Ṣrāvasti a sect of Buddhists who rejected Gautama, reverencing only the three previous Buddhas, and especially Kāṣyapa, whose body they believed to be buried under one of the dāgabas, at which they, as well as the orthodox, worshipped, while another was said to be built over the spot where he had died. To them, at least, there was some difference between the teachings of Gautama and those of Kāṣyapa; but Fa Hian, the Chinese pilgrim, to whom they showed their dāgabas, tells us nothing of their creed except that they claimed to be followers of Devadatta, that special object of the *odium theolo-*

[1] Sir Coomāra Swāmi's 'Sutta Nipāta,' p. 67. Compare St. Matthew xv. 10–21 and St. Mark vii. 14–23. See above, p. 131.

[2] A few striking examples of this are given above in the note to p. 149.

gicum of orthodox Buddhist writers.[1] When we turn from the discussion of such doctrines as this, to those regarding Gautama himself, we stand at once on firmer ground; for it is clear that many of the most prevalent beliefs on this point can never have formed part of the teaching of Gautama himself. A few of these have been already noticed in the chapters on the life of Gautama, but the subject is too interesting not to deserve more special consideration.

Gautama himself was very early regarded as omniscient, and absolutely sinless. His perfect wisdom is declared by the ancient epithet of *Sammā-sambuddha*, 'the completely enlightened one,' found at the commencement of every Pāli text; and at the present day in Ceylon, the usual way in which Gautama is styled is *Sarwajnan-wahanse*, 'the venerable omniscient one.' From his perfect wisdom according to Buddhist belief, his sinlessness would follow as a matter of course. He was the first, and the greatest of the Arahats. As a consequence of this doctrine the belief soon sprang up that he could not have been, that he was not, born as ordinary men are; that he had no earthly father; that he descended of his own accord into his mother's womb from his throne in heaven; and that he gave unmistakable signs, immediately after his birth, of his high character and of

[1] 'Fa Hian' (Beal's translation), pp. 82, 83; 'Foe Koue Ki,' p. 176; 'Hiouen Thsang,' p. 126. On Devadatta, see above, p. 74; and compare 'Mah.,' pp. 90, 93, 96; 'As. Res.,' xvi. 280. On Kāṣyapa Buddha, Hardy's 'Manual,' pp. 87, 97. A dāgaba is a solid dome, built over the relics of a saint, a development of the earliest form of sepulchral monument.

his future greatness. Earth and heaven at his birth united to pay him homage; the very trees bent of their own accord over his mother, and the angels and archangels were present with their help. His mother was the best and the purest of the daughters of men, and his father was of royal lineage, and a prince of wealth and power. It was a pious task to make his abnegation and his condescension greater by the comparison between the splendour of the position he was to abandon, and the poverty in which he afterwards lived; and in countries distant from Kapilavastu the inconsistencies between such glowing accounts, and the very names they contain, passed unnoticed by credulous hearers.

After seven days of fasting and seclusion the pure and holy Māyā[1] dreams that she is carried by archangels to heaven, and that there the future Buddha enters her right side in the form of a superb white elephant.[2] On her relating her dream to her husband he calls together sixty-four chief Brahmans to interpret it. Their reply is, that the child will be a son who will be a Chakrawartī, a universal monarch; or, if he becomes a recluse, will be a Buddha, 'who will remove the veils of ignorance and sin' from

[1] Cooma Korösi refers in a distant way to a belief of the later Mongol Buddhists that Māyā was a virgin (As. Res. xx. 299); but this has not been confirmed. St. Jerome says (contra Jovian. bk. 1): 'It is handed down as a tradition among the Gymnosophists of India, that Buddha, the founder of their system, was brought forth by a virgin from her side.'

[2] Fausböll's 'Jātaka,' p. 50. In the 'Lalita Vistara' (Foucaux, 61) this dream so far becomes reality that the Buddha actually descends from heaven in the form referred to.

the world (or as the Lalita Vistara has it, 'who will make all the worlds glad by the sweet taste of the Ambrosia of Nirvāna').[1] In the alternative thus prophesied we may find a key to much of the legend; which has simply transferred to the Buddha, sometimes in a spiritual sense, and sometimes without change, many of the beliefs which had clustered round the idea of a Chakrawartī. (See below, p. 220.) Many of these beliefs again were borrowed from the older sun-worship; the white elephant, for instance, like the white horse, being an emblem of the sun, the universal monarch of the sky. M. Senart, in his learned work, 'La Légende du Buddha,' has attempted to trace many of these coincidences, and has certainly established enough to show that in this direction an explanation may be found of much that appears at first sight bizarre and unnecessary in our legend of the Buddha. The idea that a man should enter his mother's womb in the form of a white elephant seems a most grotesque folly, until the origin of the poetical figure has been thus ascertained.[2]

At the conception of the Buddha, thirty-two signs take place; the 10,000 worlds are filled with light, the blind receive their sight, the deaf hear, the dumb speak, the crooked become straight, the lame walk, the imprisoned are set free, and so on, all nature blooming, and all beings in earth and heaven being filled with joy; while by a bold figure of speech even

[1] 'Jātaka,' p. 51; Foucaux, p. 63.

[2] This form was deliberately chosen by the future Buddha because it was the form indicated by an angel who had in a previous birth been one of the Rishis, the mythical poets of the Rig Veda! (Foucaux, 52.)

the fires of hell are extinguished, and the tortures of the damned are mitigated. During the ten months of his life in the womb the child is distinctly visible, sitting cross-legged, unsoiled, and dignified; and he preaches to the angels who guard him, stretching out his hand to do so without wounding his mother.[1]

As a dāgaba holding sacred relics cannot be used to guard any less sacred object, so his mother can bear no other child, and on the seventh day after his birth she dies. When the child is born it takes seven steps forward, and exclaims with lion's-voice 'I am the chief of the world, this is my last birth,'[2] and again the thirty-two signs of joy appear in the earth and heaven.

An aged saint, who had retired for meditation to the Himālaya mountains, seeing these signs is guided to Kapilavastu, and the child is brought in to do him reverence; but instead of doing so its feet were miraculously placed on the matted locks of the ascetic. The sage then explains the wonder to the astonished father, and (this time without any reference to universal monarchy) prophesies that the child will become a Buddha, and weeps that he himself will not live to see the day.[3]

On the fifth day the 'name-choosing' festival takes place, when 108 Brahmans learned in the three Vedas,

[1] 'Jātaka,' 51, 52; Foucaux's 'Lalita Vistara,' 73–75.

[2] Madhuratthа Vilāsinī; Turnour, J.B.A.S. vii. 798. The 'Lalita Vistara' makes him take seven steps in each of the six directions, and makes a speech for each (Foucaux, 89); but at p. 91 we have seven steps only.

[3] 'Jātaka,' 54; 'Lalita Vistara' (Foucaux, 103–110). The Pāli name is Kaḷā-devala; the Sanskrit Asita. Both Kāḷa and Asita mean 'black.'

of whom eight were especially learned in divination, are feasted at the 'palace.' Seven of the eight, after examining the marks on the child's body, hold up two fingers, and prophesy that he will become either a Chakrawartī or a Buddha; but one, Kondanya, afterwards Gautama's first disciple, holds up one finger, and prophesies that he will assuredly become a Buddha, who will remove the veils of sin and ignorance from the world. The other four of the first converts were sons of four of these prophets; and the whole story is in glorification rather of these five disciples than of the child. The Jātaka commentator is so engrossed with the prophets that he forgets to give the child's name![1]

This episode is wanting in the 'Lalita Vistara,' but in its place (chap. viii.) are stanzas describing how the infant was presented at the temple, and how all the gods of the then Hindoo Pantheon rose up and did obeisance to him. The two following episodes in the northern poem (the child's ornaments, and its miraculous knowledge of sixty-four alphabets, chaps. ix. and x.) are also wanting in the Pāli books.

Then comes the curious story of the ploughing festival, found both in the Nepalese and Ceylonese accounts. The 'great king' Suddhodana goes out to celebrate the opening of the season, and the 'prince' is taken with him. In the rejoicing, the baby is neglected. It then seats itself cross-legged on the couch, and falls into the mystic trance of Dhyāna. Though the shadows of all other trees had

[1] 'Jātaka,' p. 56; 'Madhurattha Vilāsinī,' *loc. cit.*

turned, the tree under which it sat still shaded the child. The 'Lalita Vistara,' which differs in all the details, adds that five rishis (p. 184, n. 2), flying through the air, were miraculously stopped as they passed above him. They sing stanzas in his praise, saying that by him, the Water appearing in the midst of the Fires of sin devouring the world, the Light appearing in the Darkness of the world's ignorance, the Ship appearing amidst the perils of the Ocean of human misery, the Liberator of those enchained in the bonds of sin, the Physician of those tormented by decay and disease — by him would be obtained the truth which would be the salvation of sentient beings.[1]

To the same category as the legends of the infancy of the Buddha belongs the story of his surpassing all others in youthful prowess, and teaching even his masters in the arts and sciences.[2] So the splendid accounts of his equipages, and servants, and harems, and palaces (one for each of the three seasons), are all invented to harmonize with the notion that if he had not become a Buddha, he would have become a universal monarch; and the horse Kanthaka, on which he finally rides away from his father's house, is the sun-horse of the ancient mythology.[3] It is otherwise, I think, with the four visions, and the temptation of Māra; though many of the details of the latter are doubtless derived from the ancient myths arising from the victories of the sun over the clouds of darkness. These episodes seem to me to

[1] 'Lal. Vist.,' chap. xi.; 'Jātaka,' 57, 58. See 'Sutta Nip.,' p. 119.

[2] See above, pp. 13, 29.

[3] Compare Senart, 27–31, and 428.

rest on a substratum of fact, and to relate, in the language of the time, those mental struggles which I have endeavoured to translate into the language of the nineteenth century.[1]

The title given to the first sermon, the rolling onward of the royal chariot-wheel of righteousness,[2] may be derived from, or it may be the origin of, the Chakrawartī parallel, which has had so marked an influence on the legend of the Buddha's early life.

Very few of the miraculous incidents during the forty-five years' ministry seem to be explicable from the same source. They have mostly the appearance of being due entirely to the love of exaggeration and of mystery universal among rude peoples. Gautama's display of miraculous power, and his journey to heaven to preach the law to his dead mother, related at the end of the sixth year after his enlightenment, form perhaps an exception; but these episodes cannot be discussed with profit till we have much more authentic accounts of them than are at present accessible.

The 'Parinibbāna Sutta,' the Pāli account in the Pitakas of the Buddha's death, contains much less of the miraculous. The prophecy concerning the future greatness of Pāṭaliputra, the modern Patna,[3] shows that the book as we have it is later than the time when the capital of Magadha was moved from Rājagriha to the banks of the great river. The temptations of Māra[4] are merely the form in which

[1] Above, pp. 30, 36–38.

[2] Above, p. 45. Compare Senart, 413–422.

[3] 'Parinibbāna Sutta,' J.R.A.S. vii. 62.

[4] Ib., *loc. cit.* vii. 77.

Gautama's thoughts of his approaching death are expressed. The timely purifying of the stream from which he wished to drink, with the connected story,[1] is an ordinary exaggeration. The episode of the transfiguration[2] would fit in very well with Senart's idea of the last glow of the setting sun; but I do not think it at all necessary to call in the aid of sun myth to explain the rise of so graceful and probable a tradition. Sāla-trees also assisted at his birth, and sāla-trees render him homage at his death, letting fall upon him fragrant flowers out of season, and bending lovingly over him their branches which gave him shade; and who can wonder that angels in the sky drop heavenly flowers and sing heavenly songs to strengthen him? After his death the miracles and exaggerations increase, and the former especially are evidently influenced by the desire to make the Buddha's funeral rites as splendid as those of a Chakrawartī king. The body refuses to be moved until the wish of the gods as to the direction in which it should be carried is ascertained and followed; and it refuses to burn till the venerable Kāṣyapa, the old and faithful head of the Order of mendicants, arrives.[3] Three times with his monks he paces reverently round the pile on which the dead body of his master lies, and stands with bent head opposite the feet. Then the pile takes fire of itself; and when everything except the bones has been consumed, showers from heaven extinguish it.[4]

The latter accounts relate that as Kāṣyapa stood

[1] Ib. viii. 233–235.
[2] Ib. viii. 237.
[3] Ib. viii. 254, 257.
[4] Ib. viii. 258.

by the feet of the revered teacher, he fell into the mystic trance of Dhyāna; and when he recovered from the trance prayed to see once more the sacred feet on which the thirty-two signs of a Chakrawartī were visible. He had scarcely uttered his prayer, when the coverings unrolled themselves, the coffin opened, and the feet came out like the full moon emerging from the bosom of a dark cloud. The whole assembly burst into loud applause on seeing this matchless prodigy. Kāṣyapa and his monks reverently placed the feet on their heads, after which the feet withdrew, the coverings replaced themselves, and the coffin and the pile resumed their natural position.[1] This legend seems to M. Senart to have arisen from the myth of the last glow of the dying sun; and he derives from the Krishṇa myth the statements that the Buddha's death took place among the 'wrestlers' of the town of Kusi, on the bank of a river, among trees, and soon after the destruction of the Ṣakya clan.[2]

As M. Senart's theory of the almost complete dependence of the Buddhist legend on these myths is most interesting and ingenious, I here add his summary, though it will be seen from what has been written above that I can only accept it to a certain modified extent. Dividing the legend, according to old tradition, into twelve divisions, M. Senart thus sums up the history of the Sun-Buddha:—[3]

'1. *Resolution to quit Heaven.*—The Buddha, before his birth, is a god, the chief of the gods; to speak

[1] Bigandet, 337; Hardy's 'Manual,' 348.
[2] 'La Légende du Buddha,' p. 389.
[3] Ib. pp. 504–507.

correctly, he is not born, he incarnates himself among men for their good and their salvation.

'2. *Conception.*—His conception is altogether miraculous. He has no mortal father; his descent from heaven takes place under the symbols of a god of light, veiled in the cloud-womb of his mother; his presence reveals itself there by his first rays, which call all the gods to prayer and awaken them to life.

'3. *Birth.*—He is born, as hero of light and fire, from the fire-producing tree, by the aid of Māyā. That virgin-mother, representative of the sovereign creative power, and at the same time half-obscure goddess of the vapours of the morning, dies away from the first hour in the dazzling radiance of her son. In reality, she survives under the name of the creatress, the nurse of the universe and of its god. Her son, powerful, irresistible from his birth, advances in space, illuminating the world, and proclaiming his supremacy, to which all the gods form a retinue and render homage.

'4. *Trials.*—Growing up amidst the 'young daughters' of the air, among whom his power and his splendour are hidden and unknown, or only reveal themselves at rare intervals, the day comes when he makes himself known, tries himself in his first battles against his gloomy foes, and shines without a rival.

'5. *Marriage and pleasures of the harem.*—With him the young nymphs have grown up; the companions of his games become now his wives and lovers; the god delays and forgets himself in his heavenly palaces, amidst the delights of his cloudy harem.

'6. *Departure from his father's house.*—But his hour has come; he tears himself violently, miraculously away from his splendid prison; the heavenly charger leaps over the walls of the demon fortresses, and traverses the river of the air.

'7. *Austerities.*—From that moment begins the struggle. The hero first appears tried and enfeebled, wandering as he is in the forests of space. Soon he regains his might in the heavenly pastures, where he drinks ambrosia, and bathes in the water of immortality.

'8. *Defeat of the Demon.*—He is ripe for his destined mission, the conquest of ambrosia and of the wheel, fertilising rain and light. He takes possession of the divine tree; the demon of the storm runs to dispute it with him in the duel of the storm; in this struggle against darkness the beneficent hero remains the conqueror; the gloomy army of Māra, broken and rent, is scattered; the Apsaras, daughters of the demon, the last light vapours which float in heaven, try in vain to clasp and retain the vanquisher; he disengages himself from their embrace, repulses them; they writhe, lose their form, and vanish.

'9. *Perfect Enlightenment.*—He appears then in all his glory, and in his sovereign splendour; the god has attained the summit of his course: it is the moment of triumph.

'10. *Putting the Wheel in motion.*—Free from every obstacle, and from every adversary, he sets in motion across space his disk with a thousand rays, having avenged the attempts of his eternal foe.

'11. *Nirvāna.*—A little later, he reaches the end of

his career; he is on the point of extinction, victim in his turn of the demon, the glowing wild boar; but first he sees all his race, his retinue of light, disappear in the sanguinary mêlée of the clouds of evening.

'12. *Funeral rites.*—He himself disappears in the west, glowing with his last rays, as on a huge pyre; and only the milk of the clouds is able to extinguish on the horizon the last flames of these divine funereal rites.'

In M. Senart's hands, at least, the myth has marvellous grace and beauty; but the reader would do wrong to conclude from the above poetical language that M. Senart regards the whole story of Gautama's life as a sun-myth debased into prose, or the whole of Buddhism, though its adherents knew it not, as a worship of the sun. He propounds no theory of the rise of Buddhism, and only strives to show that much of the old sun-myth has been incorporated into the legend of the Buddha, and has almost driven out the historical basis on which it rests. But that the historical basis, is, or once was, there, he does not doubt; and he holds that Buddhism, like every other system, must have had a human founder, and an historical origin.

In this chapter only the earlier forms of the legend have been considered. The principles which have guided us in their interpretation are sufficient, if we add the influence of local and sectarian jealousies, to explain all the later developements; and it would be impossible in the space at our command to point out in any detail the differences between the older and any one of the later forms of the biography. The general relation of the various accounts to one another has been already illustrated by the example given above, at p. 13: and it may be laid down as a general rule that the later forms of each episode differ chiefly from the former in the way in which they further exaggerate the details of the stories so as to make them more consistent either with the imperial wealth and power ascribed to Gautama or his father by the Chakrawartī parallel; or with the belief in Gautama's omniscience and omnipotence.

As an instance of the effect of local prejudice may be cited the legend of the Buddha's three visits to Ceylon, one of the few new episodes which have been invented. The fullest account of this visit is given in the Rev. Cornelis Alwis's translations of the 24th chapter of the Sarwagnyā Gunālankāra,[1] a Sinhalese work classed by Mr. James Alwis among 'ancient books.'[1] The tradition has not at present been traced further back than the Dīpavansa, a history of Ceylon, written about the end of the fourth century A.D.; but the account given in the opening chapters of that work shows that the tradition must have then been old. The same conclusion is forced upon us by the short reference made to the Buddha's visit by Fa Hian, who was in Ceylon about 410 A.D.; but he seems to know only of two instead of three visits.[2] From the nature of the legend it seems very probable that it has merely been adapted to the Buddha myths previously

[1] The translation is printed in Skeen's 'Adam's Peak,' pp. 301–325. Compare Jas. Alwis, in the 'Sidat Sangarāwa,' p. 191, note.

[2] Beal's 'Fa Hian,' p. 150.

current regarding the sun-god Sumana, worshipped both on Adam's Peak, and at the great cave of Dambulla, whose ancient name was Sumana Lene.[1]

The worship of local relics has also brought about local additions to the legend. Thus the worshippers of the supposed Buddha's tooth in Ceylon have added to the account of Gautama's death the incident of the Arahat Kshema having taken the tooth from the ashes of the funeral pile.[2] So the Burmese have related that the Brahman Drona, who divided the relics, stole another tooth;[3] and the Sinhalese who pretend that the Buddha's neck relic is still preserved under the Mahiyangana Dāgaba, add that the elder named Sarabhu abstracted that relic on the same occasion.[4] None of these incidents are given in the Parinibbāna Sutta, though Drona's division of the relics is described at length, and it is evident that relic worship was already in full favour when that book assumed its present shape.[5]

It is a curious part of the history of the Legend of the Buddha, that it should have been adapted into a Christian form by a father of the Christian Church, and have been found so agreeable to the Catholic lovers of saints, that the hero of it has been entered in the Roman Calendar, and is ordered to be worshipped as a saint on every 27th of November, under the title

[1] See the inscription published by me in the 'Indian Antiquary' for May, 1872.

[2] 'Dāṭhāvansa,' ii. 52.

[3] Bigandet, p. 343 (second edition).

[4] 'Dāthāvansa," ii. 51.

[5] 'Parinibbāna Sutta,' J.R.A.S., viii. 259, 260.

of St. Josaphat.[1] How this came about has been told by Professor Max Müller in his paper on the Migration of Fables in the 'Contemporary Review,' for July, 1870. A certain St. John of Damascus, who wrote in the eight century, was the son of Sergius, minister at the Court of Khalif Almansūr. St. John became a monk, and wrote many books. Among other works ascribed to him is a religious romance called the 'Life of Barlaam and Jōasaph,' which has been distinctly proved [2] to be derived as to the narrative part of it from the story of Buddha, as told in the Jātaka commentary, or the Lalita Vistara. The Greek text of St. John's romance will be found in Migne's Patrology, with a Latin translation. The bulk of the work consists of long theological and moral instructions to the Prince Joasaph by his teacher, Barlaam, in the course of which some Buddhist Jātaka stories are inserted. As the moral tone of the book, which here and there seems to betray Buddhist influence, was so popular in the Middle Ages that the romance was translated into several European languages, we need not wonder that the hero was subsequently canonized.

To have been made a Christian saint is not the only

[1] He is not mentioned by Butler in his standard work on the saints (under St. Balaam of the 19th of November is given quite another story); but see the 'Bibliothèque Sacrée' of Fathers Richard et Giraud, Paris, 1822, s.v. Barlaam.

[2] See especially Liebrecht 'Jahrbuch der Romanischen und Englischen Literatur,' vol. ii. He compares the Catholic romance with the 'Lalita Vistara,' and the likeness to the 'Jātaka' story is still closer.

curious fate which has befallen the great Teacher. He takes his place also in the 'Dictionnaire Infernel' of M. Collin de Plancy,[1] a quaintly illustrated dictionary of all matters relating to devils, fairies, magic, astrology, and so on. There he appears in a curious woodcut as 'Sakimuni, génie ou dieu,' in the character of the Man in the Moon; or, rather of the Hare in the Moon. M. de Plancy quotes as his authority a Kalmuk story given in the 'Travels' of Pallas,[2] that after the hare had given himself to be eaten by a hungry man, 'the spirit of the earth (!) pleased with the beautiful action, placed the soul of that hare in the moon—where he is still to the Kalmucks plainly visible.'

I think I can trace the origin of this legend, which is very old. In one of the Jātaka stories the future Buddha is a holy hare, who keeps the Sabbath, and exhorts his friends, carnivorous animals, to charity and piety. One Sabbath day after exhorting them to give to any hungry person part of their food, and recollecting that men cannot eat his food, which is grass, he resolves, if the opportunity arises, to give away his own body. The god Ṣakra becoming aware of this high resolve comes in the form of a Brahman, and begs; but when the hare really offers himself, and jumps into the fire, the fire does not burn him. Then Ṣakra saying, 'O wise hare, let your virtue be known through all the Kalpa' (the period till the world will be next destroyed), splits

[1] Paris, 1863 (sixth edition).

[2] 'Reisen durch verschiedene Provinzen des Russischen Reich's, 3 vols. 4to. St. Petersburg, 1771—1776.

open a mountain, and taking the sap of the mountain (!) draws a picture of the hare on the disk of the moon. If Mr. Fausböll had not published the text of this Jātaka[1] we might have found it difficult to discover the connection between our Gautama and the Man in the Moon!

[1] It is given both in Pāli and Sanskrit in the 'Five Jātakas,' pp. 51–68.

CHAPTER VIII.

DEVELOPMENTS IN DOCTRINE—(*continued*).

Northern Buddhism.

APART from the legend of the Buddha, there is little evidence of any development from the doctrines of the Pitakas in Burma, Siam, or Ceylon; but the case is very different with Nepal, Tibet, China, Japan, and Mongolia.

The development of the Buddhist doctrine which has taken place in the Panjab, Nepal, and Tibet is exceedingly interesting, and very valuable from the similarity it bears to the development which has taken place in Christianity in Roman Catholic countries. It has resulted at last in the complete establishment of Lāmāism, a religion not only in many points different from, but actually antagonistic to, the primitive system of Buddhism; and this not only in its doctrine, but also in its church organization. The hierarchical system of Lāmāism will be briefly considered in the next chapter; its doctrinal system, with which we have now to deal, has been chiefly modified by the gradual additions to its theory of the Buddhas, in which the legends regarding Gautama play little or no part.

The development starts from the theory as given at the beginning of the last chapter. According to it, the spirit of kindness out of which all virtues rise, and by the strength of which the Buddhist church will once more triumph throughout the world and conquer all sin and unbelief,[1] has been personified as *Maitreya Buddha*, the future Buddha of kindness. This doctrine already forms part of the system of the *Little Vehicle* (*Hīnāyana*), the name by which the later school, not without some contempt, calls the doctrine of the Pitakas, as distinguished from the *Great Vehicle* (*Mahāyana*), the name it gives to itself. The Little Vehicle already talks also of the *Pacceka Buddhas* (Sanskrit Pratyeka), the Personal Buddhas; and of the *Bodhisatwas*, the Buddhas Elect, or future Buddhas. The first are those who have sufficient wisdom and holiness not only to become Arahats and attain Nirvāna, but also to attain Buddhahood themselves; while they are not able to explain the truth to others. Bodhi-satwa, or Buddha Elect, is the title given to each of the beings (man, angel, or animal) who, in each of the 500 Jātaka stories, is held to be the future Buddha in one of his former births; and generally Bodhisatwa is the name given to a being whose Karma will produce other beings in a continually-ascending scale of goodness, until it becomes vested in a Buddha.

Now, as the Buddha himself has reached Parinirvāna, has passed completely away, the pious Buddhist

[1] Maitreya is therefore also called Ajita, the Unconquerable One—a name also given to the second of the twenty-four saints or Tīrthahara's of the 'Jainas.' Compare Köppen, ii. 17.

naturally turned with peculiar reverence and longing to those Bodhisatwas supposed to be now living as angels in heaven, who are the present result of the Karma which will produce the Buddhas of the future. Thus, in southern Buddhist temples the pure white image of Maitreya is sometimes found by the side of Gautama's idol; and among the followers of the Great Vehicle, at least as early as the time of Fa Hian, 400 A.D., the worship of two Bodhisatwas, named *Manju-ṣrī* and *Avalokiteṣvara*, had already become general.

It is difficult at present to explain the origin of the belief in these hypothetical beings, who are not even mentioned in the Pitakas, or in the 'Lalita Vistara,' or in the older Nepalese and Tibetan books. They will probably be found to be the invention of Buddhists, whose minds were steeped in Brahman philosophy and mythology; and who were so imperfectly converted to Gautama's system of salvation by self-control and moral culture, that their hearts craved after Buddhist gods to fill the place of the dead gods of the Hindu Pantheon, or to make them live again in their descendants.

Manju-ṣrī is the personification of Wisdom,[1] and especially of the mystic religious insight which has produced the Great Vehicle. *Avalokiteṣvara* is the personification of Power, the merciful protector and preserver of the world and of men. Both are frequently mentioned in the 'Saddharma-puṇḍarīka,' 'the Lotus of the good Law' (which is a mystic name for

[1] 'Csoma Korösi, 'Tibetan Grammar,' p. 193.

this kosmos) translated by Burnouf,—the only one of the nine great books of the Great Vehicle as yet accessible, except in MS. Manjusrī is the mythical author of the 'Saddharma-puṇḍarīka,'[1] and a whole chapter of that work (the 24th) is devoted to a glorification of the character, the power, and the advantages to be derived from the worship of Avalokiteṣvara.[2]

It is not impossible that the name of the Bodhisatwa Manjuṣrī may be derived from that of the Indian mendicant, who, according to tradition, introduced Buddhism, and with it civilisation, into Nepal. The former part of the name, at least, sounds more human than divine, *manju* meaning 'charming, lovely,' while *ṣrī*, 'good luck, prosperity, glory,' is a common part of names of gods and men. Manjuṣrī, the missionary, seems to have lived about two hundred and fifty years after the Buddha attained Parinirvāna; and as he is looked upon as the founder of that school of thought which ended in the Great Vehicle, it is quite likely that his name may have been preserved as that of the mystic wisdom by which the world was created and organized. Burnouf has, at least, clearly shown that in the books of all sects of northern Buddhists there rules the greatest confusion between the metaphysical Being and the legendary civiliser and teacher of Nepal.

The name Avalokiteṣvara, which means 'The

[1] So says the work itself, p. 160 of Burnouf's translation.

[2] Ib., pp. 261–268; also translated by Beal through the Chinese ('Catena,' pp. 389–396). For other details as to his power, see Burnouf's 'Introduction à l'Histoire,' &c., pp. 220–224.

Lord who looks down from on high,' is a purely metaphysical invention.[1] The curious use of the past participle passive *avalokita* in an active sense is clearly evident from the translations into Tibetan and Chinese.[2]

Somewhat later the power of Avalokiteṣvara was separated from his protecting care and providence; and the former more specially personified as the Bodhisatwa *Vajradhara*, 'the bearer of the thunderbolt,' or *Vajrapāṇī*, 'the thunderbolt-handed,' both formerly used as epithets of the god Indra; and this new being, together with the other two Bodhisatwas, forms the earliest Trinity of northern Buddhism.[3] In this Trinity Vājrapāṇi is the Jupiter Tonans, Manjuṣrī is the deified teacher, and Avalokiteṣvara, as we shall presently see, is the Spirit of the Buddhas present in the church. These beings, and one or two other less conspicuous Bodhisatwas, had become practically gods; and it need not be pointed out how utterly contrary their worship was to the original teaching of Gautama, which knew nothing of God, taught that Arahats, holy men, were better than gods, and acknowledged no form of prayer. But Fa Hian prays to Avalokiteṣvara just as a Hindu might to Indra or to Siva.[4]

And Northern Buddhism did not stop here. There

[1] Beal's 'Fa Hian,' p. 167.

[2] See his learned note, 'Lotus de la bonne Loi,' pp. 493–511.

[3] Burnouf, 'Introduction,' p. 226.

[4] Compare 'Foe Koue Ki,' p. 21, on the Trinity; and pp. 56, 121, on the images of these gods.

is one step still further removed from Gautama's doctrines—the step from polytheism to monotheism, and this step it also afterwards took. I have spoken above (pp. 174-177) of the four stages of Dhyāna, or mystic meditation. The Great Vehicle teaches five instead of the four stages found in the Pitakas and the Lalita Vistara. The earlier Buddhism teaches that above the worlds of the gods are 'sixteen worlds of Brahma' (*Brahma-loka's*), one above another; those who attain on earth to the first, second, or third Dhyāna, are reborn in the lower of these worlds, three worlds being assigned to each Dhyāna. Those who attain the fourth Dhyāna enter the tenth or eleventh Brahma-lokas; the remaining five being occupied by those who attain to the third path here on earth, and who will reach Nirvāna in this new existence. To each of these five groups of worlds the Great Vehicle assigns a special Buddha, called Dhyāni Buddha: these five Buddhas corresponding to the last four Buddhas, including Gautama, and the future Buddha Maitreya—the five Buddhas, that is, who belong to the present Kalpa, the age since the Kosmos was last destroyed.

The idea seems to be that every earthly mortal Buddha has his pure and glorious counterpart in the mystic world, free from the debasing conditions of this material life; or rather that the Buddha under material conditions is only an appearance, the reflection, or emanation, or type of a Dhyāni Buddha living in the ethereal mansions of those worlds of idea and mystic trance.[1] The number of Dhyāni Buddhas is accordingly, in theory, infinite, like the number of

[1] Compare Köppen, ii. 26.

the Buddhas, but only the five are practically acknowledged. These Dhyāni Buddhas, like their types or antitypes the Buddhas, must have their Bodhisatwas also, and the following three sets of five are thus co-ordinated.[1]

The Dhyāni Buddhas :—

1. Vairochana.
2. Akshobya.
3. Ratna-sambhava.
4. AMITĀBHU.
5. Amogasiddha.

Their Bodhisatwas :—

1. Samanta-bhadra.
2. Vajrapāṇī.
2. Ratnapāṇī.
4. PADMAPĀNI—AVALOKITEṢVARA.
5. Viṣvapāṇī.

The Mānushi (human) Buddhas :—

1. Kraku-chanda.
2. Kanaka-muni.
3. Kāṣyapa.
4. GAUTAMA.
5. Maitreya.

This theory of the Dhyāni Buddhas is unknown, not only to the Pitakas and the Lalita Vistara, and even to the Saddharma Puṇḍarika,[2] but also, if we may judge from negative evidence, to the Chinese Buddhist

[1] Burnouf, 'Introduction,' p. 117.

[2] Two of them, however, the first and fourth, are mentioned in that work. Burnouf, p. 113.

pilgrims, Fa Hian and Hiouen Thsang, who visited India in the beginning of the fifth and in the seventh century respectively. Among these hypothetical beings,—the creations of a sickly scholasticism, hollow abstractions without life or reality,—the fourth, *Amitābha*, 'Immeasurable Light,' whose Bodhisatwa is Avalokiteṣvara, and whose emanation is Gautama, occupies, of course, the highest and most important rank. Surrounded by innumerable Bodhisatwas, he sits enthroned under a Bo Tree in Sukhavatī, *i.e.*, the Blissful,[1] a paradise of heavenly joys, whose description occupies whole tedious books of the so-called Great Vehicle.[2] By this theory, each of the five Buddhas has become three, and the fourth of these five sets of three is the second Buddhist Trinity, the belief in which must have arisen after the seventh century of our era.

But all this was not enough to satisfy the Tibetan and Nepalese hankering after gods many, and lords many. In the tenth century A.D.,[3] a new being—this time infinite, self-existent, and omniscient—was invented, and called *Ādi-Buddha*, the Primordial Buddha. He was held to have evolved out of himself the five Dhyāni Buddhas by the exercise of the five meditations; while each of these evolved out of himself by wisdom and contemplation the corre-

[1] Gunā Karanda Vyūha, in Burnouf, 'Introduction,' p. 222.

[2] *e.g.* 'Sukhavatī Vyūha,' analysed by Burnouf, ib., pp. 99–101; and 'Kumārajīva,' translated by Beal through the Chinese 'Catena,' pp. 378 *et seq.*

[3] For this date, see Csoma Korösi, 'Tibetan Grammar,' p. 192; 'Asiatic Researches,' vol. xx. p. 488.

sponding Bodhisatwas, and each of them again evolved out of his immaterial essence a kosmos, a material world. Our present world is supposed to be the creation of the fourth of these, that is of Avalokiteṣvara.

It will be noticed that these emanations bear a distant resemblance to the Eons or Emanations of the Gnostic Church; and it is not impossible that these gods owe their existence to the influence of Persian Christianity. In any case the whole theory, though in some sense based upon the teachings of Gautama, is the greatest possible contradiction to the Agnostic Atheism, which is the characteristic of his system of philosophy; and, indeed, the Ādi Buddha Theism has never been considered orthodox even in Tibet.

It is needless to add, that under the overpowering influence of these sickly imaginations the moral teachings of Gautama have been almost hid from view. The theories grew and flourished; each new step, each new hypothesis demanded another; until the whole sky was filled with forgeries of the brain, and the nobler and simpler lessons of the founder of the religion were smothered beneath the glittering mass of metaphysical subtleties.

As the stronger side of Gautama's teaching was neglected, the debasing belief in rites and ceremonies, and charms, and incantations, which had been the especial object of his scorn, began to live again, and to grow vigorously, and spread like the Bīrana weed warmed by a tropical sun in marsh and muddy soil. As in India after the expulsion of Buddhism the degrading worship of Siva and his dusky bride

P 2

had been incorporated into Brahmanism from the wild and savage devil-worship of the dark non-Āryan tribes; so as pure Buddhism died away in the north, *the Tantra system*, a mixture of magic and witchcraft and Siva-worship, was incorporated into the corrupted Buddhism.

The founder of this system seems to have been *Asanga*, an influential monk of Peshāwar, in the Panjāb; who lived, and wrote the first text book of the creed, the *Yogāchchāra Bhūmi sāstra*, about the sixth century of our era. Hiouen Thsang, who travelled in the first half of the seventh, found the monastery where Asanga had lived in ruins, and says that he had lived 1,000 years after the Buddha.[1] He managed with great dexterity to reconcile the two opposing systems by placing a number of Saïvite gods or devils, both male and female, in the inferior heavens of the then prevalent Buddhism; and by representing them as worshippers and supporters of the Buddha, and of Avalokitesvara. He thus made it possible for the half-converted and rude tribes to remain Buddhists while they brought offerings, and even bloody offerings, to these more congenial shrines; and while their practical belief had no relation at all to the Truths or the Noble Eightfold Path, but busied itself almost wholly with obtaining magic powers (*Siddhi*), by means of magic phrases (*Dhāraṇi*), and magic circles (*Maṇḍala*).

Asanga's happy idea bore but too ample fruit. In his

[1] Rémusat's translation, 'Mémoires sur les Contrées Occidentales,' p. 270; and 'La Vie de Hiouen Thsang,' p. 94.

own country and Nepāl the new wine, sweet and luscious to the taste of savages, completely disqualified them from enjoying any purer drink ; and now in both countries Saivism is supreme, and Buddhism is even nominally extinct, except in some outlying districts of Nepāl. But this full effect has only been worked out in the lapse of ages ; the Tantra literature has also had its growth and its development, and some unhappy scholar of a future age may have to trace its loathsome history. The nauseous taste repelled even the self-sacrificing industry of Burnouf, when he found the later Tantra books to be as immoral as they are absurd. 'The pen,' he says, 'refuses to transcribe doctrines as miserable in respect of form, as they are odious and degrading in respect of meaning.'[1]

I have only to add, that as the Dhyāni and Tantra systems grew, the idols of the Dhyāni Trinities and the Tantra gods and goddesses took their place in the monasteries and the temples, and their hideous figures with many eyes, and heads, and hands are painted in the books and on the walls, and put up on the sides of roads. The belief in mystic charms and phrases also re-acted even on the purer Buddhism; for the supposed efficacy of endless repetitions is one of the most striking features of the modern religion of Tibet. Every Tibetan has a rosary of 108 beads, that he may keep a reckoning of his good words, which supply to him the place of good deeds ; and in both public and private worship the greatest importance is attached to

[1] 'Introduction, &c.,' p. 558, speaking of Pañca-khama. Comp. pp. 553, 554 ; and Csoma, As. Res. xx. 488.

the multitude of words. Though we know something of such doctrines nearer home, the Tibetan carries them out with a fearless logic which may gain our wonder, if not our admiration. Perhaps the most marvellous invention which he has devised for drawing down blessings from the hypothetical beings with which his childish fancy has filled the heavens, are the well-known praying wheels,—those curious machines which, filled with prayers, or charms, or passages from holy books, stand in the towns in every open place, are placed beside the footpaths and the roads, revolve in every stream, and even (by the help of sails like those of windmills) are turned by every breeze which blows o'er the thrice-sacred valleys of Tibet.[1] So in the public divine services the hymns and anthems are sometimes chanted in unison, sometimes antiphonally—one verse by one choir, one by the other. But this takes time; and occasionally the hymns are actually chanted in a quite original manner, each monk intoning a different line; so that the whole body can chant an entire chapter in the time it takes to chant a single verse,—a plan which has its manifest advantages when the object is to get through as many holy words as possible.

So, also, these simple folk are fond of putting up what they call 'Trees of the Law,' that is, lofty flagstaffs with silk flags upon them emblazoned with that mystic charm of wonder-working power, the sacred words, '*Om Mani padme hum*,' 'Ah, the jewel is in

[1] Huc et Gabet, 'Voyages,' i. 324; General Cunningham's 'Ladak,' p. 374; Davis, 'Transactions of the Royal Asiatic Society,' ii. 494; Klaproth, 'Reise in den Kaukasus,' i. 181.

the lotus' (*i.e.* the Self-creative force is in the Kosmos). Whenever the flags are blown open by the wind, and 'the holy six syllables' are turned towards heaven, it counts as if a prayer were uttered; a prayer which brings down blessings not only upon the pious devotee at whose expense it was put up, but also upon the whole country-side. Everywhere in Tibet these praying flag-staffs meet the eye; and one may be glad in closing this outline of the theological doctrines peculiar to North-Indian Buddhism to have met with a custom which, however foolish, is not without its graceful side.[1]

[1] On Lāmāism may be compared also the few remarks below, pp. 248-250.

CHAPTER IX.

ON THE HISTORY OF THE ORDER.

THE first question that arises in giving a sketch of the history of Buddhism is that of the date of Gautama's death—a question so intricate and uncertain that I have decided not to enter upon it at any length in this little work; partly, because it would be impossible to discuss it with that fulness which is necessary to make a chronological discussion of much value; partly, because it would be difficult in any case to make the subject clear. Similar objections apply, perhaps, with almost equal force to the sketch of Gautama's life, and to the sketch of Buddhist metaphysics, which I have above attempted to give. In both cases I have been compelled to state the results to which I have been led, without combating the possible objections to them, and without giving at sufficient length the processes by which they have been reached: and in the constant endeavour to make the discussion of these abstruse matters as clear and simple as I possibly could, I must have omitted to touch upon points which ought to have been noticed. But there is not sufficient space at our disposal to make the question of the Buddhist era even clear. I can only refer, therefore, to the full statement of the argument which will be found in my 'Ancient Coins and Measures of Ceylon,' and merely state here the final conclusion—that the Buddha died within a few years of 412 B.C.

After Gautama's death, the Buddhist church, that is, the members of the Order, did not at once fall asunder into numerous sects; though doubtless from the very first there must have been some among them who retained more than the rest the influence of the Brahmanism in which they were brought up. This was owing to the wisdom of the older members, who, as both Northerns and Southerns agree, determined immediately after the death of the Teacher to hold a council in order to settle the rules and doctrines of their Order—the first, as it has been the most abiding and influential, and by far the largest in numbers of all the religious orders which the world has seen.

The first council was accordingly held near Rājagriha in the season of *was* following the death of the Buddha, and under the presidency of the aged Mahā Kāṣyapa, one of the first members of the Order, with whom the Buddha had once exchanged robes as a symbol of the unity of feeling between them.[1] The council consisted of 500 members of the Order, and was held in the Sattapaṇṇi cave, which still exists in the Vaihara hill, near Rājagriha, and which was prepared for the occasion by King

[1] On Kāṣyapa, see above, pp. 89, 189, and 'Mahāvansa,' p. 11. On the first council, see Mahāv., chap. iii. pp. 11–14; Dīpavansa, canto iv.; and the account given by Turnour, J.B.A.S., vi. pp. 510 and following from the 'Sumangala Vilāsinī,' Buddhaghosha's commentary on the 'Dīgha Nikāya.'

Ajātaṣatru of Magadha. There the whole council is said to have chanted together[1] the words of their revered Teacher, preserved in the Theravāda or doctrines of the Elders; following Upāli when the subject was the rules of the Order (Vinaya), and Ānanda when the subject was those more general precepts applicable to the Order and the laity alike (Dharma).

The Southern Buddhists believe that the Thera Vāda is identical with the Three Pitakas as now existing in Ceylon. This cannot, however, be the case. Some parts of the Pitakas, however much of the Thera Vāda other parts may contain—and this question cannot even be discussed until the Pitakas are published—bear evident marks of later composition. But that at the time of the Council of Rājagriha the doctrines of Buddhism had already been formulated into treatises which could be, and which had been, learnt by heart, is not only not impossible but highly probable.[2] The divisions of the Thera Vāda, however, as detailed in the Dīpavansa,[3] are quite different from those of the Pitakas, and no mention is made of Abhidharma or philosophy as a special division of the Scriptures. The divisions are as follows:[4]—

[1] Hence the Pāli word for council is *Sangīti*, 'the chanting together.'

[2] Compare the remarks above, p. 36, and below, p. 235.

[3] Canto iv. ṣloka 17 of my MS.

[4] See Childers, Dict. s. v.; Burnouf, Introd., pp. 51-63; 'Lotus,' pp. 355, 356; Alwis Pāli Grammar, pp. 60, 61; Hardy, 'Manual,' p. 175; Hodgson, 'Essays' (1874), p. 15; and 'Dīpavansa,' canto iv. ṣloka 17.

1. Sutta; Discourses.
2. Geyya; Mixed prose and verse.
3. Veyyākarana; Exposition.
4. Gāthā; Verse.
5. Udāna; (see above p. 20).
6. Itivuttaka; (see above p. 20).
7. Jātaka; (see above p. 21).
8. Abbhuta; Mysteries.
9. Vedalla;[1] Long treatises.

The Nepāl pandits attempt to bring all the later works of Northern Buddhism under the above and three other[2] heads, and Buddhaghosha attempts to bring all the Pitakas within these divisions; but both, as it seems to me, with very little success. Both the Ceylon chronicles say that the first council lasted seven months, and the Dīpavansa (iv. 4, 5) gives the names of eight of its principal members.

After this we have no details of the history of the Order till the time of the second council of Vaiṣāli, about 100 years after the first.[3] Some of the monks

[1] Means the same as the Vaipulya of the Northerns. Burnouf, 'Lotus,' pp. 754–757. Comp. Par. S., p. 238.

[2] The three others are Nidāna, Avadāna, and Upadesa (Hodgson, *loc. cit.*). Apadāna is one of the divisions of the second Pitaka. See above, p. 19.

[3] On the second Council, see 'Dīpavansa,' canto iv. end, and v.; Mahāv., ch. iv.; and Buddhaghosha in Turnour, *loc. cit.*, Sept., 1837. Short notices of it are given by the Chinese Buddhists, 'Fa Hian,' chap. xxv. (Beal, p. 99); Julien's 'Vie de Hiouen Thsang,' p. 158; 'Voyages,' i. 397–399; Sanang Setsen, in Rémusat's 'Foe Koue Ki,' p. 248; by the Mongolians (ibid. p. 248); and by the Tibetans, Schiefner, p. 310; Tāranātha's 'History of Buddhism,' p. 41.

at Vaiṣāli maintained what are called the Ten indulgences, which were opposed by others. They were:

1. That salt might be preserved in horn, whereas salt like other edibles might not according to the Winaya be laid aside for use.

2. That solid food might be taken, not only up till noon, but till the sun threw shadows two inches long.

3. That the rules of the Winaya might be relaxed in the country, away from the conveniences of the monasteries.

4. That ordination, confession, &c., might be performed in private houses, and not only in the *uposatha* halls attached to the monasteries.

5. That where the consent of the Order was necessary to any act, that consent might be obtained after, and not only before the act.

6. That conformity to the example of others was a good excuse for relaxing rules.

7. That whey might be taken after noon, and not only liquids such as water or milk.

8. That fermented drinks, if they looked like water, were allowed to be drunk.

9. That seats covered with cloths were allowed, so long as the cloths had no fringes.

10. That gold and silver might be received by members of the Order.[1]

After a severe struggle, the more orthodox party succeeded in getting these indulgences condemned; and forthwith under the leadership of Yasa, son of Kākandaka, and of Revata, a second council, this

[1] Tāranātha's list differs, especially as to Nos. 2, 3, 4, 5, 6.

time of 700, was held during eight months at Vaiṣāli, and the rules of the Order and the doctrines of the Faith[1] again settled and vindicated. But the decisions of the council were not universally acknowledged. The other party also held a council, much more numerous than that of their stricter opponents, and hence called the Mahā Sangīti, the Great Council. It is to be regretted that we have not as yet any detailed account of this struggle from the side of the seceders; for it is difficult without such assistance to decide how much truth there may be in the partial descriptions before us. The Dīpavansa[2] says of the 'heretics,' as the Southern Church calls them:

The monks of the Great Council overturned religion,
They broke up the old Scriptures and made a new recension,
A discourse put in one place they put in another,
And distorted the sense and the doctrine of the five Nikāyas—
These monks who knew not what had been spoken in order,
And what had been spoken separately,
What was the obvious and what the higher meaning.—
What had been spoken in one connection they put in another,
And destroyed much of the spirit by holding to the shadow of the letter.
They partly rejected the Sutta and Vinaya so deep,
And made a different Sutta and Vinaya and text,
The Parivāra,[3] and the commentary, and the six books of the Abhidhamma,
The Paṭisambhidā,[4] the Nidesa,[4] and a portion of the Jātaka[4]—
So much they put aside, without even making them afresh!

---

[1] The whole of the 'Sāsana,' the Dharma' and 'Vinaya' (Bhuddhaghosha, *loc. cit.*). [2] Bhānavāra V.

[3] The last book in the 'Vinaya Pitaka.' See p. 20.

[4] These are Nos. 10–12 in the 'Khuddaka Nikāya.' See p. 21.

This was the first open and declared schism. Both the Ceylon chronicles go on to give the names of 18 sects (or rather of 17 besides the orthodox) into which these two afterwards divided; but the lists differ as to five or six names from one another, and from the list of eighteen sects given by the Tibetans.[1] We know almost nothing at present of the differences which divided these sects from one another; but they all belonged to the Little Vehicle in contradistinction to the Great Vehicle of the later Northern School.[2] It is doubtful whether the eighteen sects were sects in the modern sense, whether, that is, they formed different church governments, and their adherents lived apart from one another in different monasteries. Some of them at least, must have differed only slightly from the rest; and though the dispute between the two great divisions of the laxer and the stricter bodies may have been bitter, they each and all acknowledged that the others could attain the same salvation as themselves. In the words of the learned Chinese Buddhist Hiouen Thsang—[3]

"The schools of philosophy are always in conflict, and the noise of their passionate discussions rises like the waves of the sea. Heretics of the different sects attach themselves to particular teachers, and by different routes walk *to the same goal.*"

---

[1] Csoma in As. Res., xx. 298.

[2] On the 18 sects, see Burnouf, 'Lotus,' pp. 356–359; and Köppen, 'Religion des Buddha,' pp. 150–159. Fa Hian (Beal, p. 96) mentions 96 sects. Comp. the 32 heresies above, p. 98.

[3] Julien, 'Mémoires,' &c., i. 77. Thsang, himself an adherent of the Great Vehicle, calls all the others heretics. In the next paragraph he gives the number of the sects as eighteen.

It is instructive to notice that this rapid growth of the Buddhist sects is placed just at the time when the political history of the Eastern valley of the Ganges would have been most likely to favour and strengthen it. The old Aryan civilisation had begun even at the time of Gautama to yield to changing circumstances. The influence of the priesthood was becoming more exclusively spiritual, while the temporal power of the chiefs was growing. Some of the latter had even then become kings, and the oligarchies of the clans were more and more merging into despotisms. Shortly after Gautama's death Ajātaṣatru, king of Magadha, destroyed the Confederation of the Wajjian clans on the opposite side of the Ganges; and then ensued a series of struggles between Magadha and the neighbouring kingdoms of Kosāmbi and Ṣrāvasti. The lesser chiefs had to take sides with one or other of the powerful combatants, while each country became the scene of intrigues for the coveted possession of the throne. These struggles gave a chance to men of the lower castes which they could never have in the old system of the clans—a system which, at the time of the Councils of Vaiṣāli, must almost have ceased to exist.

The kingdom of Magadha had by that time become supreme, and either just before or just after the councils had assembled in the old capital of the Wajjians, that important revolution took place, which raised a low-caste adventurer to be the first king of all India—or as both Buddhists and Brahmans would call it, to be the first Chakravarti, the first Universal Monarch. To them India was 'the world,' just as

European writers till quite recently talked complacently of 'the world,' while they were ignoring more than three-fourths of the human race. Is it surprising that this unity of power in one man made a deep impression upon them? Is it surprising that like Romans worshipping Augustus, or Greeks adding the glow of the sun-myth to the glory of Alexander, the Indians should have formed an ideal of their Chakravartī, and transferred to this new ideal many of the dimly sacred and half-understood traits of the Vedic heroes? Is it surprising that the Buddhists should have found it edifying to recognise in *their* hero the Chakravarti of Righteousness, and that the story of the Buddha should be tinged with the coloring of these Chakravarti myths?

It was in 325 B.C. that Alexander stopt his victorious career on the banks of the Hyphasis, and there a defeated rebel escaping from the hands of the king of Magadha visited his camp. When Alexander had turned away, that despised and rude adventurer, whom he had almost determined to kill, gathered round him the tribes of the Panjāb, and gradually extended his power till, about 315 B.C.,[1] when Nanda, the Rāja of Magadha, was murdered in his palace, the low-born robber chief stept into the vacant throne; and shortly afterwards, under the title or name of Chandragupta, drove the Greeks out of India, defeating Seleukos, the Greek ruler of the Indus provinces. Is it possible that he was

[1] He began to count his reign seven or eight years before, when he became king of the western provinces.

the Aṣoka in whose reign both Northern and Southern Buddhists place the Vaiṣāli Councils? It is certain that the Southerns are wrong in identifying this Aṣoka with Kākavarṇa; Chandragupta, the moon-protected—like Piyadasi, the name by which his grandson the great Aṣoka, invariably styles himself—is not a name at all, properly speaking, but an epithet, adopted probably after the rise of his power; and probability is also in favour of the name Aṣoka being twice found rather in one family than in two. This would seem to be confirmed by Tāranātha, who, while placing the Vaiṣāli Council in the time of Aṣoka, adds that its members were supported by King Nanda. However this may be, it is clear that it was just when Chandragupta and his low caste followers from the Panjāb came into power, just when the old order of things had given place to new, that the Buddhists, the party of reform, the party who made light of caste distinctions, began to rise rapidly in numbers and in influence.

Neither Chandragupta nor his son Bindusāra[1] were Buddhists; but the third of the race, Piyadasi, best known under the name of Aṣoka (in Pāli Asoka), openly adopted the now popular creed. His name is honoured wherever the teachings of the Buddha have spread, and is reverenced from the Volga

[1] If any proof were wanted that Indian, like other Oriental, kings had an official epithet which often took the place of their more proper name, it would be found in the fact that the Greeks only know Bindusāra as Amitrochates—a difference unexplained till Lassen pointed out that Amitrochates is the Sanskrit Amitraghāta, 'Foe-slayer,' doubtless the official epithet of Bindusāra.

to Japan, from Ceylon and Siam to the borders of Mongolia and Siberia. 'If a man's fame,' says Köppen, 'can be measured by the number of hearts who revere his memory, by the number of lips who have mentioned and still mention him with honour, Aṣoka is more famous than Charlemagne or Cæsar.'

Like his Christian prototype Constantine, he was converted by a miracle, so highly do the Buddhist scribes estimate his adhesion to their cause. And yet it cannot be doubted that it was the first great step on the downward path of Buddhism, the first step to its expulsion from India; not, of course, that the conversion itself injured the church, but Buddhist writers have cause to use, without much change, the words of Dante :—[1]

> Ah ! Constantine, of how much ill was cause,
> Not thy conversion, but those rich domains
> That the first wealthy Pope received of thee.

After his conversion, which took place in the 10th year of his reign, he became a very zealous supporter of the new religion. He himself built many monasteries and dāgabas, and provided many monks with the necessaries of life; and he encouraged those about his court to do the same. He also established gardens and hospitals for man and beast, and published edicts throughout his empire, enjoining on all his subjects morality and justice.

Within the last 50 years a most important and interesting discovery has been made of several of

[1] 'Inferno,' canto xix. ; 'Paradiso,' canto xx. The translation is Milton's.

these edicts, engraven in different Prākrit dialects on pillars or rocks, whose wide distance from one another is sufficient to show the great extent of Aṣoka's empire. The pillars are at Delhi and Allahabad; the rocks at Kapur da Giri near Peshaur, at Girnar in Guzerāt, at Dhauli in Orissa, and at Babra, on the road running S.W. from Delhi to Jayapura.[1] They were first published and translated by James Prinsep, then republished by Wilson, and have been since then further explained by Burnouf and Professors Westergaard and Kern. Their general sense is not at all doubtful, but the facsimiles which have hitherto reached Europe have been imperfect, and the text is by no means settled. It were much to be wished that the Indian Government would have a correct edition published of these noble memorials of a byegone time, records unique of their kind in the history of the world.

It is clear from these most valuable inscriptions that Buddhism in the time of Aṣoka was still comparatively pure. We hear nothing of metaphysical beings or hypothetical deities, nothing of ritual, or ceremonies, or charms; the edicts are full of a lofty spirit of tolerance and righteousness, reminding us often of the wise and simple teachings of the Sigālovāda Sutta.[2] Obedience to parents; kindness to children and friends; mercy towards the brute creation; indulgence to inferiors; reverence towards Brahmins and members of the Order; suppression

[1] In the edicts themselves he claims to rule also over South India and Ceylon.

[2] See above, pp. 143–148.

of anger, passion, cruelty, or extravagance; generosity, and tolerance, and charity—such are the lessons which 'the kindly king, the delight of the gods,' inculcates on all his subjects.

One of these edicts is addressed to the Buddhist monks in council assembled—the council held at Patna in the 18th year of Asoka's reign. The increased respect paid to the Order had attracted to its ranks many unworthy members; and 'heretics,' says the Mahāvansa, 'assumed the yellow robe in order to share in its advantages; whenever they had opinions of their own they gave them forth as doctrines of the Buddha, they acted according to their own will, and not according to what was right.'[1] Accordingly, a formal council of 1,000 elders, lasting nine months, was held under the presidency of Tissa, son of Moggali; and once more the rules of the Order and the doctrines of the Faith were solemnly rehearsed and settled. The edict referred to, that of Babra, says as follows:[2]—

King Piyadasi (the kind-hearted), of Magadha, greeting the Council, wishes it health and happiness. You know, reverend sirs, how great is my respect and reverence for the Buddha, the Law, and the Church. All those things, reverend sirs, which were spoken by the Blessed Buddha, were well spoken; by looking upon them, reverend sirs, as authority, the true Law will long endure. I honour, reverend sirs, as such, the follow-

[1] Pp. 38, 39.

[2] Captains Burt and Kittoe, J. of the Bengal As. Soc., ix. 616. Burnouf, 'Lotus,' pp. 718–730. Kern, Jahrtelling, pp. 32-43.

ing Scriptures of the Law :—The substance of the Vinaya,[1] the State of the Just,[2] the Fears of the Future,[3] the Poems on (or of) the Wise,[4] the Discourse on Conduct Befitting the Wise,[5] the Questions of Upatissa,[6] the Exhortations to Rāhula regarding Falsehood[7] spoken by the Blessed Buddha. These scriptures of the Law, reverend sirs, I hope that the honourable monks and nuns may constantly learn and reflect upon ; and so also the laity of either sex. To that end, reverend sirs, I cause this to be written, and have uttered my desire.

I think it would be evident from this inscription alone, that the belief of the Southern Buddhists, that the whole of the Three Pitakas was spoken by Buddha, is quite unfounded; for a comparison of it with the list given above pp. 18-21, will show the reader that the list is far shorter than that of the Pitakas. Asoka's list, moreover, shows us that books agreeing to these descriptions were then extant, and if we do not find them somewhere in the present Pitakas, the conclusion is inevitable that these cannot have preserved to us the recension made by the Council of Patna. The pious editors may have described them by other titles, or may have inserted them in other later books which they regarded as sacred, but they never could have omitted them from their canon.

[1] Vinaya-Samākase = V.-samākassa, the contraction, summary of the Vinaya.

[2] Aliya (=ariya) vasāni. There is much doubt about the real meaning of vasāni.

[3] Anāgata-bhayāni.

[4] Muni-gāthā. Comp. Thera- and Theri-gātha above, p. 21.

[5] Monēya-sūta = moneyya-sutta. Comp. Child. Dict., p. 617.

[6] Upatissa is the name of the monk usually called Sāri-putta, the son of Sāri. See above, p. 62.

[7] Rāhula was Gautama's son. Above, pp. 30, 50, 72.

The Vinaya-samākasa is exactly the same in meaning as the Parivāra-pāṭha, the 5th Division of the 1st Pitaka; and the Muni-gāthā, possibly the same as the Thera-gāthā, the 8th Book of the 5th Division of the 2nd Pitaka, and it may also have included the 9th. The differences in the names need not surprise us. We should expect to find slight differences, as the two lists are in different dialects. It must be borne in mind that we only know the contents of a few of the books in one division of the Sutta Pitaka; and the subjects of those books in Aṣoka's List, which we cannot at present trace, are such that we should expect to find them, if we find them at all, in those Divisions, the Books of which are at present unknown. The Ariyavasāni seems to be a description of Nirvāna, the Ariyas being the same as the Arahats who have entered the 4th Path. The Terrors of the Future seems to be a description of the different worlds of purgatory, one of which is described in the Petavatthu, the 7th Book of the 5th Division of the 2nd Pitaka. More than one Sutta purports to have been delivered by Gautama in answer to questions by Sāriputta; and several purport to have been addressed to Rāhula, but nothing has yet been heard of one on the subject of Falsehood.

At the close of the Council of Patna,—of which, it should be noticed, the Northern Buddhists are perhaps ignorant[1], — missionaries were sent into

[1] It is not known to be mentioned in any northern Buddhist work, and is not referred to in Csoma's 'Analysis of the Tibetan Scriptures' ('As. Res.,' xx. 41, 297 seem to refer to the second Council); but it is mentioned, with both the former ones, in

different countries; and the 8th chapter of the Dipavansa and the 12th chapter of the Mahāvansa give us the details comprised in the following table:—

To Kashmīr and Gandhāra	went	Majjhantika.
,, Mahīsa [1]	,,	Mahādeva.
,, Vanavāsi [2]	,,	Rakkhita.
,, Aparantaka [3]	,,	the Bactrian Dhammarakkhita.
,, Mahāraṭṭha [4]	,,	Mahā Dhammarakkhita.
,, Yonaloka [5]	,,	Mahā Rakkhita.
,, Himavanta [6]	,,	Majjhima.
,, Suvaṇṇa-bhūmi [7]	,,	Sena and Uttara.
,, Lankā (Ceylon)	,,	Mahinda and others.

In the time of the Ceylon chronicles it was no uncommon thing for boats to cross the Indian Ocean, even at its broadest part;[8] whether this could have

Palladji's 'Historische Skizzen des alten Buddhismus,' in Erman's 'Archiv,' pp. 206 and following, *teste* Köppen, i. 139. Palladji drew his materials from Chinese sources.

[1] The most southerly settlement of the Āryans, south of the Godāvari, in the Nizam's dominions (Lassen, i. A. 1, 681).

[2] That is, the Wilderness. It surely cannot mean Tibet (see Childers, 'Dict.'). Perhaps it was on the borders of the Great Desert in Rajputāna.

[3] The Border land; that is, the west of the Panjāb.

[4] The ancient seat of the Mahrattas at the sources of the Godāvari, 150 miles north-east of Bombay.

[5] Bactria.

[6] The central Himālayas. Majjhima returned to India, and was burned under one of the Sānchi Topes, where his relics were lately discovered! (Cunningham, J.R.A.S., xiii. 111).

[7] The Golden Land. Perhaps the Malay Peninsula is meant, which the classical geographers, *teste* Lassen, ii. 249, call the Golden. More probably the whole coast from Rangoon to Sincapore, which is still so called in Ceylon.

[8] Parākrama the Great, of Ceylon, actually sent an army

been thought of in the time of Aṣoka is doubtful. The other items are not improbable; and it is certainly very curious that the inscription in the same characters as those used in most of the Aṣoka Edicts found on the tomb of Majjhima, should so entirely confirm that one of them which would, if unconfirmed, have been least likely to be true.

In the same year, Aṣoka founded an office, that of *Dharma Mahāmātra*, chief Minister of Justice or Religion, whose duty it was to preserve the purity of religion, and to overlook and care for the right treatment and the progress of the aborigines and the subject races—a striking conjunction of duties. Similar officials were appointed in the dependent courts, and others to promote the education of the women in the harems and elsewhere in the principles of the religion of Gautama; and these appointments were also recorded in the edicts.

The Edicts also show us that Aṣoka was not content with spreading the precepts of Buddhism within his own territories, large as they were. He is stated in them to have established in neighbouring lands hospitals for man and beast; to have planted medicinal plants and fruit-bearing trees where such did not naturally grow; and to have dug wells and planted trees on the roadsides for the use of man and beasts.[1] As the foreign countries where these orders

across to Cochin China about A.D. 1180. See 'Coins and Measures of Ceylon,' p. 24.

[1] For similar acts by Buddhist kings of Ceylon, see my article "On Two Old Sinhalese Inscriptions," J.R.A.S., p. 3, 1875; Mah., ch. lxxx. sl. 25; Turnour, Mah., pp. 242, 245.

were carried out are mentioned Chola,[1] Pāndya,[2] Satyaputra,[3] Kerala,[4] Ceylon, and the land of the Greek king Antiochus. In another edict, Aṣoka claims to have sent embassies to four Greek kings—whose names enable his date to be fixed within a few years—and to have 'won from them a victory, not by the sword, but by religion.'

The most important of Aṣoka's embassies or missions was, undoubtedly, as far as our present purpose is concerned, that which he sent to Ceylon. The king of Ceylon at that time was Tissa (250–230 B.C.), called in the chronicles 'Tissa, the delight of the gods,' a title he probably adopted from his great contemporary. To him, as we have seen above, Aṣoka's own son Mahinda,[5] who had been admitted into the Order 12 years before, was sent immediately after the council to introduce Buddhism into that island. He did not, however, start till the next year. When he did so, he took with him a band of monks,[6] and also, in

[1] Tanjūr. The Koromandel coast is the *maṇḍdala*, or province of Chola. Chola, Pāṇḍya, and Kerala together are used in later Ceylon inscriptions to describe all South India. See my articles in the J.R.A.S. for 1874 and 1875.

[2] Madura and Tinnivelli. I read Pāḍā in accordance with Kern, 'Jahrtelling,' p. 89.

[3] The modern Satpura mountains (Holkar's dominions), south of the Narmada.

[4] The Malabar coast.

[5] Mahinda and his sister Sanghamittā were born at Wessanagar, the modern Besnagar, close to which are the Bhilsa Topes, where General Cunningham has made such interesting discoveries.

[6] Four of the names are given ('Mahāv.,' p. 71) Iṭṭhiya, Uttiya, Sambala, and Bhaddasāla; and two others, Sumana and Bhaṇḍu, pp. 76, 77.

the memory of himself and of his followers, the Piṭakas as just settled at the Council of Patna, together with the commentaries upon them. These commentaries he subsequently translated from the Pāli into the Sinhalese Prākrit.

He was received with great favour by king Devānam Piya Tissa, who became a very zealous ad herent and supporter of the new religion—probably because it was the religion of Aṣoka. He had already sent an embassy to Aṣoka, and had received an embassy in return, and had even allowed himself to be crowned by Aṣoka's ambassador. The king was persuaded by Mahinda to build the Thūpārāma Dāgaba, which is still one of the glories of the ruined city of Anurādhapura. Under it both the chronicles say that the right collar-bone of Gautama was buried, but the details prove that the relic is fictitious. Close by it the king also erected a monastery for the Indian monks, and another on the beautiful hill of Mihintale, eight miles to the east of the city.

It was on this hill, the three peaks of which, each now surmounted by a Dāgaba, form so striking an object from the central trunk-road which runs along its side, that the famous missionary spent most of his after years. Here on the precipitous western side of the hill, under a large mass of granite rock, at a spot which, completely shut out from the world, affords a magnificent view of the plains below, he had his study hollowed out, and steps cut in the rock over which alone it could be reached. There also the stone couch which was carved out of the solid rock still exists, with holes either for curtain rods, or for a protecting balustrade beside it. The great rock effectually protects the cave from the heat of the sun, in whose warm light the broad valley below lies basking; not a sound reaches it from the plain, now one far-reaching forest, then full of busy homesteads; there is only heard that hum of the insects which never ceases, and the rustling of the leaves of the trees which cling to the side of the precipice. I shall not easily forget the day when I first entered that lonely, cool, and quiet chamber, so simple and yet so beautiful, where more than 2,000 years ago the great teacher of Ceylon had sat, and thought, and worked through the long years of his peaceful and useful life.[1] On that hill he afterwards died, and his ashes still rest under the Dāgaba, which is the principal object of the reverence and care of the few monks who still reside in the Mahintale Wihāre.

Shortly after the building of the Thūpārāma Dāgaba had commenced, some of the king's female relations expressed a wish to become nuns. Mahinda accordingly sent for his sister Sanghamittā, who had entered the Order at the same time with himself. Taking leave of her father, she brought over with her a band of nuns,[2] and instructed the new disciples in the precepts of Buddhism, their principal occupation being the hearing and repeating of the sacred books.

Sanghamittā also brought over with her a branch of the sacred Bo Tree, the tree then growing at

[1] Compare 'Mahāv.,' p. 123.

[2] The names of nine of them, and of several of their most learned pupils are given in the Dīpav, ch. 18.

Buddha Gāyā on the site of the present temple, and then believed, not, perhaps, without reason, to be the very tree under which Gautama had experienced that mental conflict which is called his attainment of Buddha-hood. That precious memorial of their revered teacher was planted at Anurādhapura, a little to the south of the Ruwanwæli Dāgaba; and, strange as it may seem, there it still grows. Sir Emerson Tennent says of it :—

"The Bo Tree of Anurādha-pura is, in all probability, *the oldest historical tree in the world.* It was planted 288[1] years before Christ, and hence is now 2,147 years old. Ages varying from one to four thousand years have been assigned to the *Baobabs* of Senegal, the *Eucalyptus* of Tasmania, the *Dragon tree* of Orotava, the *Wellingtonia* of California, and the chestnut of Mount Etna. But all these estimates are matter of conjecture; and such calculations, however ingenious, must be purely inferential: whereas the age of the Bo Tree is *matter of record,* its conservancy has been an object of solicitude to successive dynasties, and the story of its vicissitudes has been preserved in a series of continuous chronicles, among the most authentic that have been handed down by mankind. Compared with it the Oak of Ellerslie is but a sapling, and the Conqueror's Oak in Windsor Forest barely numbers half its years. The Yew trees of Fountain's Abbey are believed to have flourished there 1,200 years ago; the Olives in the garden of Gethsemane were full grown when the Saracens were expelled from Jerusalem; and the Cypress of Sorna, in Lombardy, is said to have been a tree in the time of Julius Cæsar: yet the Bo Tree is older than the oldest of these by a century; and would almost seem to verify the prophecy pro-

---

[1] This should be 245; Tennent adhered to the now-rejected chronology. The Bo Tree is now (1877) 2,122 years old.

nounced when it was planted, that it would "flourish, and be green for ever." [1]

The tree could scarcely have lived so long had it not been for the constant care of the monks. As it showed signs of decay terraces were built up around it, so that it now grows more than twenty feet above the surrounding soil; for the tree being of the fig species—its botanical name is *ficus religiosa*—its living branches could then throw out fresh roots. Where its long arms spread beyond the enclosure, rude pillars of iron or masonry have been used to prop them up; and it is carefully watered in seasons of drought. The whole aspect of the tree and its enclosure bears evident signs of extreme age; but we could not be sure of its identity were it not for the complete chain of documentary evidence which has been so well brought together by Sir Emerson Tennent.[2]

Dewānam-piya Tissa, who reigned for 20 years,[3] died just before Mahinda; and soon after his death Ceylon was for the first time overrun by the Tamils, who for some 60 years retained the Northern provinces and the kingly power in their hands. They were driven out, about B.C. 164, by Dushṭa Gāmini, a grandson of Tissa's brother, who had fled to the south of the island. This king also was a zealous supporter of Buddhism. He built two of the large Dāgabas at Anurādhapura, the Miriswœti, 150

[1] Ceylon, ii., pp. 613, and foll. The italics are his own.

[2] In the appendix to the chap. quoted. See also above, p. 39, note.

[3] Not 40. See Westergaard 'Ueber Buddha's Todesjahr,' p. 105. The whole discussion here on this period of Sinhalese history is most valuable.

feet high, and the Mahā Thūpa, 200 feet high; and also the huge monastery (called the Great Brazen Palace, from its having been roofed with metal,) whose 1,600 granite pillars still stand just outside the sacred enclosure round the Bo Tree.

Thirty-four years after his death the Dravidians again conquered the island, but were a second time driven out by Waṭṭa Gāmiṇi, a son of Dushṭa Gāmiṇi's brother, in about 88 B.C. He built the largest Dāgaba in Ceylon, called the Abhaya-giri Dāgaba, 250 feet in height; and it was in his reign, about 160 years after the Council of Patna, and 330 years after the death of Gautama, that the Three Pitakas were for the first time reduced into writing.[1] The Mahāvansa relates this important event in a stanza, which it quotes from the Dīpavansa:—

'The wise monks of former days handed down by word of mouth
The text of the Three Pitakas, and the Commentary upon them;
Seeing the destruction of men, the monks of this time assembled,
And, that the Faith might last long, they wrote them in books.'[2]

To understand the real significance of this record it is necessary, in the first place, to get rid of the European notion that books can only be preserved in writing. The Indian opinion is just the other way. Even at the present time, if all the printed copies of the Vedas were destroyed, the Vedas would still be preserved in the memory of the priests, as they have been for certainly more than 3,000 years; and those priests look

[1] At Alu Lene, 3 m. S. of the modern town of Mātale, a cave still well-known, which lies close to the great central road, and is well worth a visit.

[2] Mahāv, p. 207. Dīpav, ch. 19.

upon the Veda, thus authenticated, as the test to which all printed or written copies must give way. If you depend upon written copies, they would argue, you are sure to make, and to perpetuate mistakes; but the text as handed down by word of mouth is preserved, not only by being itself constantly repeated, but by the assistance of the commentaries, in which every word of the text is carefully enshrined.[1] So long as reliance can be placed on the succession of teachers and pupils this argument may not be so far wrong; but when a text has to be preserved in a small country liable to be overrun by persecuting enemies, the condition of things is changed, and it becomes necessary to preserve it also in writing. Mahinda could have written the texts, had he so chosen. We know that the square alphabet which Asoka used was at least known in Ceylon, if it did not originate there.[2] That he did not choose to do so ought to throw no doubt upon the identity of the existing version of the text with that which he brought to Ceylon. On this question, as on so many others, we must wait for the publication of the Piṭakas before we form a definite conclusion; but probability is in favour of our present text having been handed down correctly during the 160 years between Mahinda's arrival, and the time when it was reduced to writing; and since that time it has been preserved in the same manner as the classical writings of whose authenticity there is no doubt.[3]

[1] Compare the remarks above pp. 10, 86.

[2] See Dr. Goldschmidt's letter to the *Academy*, 17th February, 1877.

[3] I once tried in vain to persuade my friend and tutor, the learned and high-minded monk Yātrāmulle Unnānse, that it

As this is the last place in which the text will be discussed, it may be of interest to add that a Revision Committee of the most learned monks met at Ratnapura during 1875, under the presidency of the learned Chief Priest, Sumangala, and went carefully through the whole of the Pitaka Texts.

The only other event in the history of Ceylon Buddhism which we need here record, is the work of Buddhaghosha. This celebrated monk was born near the Bo Tree, at Buddha Gāyā, and came to Ceylon about 430 A.D. There by his great work, the *Visuddhi Magga* or *Path of Holiness*, a cyclopædia of Buddhist doctrine, he quickly proved himself to be a master of all Buddhist knowledge; and he was employed by the rulers of the Order in Ceylon to rewrite in Pāli the commentaries which had till then been handed down in Sinhalese.[1] Almost all the commentaries now existing are ascribed to him, and his work was at least complete enough to drive the Sinhalese version so completely out of use, that every trace of it has now been lost,—unless, as Alwis thinks, two very ancient Sinhalese works, the Kudusika and Mulusika, should turn out to be as early as this period.[2]

would be a good thing to print the Pitakas. He said they would be no longer copied; and he would not be convinced that books printed on our flimsy paper were safer than those written on substantial palm leaves. Other influential Buddhists thought differently, but since my departure from Ceylon the project has, I am afraid, been quite neglected.

[1] Mahav, p. 250–253.

[2] Sidat Sāngarawa p. cl. This seems to me highly improbable. Compare my paper on Pali and Sinhalese literature in the 4th Annual Report of the Philological Society (1875), p. 75.

The following is a list of the Pāli commentaries now extant[1] :—

Samanta-pāsadikā	on the	Vinaya.
Kankhā-vitaraṇī	,,	Pātimokkha.
Sumangala-vilasinī	,,	Dīgha Nikāya.
Papañca-sūdanī	,,	Majjhama Nikāya.
Sārattha-ppakāsinī	,,	Samyutta Nikāya.
Manorattha-pūraṇī	,,	Anguttara Nikāya.
Paramattha-jotika	,,	Khuddaka Pāṭha and Sutta Nipāta.
Dhamma-pada Aṭṭhakathā	,,	Dhamma-pada.
Paramattha-dīpanī	,,	Udāna, Vimāna-vatthu, Peta-Vatthu Theragāthā, and Theri-gathā.
Abhidhammattha-dīpanī	,,	Iti-vuttaka
Jātaka Aṭṭhakathā	,,	Jātaka.
Saddhamma-ppajotikā	,,	Niddesa.
Saddhamma-ppakāsinī	,,	Patisambhidā.
Visuddha-jana-vilāsinī	,,	Apadāna.
Madurattha-vilāsinī	,,	Buddhavansa.
Cariyā-piṭaka Atthakathā	,,	Cariyā Piṭaka.
Attha-sālinī	,,	Dhamma-sangaṇī.
Sammoha-vinodanī	,,	Vibhanga.
Pañca-ppakaraṇa Aṭṭhakathā	,,	Five last books of the Abhidhamma Pitaka.

The other missions sent out after Aṣoka's Council have left few traces behind them, though there is every reason to believe that those sent to parts of the peninsula of India itself were not unsuccessful. Both Burma and Siam were first really converted to Buddhism from Ceylon; the former about 450 A.D., when Buddhaghosha went there after his stay in that

[1] Childers' 'Pāli Dict.' s. v. Aṭṭhakathā.

island, the latter in 638 A.D.[1] Java seems to have received its first missionaries from Kalinga in the sixth or seventh century; but the point is still uncertain[2]; it is only clear that Buddhism was the prevailing religion in the thirteenth century, when the great Temple at Boro Budor was built. About this time also Buddhism penetrated from Java into the adjoining islands Bali and Sumatra, but in the latter it never took firm hold.

Of the success of the missions towards the north we have more certain knowledge. It is clear from the coins of Huvishka and Kanishka that Buddhism became the State religion of the north-westerly parts of India at about the commencement of our era. Huvishka first reigned in Kabul, and when driven out from there founded a new kingdom in Kashmīr, and subsequently conquered the adjacent countries as far down as Mathurā, where he built a monastery.[3] His successor, Hushka, also built a Vihāra, but both of these kings seem also to have been fire-worshippers. His successor, however, Kanishka, the third of the three brothers, who began to reign about 10 A.D., was a very zealous Buddhist.

Kanishka's dominions extended from Kabul to the Hindu-kush and Bolor Mountains; over Yarkand and Khokan; throughout Kashmīr, Ladāk, and the

[1] Crawfurd 'Journal of the Embassy to the Courts of Siam and Cochin China,' p. 615.

[2] See Lassen's Indische Alterthumskunde, ii. 1076, iv. 711.

[3] Cunningham, 'Archæological Reports,' i., p. 238. Dawson, 'Ancient Inscriptions from Mathurā, J.R.A.S. New Series v., p. 182. Alexander Polyhistor, who wrote 80–60 B.C., confirms this by stating that monks (Samanaioi) 'philosophised in Baktria' (see the passage in Lassen, ii. 1092).

Central Himālayas (Himavanta); down over the plains of the Upper Ganges and Jamna as far as Agra; over Rajputāna, Guzarāt, and Sindh; and through the whole of the Panjāb—a magnificent empire, unequalled in extent from the time of Aṣoka to that of the Moguls.

On the recommendation of his tutor, Pārṣvika, Kanishka held a council of 500 learned monks, under the presidency of Vasubandhu.[1] At this council, unfortunately, nothing was done towards settling a canon of scripture which might have prevented the subsequent changes which so entirely reformed the character of Northern Buddhism. The monks satisfied themselves with drawing up three Commentaries. 1. *Upadesa* on the Sūtra Pitaka; 2. *Vinaya-vibāshā-ṣāstra* on the Vinaya; and, 3. *Abhidharma-vibāshā-ṣastra* on the Abhidharma Pitaka, each according to Hiouen Thsang in 100,000 couplets.

These three works Kanishka had engraven on plates of red copper, and carefully sealed up in a stone box, over which he built a Dāgaba. If the tradition preserved by Hiouen Thsang be correct, there they probably still lie buried; but that learned traveller wrote nearly seven centuries afterwards, and his account of the council contains incredible details.[2] None of the

[1] The only account of this council is in Hiouen Thsang's 'Travels' (Julien's trans., vol. i., pp. 173–178). That in the Chinese Life of H. T. (Julien's trans., pp. 95, 96), is taken from the 'Travels.' The council is referred to by Csoma, 'As. Res.' xx., pp. 41,2197. Schmidt 'Geschichte der Ost Mongolen, pp. 17,315. Schiefner, 'Lebensbeschreibung,' p. 310—all from sources independent of H. T.

[2] He tells a story of the miraculous completion of Vasu-

three works are mentioned in Hodgson's long list of Sanskrit Buddhist works extant in Nepāl,[1] or were known to Burnouf or Csoma, or are included in the Hodgson MSS. sent to Europe;[2] and Fa Hian says[3] that in his time, through the whole of Northern India, the various masters handed down the doctrines by word of mouth, and had no written copies of them. The *Upadesa* mentioned above (p. 215) is evidently a different and older work. Hiouen Thsang had the Abhidharma-vibāshā-ṣastra explained to him during his residence in Kashmīr,[4] though he does not mention the others. The same work is still extant in China and Japan, and a copy is in the India Office.[5]

This council is unknown to the Southern Buddhists. As it was held before the rise of the school of the so-called Great Vehicle, the works then held sacred, many of which are still extant, must preserve the ancient Buddhism; and from the meagre accounts of them, from which, and from the Lalita Vistara, all our knowledge of early Northern Buddhism is derived, it would seem that there was but very little difference between it and the Buddhism of the Pitakas.

When at his death Kanishka's empire fell to pieces,

bandha's Arahatship just after the council met, and before it sat, evidently due to a reminiscence of the similar story about Ananda; and the detail about the 100,000 *slokas* sounds legendary.

[1] Essays (1874 Edition), pp. 36–39, com. 49.

[2] See the catalogue drawn up by Professors Cowell and Eggeling, J.R.A.S., 1876.

[3] Ch. 36.

[4] Life, p. 164.

[5] Beal's Catalogue, p. 79, 80.

succeeding dynasties again favoured Brahmanism, till Megha-vāhana became King of Kashmīr, A.D. 104-144, and extended his power down the valley of the Ganges as far as Kalinga and Orissa.[1]

Buddhism had long before this penetrated to China, along the fixed route from India to that country, round the north-west corner of the Himālayas and across Eastern Turkestan. Already in the 2nd year B.C., an embassy, perhaps sent by Huvishka, took Buddhist books to the then Emperor of China, A-ili;[2] and the Emperor Ming-Ti, 62 A.D., guided by a dream, is said to have sent to Tartary and Central India, and brought Buddhist books to China.[3] From this time Buddhism rapidly spread there. Monks from Central and North-Western India frequently travelled to China; and the Chinese themselves made many journeys to the older Buddhist countries to collect the sacred writings, which they diligently translated into Chinese. In the fourth century Buddhism became the state religion; and there have been, and still are, monks in China belonging to most of the different schools of later Northern Buddhism, though no new sects seem to have been formed.[4]

[1] He is also said in the Rāja Tarangini, iii., 29–79, to have conquered Ceylon, but the native histories know nothing of this. An inscription by him, very Buddhistic in its morality, has been found in Orissa.

[2] Rémusat's 'Foe Koue Ki,' p. 41.

[3] Beal's 'Fa Hian,' pp. xx.–xxii. 'Foe Koue Ki.,' p. 44.

[4] A valuable sketch of the history of Chinese Buddhism is given by Beal in the introduction to his translation of Fa Hian.

Into the Korea Buddhism was introduced from China as early as 372 A.D.;[1] and thence into Japan in 552, in the thirteenth year of King Kin Mei Teno.[2] The old religion of Japan was a worship of the powers of nature, the latest development of which has been preserved in the work on Sin To, by a learned Japanese woman of the twelfth century; and in the thirteenth century, a monk named Sin Ran, who died in 1262, founded a new Buddhist sect, which incorporates into its belief much of the old creed, and the monks belonging to which wear the ordinary dress, and marry.[3] Many of them are thus allied to noble and even to the royal family, and all the Buddhists in Japan—that is, the great mass of the people—belong to this sect; but the fashionable religion of the chiefs is still the system of Sin To.

Kochin China and Ava, the island of Formosa, and Mongolia, probably received their Buddhism from China, during the fourth and fifth centuries; and before that it had spread westwards and northwards from Kabul and Yashkand to Balk, Bokhāra, the Balkash or Dengis Lake, and into China again by way of Jungāria (Ili) and Kobdo. In the course of the twelfth century Muhammadamism drove Buddhism out as far as the west frontiers of China and India; but even before then it had become weak and corrupt.

In India itself, Brahmanism, from the commencement of our era, carried on a continual struggle against Buddhism. The latter gained ground all

[1] Rémusat, 'Foe Koue Ki,' p. 43.

[2] Klaproth, 'Annales des Empereurs de Japan,' p. 25.

[3] Ibid., p. 255.

down the Ganges valley and in Central India, till the fifth century, and for some time longer in the south of the peninsula. Almost all that we know of it is derived from the accounts of the Chinese pilgrims Fa Hian, 400 A.D., Sung Yun, 518 A.D., and Hiouen Thsang, 629-648 A.D.; from Indian coins and inscriptions we can only gather a few vague data, as, for instance, that the later kings of the Gupta dynasty, whom Lassen[1] places from 435-540, and Thomas,[2] two centuries earlier, were supporters of Buddhism.

It is impossible here to compare at any length the data of the Chinese travellers. Fa Hian found Buddhist monks belonging to both Vehicles, and monasteries, and dāgabas in great numbers, all the way from Kabul down to Magadha; but Brahman priests and Hindu temples were scarcely less numerous, and princes and people honoured both.

Sung Yun's account is very short.[3] He came by the usual route, and mentions that the king of Khoten was not a Buddhist, though monks from India had visited the country. Balk was Buddhist; but in Kaferistān, west of the Indus, a heathen Tartar conqueror was persecuting the believing people. East of the Indus all was Buddhist, and Sung Yun did not penetrate further than Peshāwur.

Hiouen Thsang found the powerful Buddhist king Kapisa, ruling over ten kingdoms in Afghanistān; but

[1] iii. p. 657, and iv. pp. 654, 660.
[2] Records of the Gupta Dynasty (1876), p. 55.
[3] It will be found translated in Beal's Fa Hian, pp. 174-208.

many of the monasteries that he saw were in ruins, owing to constant wars and the shifting of the population, never very dense in those regions. Gandhāra was in much the same state, and in the ancient capital, Peshāwar, the great monastery built by Kanishka was deserted; but the people were Buddhists still, and mostly adherents of the Great Vehicle. This was also the case in Kashmīr, where king and people were zealous Buddhists, and where Hiouen Thsang found 500 monasteries, and 5,000 monks. In Sindh the Little Vehicle was still the favourite.

On the Upper Ganges and Jamna also the Buddhists adhered to the old school, but Brahmanism was also in great favour. At *Kanoj* there reigned the then most powerful monarch in all India, *Sīlāditya*, who was a zealous Buddhist, and himself well read in the holy books; but in his capital there were 100 Hindu temples, as well as 100 Buddhist monasteries. Whilst he staid in this country Hiouen Thsang was present at the great council of Kanoj (Kanyākubja), held under Sīlāditya in 634 A.D.,[1] at which the teachings of the Little Vehicle were formerly condemned.

In Ṣrāvasti and Kapilavastu all was in ruins; the few monks remaining only followed the Little Vehicle; Brahmans were flourishing, and heretics numerous. Even in Benāres there were only four monasteries against 100 idol temples. In Magadha and Vaisali, however, especially in the former, the true belief was

[1] On this council see the 'Life of Hiouen Thsang' (Julien's transl., pp. 242, and foll.).

still by far the most flourishing, and 50 monasteries sheltered 1,000 monks. The principal seat of learning was Nālanda, at the east end of the Rājagriha valley, to which students from all parts of India, and even from Ceylon, were attracted. Hiouen Thsang gives the names of the principal teachers, and himself studied there for years. He also describes at great length the dāgabas, the holy places, the legends, and the relics of which the Buddhist Holy Land was full. Here both Vehicles were equally honoured, and at Nālanda all the sacred books of all the sects were repeated and explained.

Further down the Ganges and in Orissa Buddhism was in full life; and on the west-side of the peninsula the powerful Vallabhi king, Dhruvasena II., ruled over a Buddhist country, which included Guzerāt, Khandesh, and the south-west half of Rajputāna. Nagpur, then called Kosala, was also Buddhist; but in Kalinga, of which the Godāvari was the south boundary, and throughout Telugu it was in little favour; further south, however, in Draviḍa, it was again in the ascendant.

On the whole Buddhism appears in Hiouen Thsang to have fallen very far below the point at which it stood in Fa Hian's time; to have been equal in power with Brahminism only where it was supported by powerful kings, and to have been generally accepted as the one religion of the country only in Kashmīr, and the upper Panjāb, in Magadha, and in Guzarāt.

Shortly after he left India the Buddhists are said to have been cruelly persecuted and oppressed by the Hindus, especially under the instigation of the learned Brahmins Khumarīla Bhaṭṭa, and afterwards Ṣankarāchārya; but the details of their extermination are not known; and in the eleventh century Harshadeva, king of Kashmīr, and Sthīrapāla, king of Orissa, still supported the religion of Gautama. The tradition of the persecution is certainly not devoid of foundation [1]; but it seems also certain that Buddhism had in the eighth and ninth centuries become so corrupt that it no longer attracted the people, and when it lost the favour of the kings, it had no power to stand against the opposition of the priests. In the twelfth century, when Kashmīr was conquered by the Moslems, there were no Buddhists left in India, except a few who preserved an ignoble existence by joining the Jain sect, and by adopting the principal tenets, as to caste and ceremonial observances, of the ascendant Hindu creeds.[2]

A few words must be added on the Lāmaism of Tibet, the only country where the Order has become a hierarchy, and acquired temporal power. Here, as in so many other countries, civilisation entered, and history began with Buddhism. When the first missionaries went there is not, however, accurately

[1] The discoveries at Sarnath show that 'all has been sacked and burnt—priest, temples, idols, altogether, and this more than once.' Major Kitto in Cunningham's Reports, 1, 126. See also pp. 121, 123, and Thomas, J.B.A.S. 1854, 472, quoted on p. 128. Wang Pū translated by Beal, Catena, p. 139, says 'The end was the streams of the Sweti (in Kabul) overflowing with blood.'

[2] The best account of the Jains is by S. Warren. 'Over de godsdienstige en wijsgeerige Begrippen der Jainas,' 1876.

known; but Nepāl was becoming Buddhist in the sixth century, and the first Buddhist king of Tibet sent to India for the holy scriptures in 632 A.D. A century afterwards an adherent of the native devil-worship drove the monks away, destroyed the monasteries, and burnt the holy books; but the blood of the martyrs was the seed of the church—it returned triumphant after his death, and rapidly gained in wealth and influence. I have already sketched above the development which took place in doctrine; and have noticed the rise of the belief in Avalokitevṣara, the Spirit of the Buddhas, present in the church. This belief did much to hasten the downward course. He is supposed to be present in the *chutuktus*, who occupy much the same position as the cardinals in the Romish church; and to be especially incarnate in the Dalai Lāma, the infallible Head of the Church, the representative on earth of Ādibuddha, the Buddhist pope. But before the doctrine was thus carried out to its logical conclusion, long and severe struggles had taken place. As the Order became wealthy, rival abbots had contended for supremacy, and the chiefs had first tried to use the church as a means of binding the people to themselves, and then, startled at its progress, had to fight against it for their own privilege and power. When in the long run, the crozier proved stronger than the sword, the Dalai Lāma became in 1419 sole temporal sovereign of Tibet.

However interesting and instructive the study of the rise of Lāmaism may be, as throwing light on the natural causes and the intimate connection of superstitious dogma, gorgeous ritual, and priestly power, it would be quite outside our purpose to enter upon it here. The following sketch of the high service in Lhassa cathedral will show the reader the stage to which Lāmaism has now reached; and the learned work of Köppen[1] will give him, should he so desire it, a full account of its rise or fall:—

The entrance to the chief Temple of the holy city is through a large hall where holy water and rosaries are sold, and in which stand four statues of the Archangels. The walls are covered with rude paintings of scenes from the legends of the Buddha, and its roof is supported by six massive pillars covered with beautiful carving, spoilt by gorgeous paint and gilding. The church itself is a long nave divided by rows of pillars from two aisles, and by silver screens of open trellis-work from two large chancels. Into the aisle on each side open fourteen chapels. At the end is the holy place, containing fifteen jewelled tablets, with mystic symbols of Sang-sāra and other creations of Buddhist metaphysics; and in the furthest niche in a kind of apse is the magnificent golden statue of the now deified Gautama Buddha. On the left is the throne of the Dalai Lāma; on the right that of the Pantshen Lāma; and in order on either side, gradually decreasing in height and splendour, the seats of the Chutuktus, the abbots, and the eighteen orders of inferior clergy. In front of the idol is the high altar, or table of offerings, raised by several stages above the floor; on the upper levels being images of gold, silver, and clay; on the lower the bells, and lamps, and censers,

[1] Vol. ii. of his 'Religion des Buddha.'

and other vessels used in the holy service. At the sound of a horn or trumpet the clergy assemble in the entrance hall, wearing the cloak and cap; and at its third blast the procession, with the living Buddha at its head, marches down the aisle. When he is seated on his throne each Lāma bows three times before him, and then seats himself cross-legged on the divan according to his rank. A bell is then rung, and all murmur the Three Refuges, the Ten Precepts,[1] and other formulas. After silence is restored the bell sounds again, and the priests now sing in choir[2] longer pieces from the sacred books. If it be a feast day, the highest point of the service is reached in the Tuisol, or prayer for sanctification, when the offerings are blest. A bell is rung, and all the monks burst out into a hymn of prayer for the presence of the Spirit of all the Buddhas. One of them raises aloft over his head a looking-glass—the idea of which seems to be to catch the image of the spirit as it comes; a second raises aloft a jug; a third a mystic symbol of the world: a fourth a cup; and others other sacred vessel or mystic symbols. Meanwhile the voices of the singers, and the sound of the bells and drums and trumpets grows louder and louder, and the church is filled with incense from the sacred censers. The monk with the jug pours several times water mixed with sugar and saffron over the mirror, which another wipes each time with a napkin of silk. The water flows over the mirror on to the symbol of the world, and is caught in the cup beneath. Thence the holy

[1] See above, p. 160. [2] Above, p. 210.

mixture is poured on to another jug, and a drop or two is allowed to trickle on to the hands of each of the worshipping monks, who marks the crown of his shaven head, his forehead, and his breast with the sacred liquid. He then reverently swallows the remaining drops; and, in so doing, believes himself to be mystically swallowing part of the Divine Being, whose image has been caught in the mirror over which the water has past.[1]

Lāmaism, indeed, with its shaven priests, its bells, and rosaries, its images, and holy water, and gorgeous dresses; its service with double choirs, and processions, and creeds, and mystic rites, and incense, in which the laity are spectators only; its abbots and monks, and nuns of many grades; its worship of the double Virgin, and of the saints and angels; its fasts, confessions, and purgatory; its images, its idols, and its pictures; its huge monasteries, and its gorgeous cathedrals, its powerful hierarchy, its cardinals, its Pope, bears outwardly at least a strong resemblance to Romanism, in spite of the essential difference of its teachings, and of its mode of thought.[2]

[1] Schlagintweit, 'Buddhism in Tibet,' pp. 227, 239. Huc et Gabet, 'Voyages,' 1, p. 29. Moorcroft and Trebeck 'Travels,' 1, pp. 344, and foll. Klaproth 'Reise in den Kaukasus,' 1, p. 203. Pallas 'Reise durch verschiedene Provinzen des Russischen Reichs,' ii., 160–190.

[2] Father Bury in Kerson's 'The Cross and the Dragon,' (1854) p. 185.

INDEX

OF THE PRINCIPAL

PROPER NAMES AND TECHNICAL TERMS.

ADAM'S Peak, 195.
Ādi-buddha, 206.
Ajataṣatru, 75.
Alāra, 33, 42.
Āmagandha Sutta, 131, 181.
Amitābha, 205.
Anam, 2.
Ānanda, 32, 68, 80, 214.
Anathapiṇḍika, 69.
Anoma river, 32, 68.
Anūpiya, 68.
Anuruddha, 52, 68.
Arahats, 109, 120, 154, 158, 174, 176, 203.
Asanga, 208.
Aśoka, 83, 220–228.
Āsava, 120.
Avalokiteṣvara, 201, 203.
BALĀNI, 173.
Bali, 3, 237.
Benāres, 25, 35, 42.
Bodhi-aṅgā, 173.
Bodhi-satwa, 200.
Bo tree, 37, 39, 169, 231.
Burma, 3, 237.
Buriats, 3.
CHAKRAVARTI, 183, 222.
Chandragupta, 219.
Channa, 29–33, 82.
China, 2, 3, 4, 240, 242.
Chunda, 79.
Council of Rājagriha, 213.
,, Vaiṣāli, 215.
,, Patna, 224.
Council of Kanishka, 238.
,, Kanoj, 244.
DĀGABA, 169, 182, 185.
Deer-park, 43, 53.
Devadatta, 52, 68, 75, 181.
Dhamma-cakka-ppavattana Sutta, 45.
Dhamma-pada, 19, 31, 62, 65, 72, 107, 108, 120, 122, 153.
Dhammika Sutta, 137, 156.
Dhāraṇi, 208.
Dharma, 45, 79.
Dhyāna v. Jhāna,
Dhyāni-Buddhas, 204.
Dina-cariyāwa, 169.
EUROPE, Buddhists in, 5.
FOUR Truths, 48, 106.
,, Paths, 108.
GHANDHAHASTI, 59.
HIRI SUTTA, 155.
IDDHI, 173, 174.
Iriyāpatha, 157.
JAINS, 4, 245.
Japan, 5, 241.
Jātaka, 12, 21, 58, 180, 197.
Java, 5, 236.
Jetavana, 69.
Jhāna, 175, 204.
KALPA, 197, 204.
Kāma Sutta, 121.
Kammavācā, 158.
Kanishka, 238.
Kapilavastu, 25, 27, 29, 243.
Karma, 101–103, 150, 175.

Kashmīr, 5, 236, 238.
Kāşyapa, 59, 61, 189, 214.
Khagga-visāna Sutta, 158, 163.
Kisāgotamī, 133.
Kohāna, 25, 70.
Koliyans, 26, 52, 70.
Kondanya, 44, 49, 186.
Kusala, 135.
Kusi-nagara, 80.
LADĀK, 5.
Lalita Vistara, 9, 11, 186.
Lāmāism, 199, 246.
MADURATTHA Vilāsinī, 11, 29.
Mahābhinishkramana Sūtra, 11.
Mahā Parinibbāna Sutta, 11, 13, 78, 81, 82, 113, 117, 120, 172, 177, 188–190.
Mahā-Nidāna Sutta, 149.
Mahinda, 228.
Maitreya, 180, 200.
Malla lingara Watthu, 11.
Manchūria, 5
Mangala Sutta, 127.
Manju-şrī, 201.
Maṇḍala, 208.
Mārd, 32, 35, 107, 187.
Metta Sutta, 109.
Milinda Praşnaya, 96, 137.
Moggallāna, 62.
Mongolia, 5.
NĀGASENA, 96.
Nanda, 52, 68.
Nāvā Sutta, 121, 155.
Nepal, 5.
Nirvāna, 111, 120, 125, 148, 149.
PACCEKA-BUDDHA, 200.
Pathama Sambodhiya, 14.
Pāti-hārika-pakkha, 139, 141.
Pātimokkha, 162.
Pāvā, 79.
Pitakas, 8, 9, 18, 20, 233, 234.
RĀHULA, 30, 50, 67, 72.
Rājagriha, 33, 50.
Ratana Sutta, 122.
Ratna-dharma-rāja, 11.
Rohini, 25, 26.
Rūpa, 90.
SAMĀDHI, 177.
Samañña-phala Sutta, 21, 177.
Sammā-sambuddha, 182.
Sammappadhānā, 172.
Saṅkhārā, 91.
Sang-yojana, 109.
Sang-sāra, 121, 137.
Saññā, 91.
Sāriputta, 62.
Sati-paṭṭhānā, 172.
Siam, 2, 237.
Siddhi, 208.
Sigalovada, Sutta, 129, 143.
Sikhim, 5.
Sīla, 121, 141.
Skandha, 93.
Spīti, 3.
Srāvasti, 26, 69.
Subhadra, 81.
Subha Sutta, 21.
Suddhodana, 26, 28, 64, 65.
Sukhavatī, 206.
Sutta Nipāta, 19, 20.
TIBET, 3, 199–210, 246.
Tooth, 195.
Trishnā, 101, 107, 113, 136.
UDRAKA, 33, 42.
Upādāna, 95, 101.
Upādi, 114.
Upāli, 68.
Uposatha, 139, 140, 164.
Uruvela, 34.
VAJJIAN clans, 78.
Vedanā, 91.
Vehicle, 200, 218, 243.
Veḷuvana, 62.
Vihāra, 169.
Vinaya, 18, 79.
Vindhya Mountains, 33.
Viññāna, 93.
YASA, 54, 215.
Yasodharā, 50, 52, 66.
Yashṭivana, 62.

WYMAN AND SONS, PRINTERS, GREAT QUEEN STREET, LONDON, W.C.

RECENT PUBLICATIONS.

s. d.

AFRICA UNVEILED. By the Rev. H. ROWLEY. With Map, and Eight full-page Illustrations on toned paper. Crown 8vo. ....*Cloth Boards* 5 0

BIBLE PLACES; OR, THE TOPOGRAPHY OF THE HOLY LAND: A Succinct Account of all the Places, Rivers, and Mountains of the Land of Israel mentioned in the Bible, so far as they have been identified. Together with their Modern Names and Historical References. By the Rev. Canon TRISTRAM. *A new and revised Edition, Crown 8vo., with Map, numerous Wood-cuts* ....*Cloth Boards* 4 0

CHINA, THE LAND AND THE PEOPLE OF. A short Account of the Geography, History, Religion, Social Life, Arts, Industries, and Government of China and its People. By J. THOMSON, Esq., F.R.G.S., Author of "Illustrations of China and its People," &c. With Map, and Twelve full-page Illustrations on toned paper. Crown 8vo. ....*Cloth Boards* 5 0

INDIA, THE HISTORY OF, from the Earliest Times to the Present Day. By L. J. TROTTER, Author of "Studies in Biography." Post 8vo. With a Map and 23 Engravings ....*Cloth Boards* 10 6

ISRAEL: THE LAND OF. A Journal of Travels in Palestine, undertaken with Special Reference to its Physical Character. Third Edition, revised. By the Rev. Canon TRISTRAM. With numerous Illustrations ....*Cloth Boards* 10 6

JEWISH NATION, A HISTORY OF THE. From the Earliest Times to the Present Day. By E. H. PALMER, Esq., M.A., Fellow of St. John's College, and Lord Almoner's Professor of Arabic in the University of Cambridge, Author of "The Desert of the Exodus," &c. &c. Crown 8vo. With Map and numerous Illustrations ....*Cloth Boards* 5 0

LESSER LIGHTS; or, Some of the Minor Characters of Scripture traced, with a View to Instruction and Example in Daily Life. By the Rev. F. BOURDILLON, M.A., Rector of Woolbeding, Sussex, Author of "Bedside Readings," &c. Post 8vo. ....*Cloth Boards* 2 6